THE
THETFORD
TREASURE

THE THETFORD TREASURE

ROMAN JEWELLERY AND SILVER

CATHERINE JOHNS AND
TIMOTHY POTTER

with contributions by

M. R. Cowell, A. K. Gregory, M. Henig
R. Holmes, K. H. Jackson, S. La Niece,
N. D. Meeks, W. A. Oddy

and drawings by

Philip Compton and Robert Pengelly

and photographs by

Victor Bowley

Published for
The Trustees of the British Museum by
British Museum Publications Limited

© 1983 The Trustees of the British Museum
Published by British Museum Publications Ltd,
46 Bloomsbury Street, London WC1B 3QQ

British Library Cataloguing in Publication Data

Johns, Catherine
The Thetford treasure,
1. Goldwork, Roman – England – Thetford (Norfolk)
2. Silverwork, Roman – England – Thetford (Norfolk)
I. Title II. Potter, Timothy
739'.2'0937   NK4707

ISBN 0-7141-1372-7

Designed by Harry Green

Text set in Erhardt Roman
and printed in Great Britain by Henry Ling Limited,
at the Dorset Press, Dorchester, Dorset.

Plates Printed in Great Britain by
the Curwen Press, Plaistow, London.

Contents

List of tables *page 6*

List of plates *page 6*

List of figures *page 6*

Foreword *page 7*
by I. H. Longworth

Preface *page 9*

Summary *page 11*

1 The Discovery of the Treasure and its Site *page 13*
(with a section by A. K. Gregory)

2 The Jewellery *page 20*

3 The Gemstones *page 30*
by Martin Henig

4 The Shale Jewellery Box *page 33*

5 The Silver Spoons *page 34*

6 The Inscriptions on the Silver Spoons *page 46*
by Kenneth Jackson

7 The Cult of Faunus *page 49*

8 The Silver Strainers *page 53*

9 The Scientific Examination of the Thetford Treasure *page 56*
by Michael Cowell, Susan La Niece, Nigel Meeks,
Andrew Oddy and Robert Holmes

10 The Significance of the Treasure *page 68*

11 Catalogue *page 77*

Bibliography *page 132*

Index *page 135*

The Plates

Tables and Illustrations

List of tables

1 The distribution of the principal decorative features in the jewellery.

2 The weights of the jewellery.

3 Frequency matrix for the duck-handled spoons.

4 The distribution of the main typological characteristics of the long-handled spoons.

5 XRF analyses of the objects.

6 Stones and backing pastes.

7 An assessment of the amount of wear on the jewellery.

8 Gold and silver objects from major 'jewellery hoards'.

List of figures

1 Late-Roman hoards of gold and silver from Britain.

2 Sites in the Thetford area.

3 Map showing the main archaeological features on Gallows Hill, Thetford.

4 Plan of the excavated late-Roman features near to the approximate findspot of the treasure.

5 Inscriptions of groups A – D.

7–45 The objects in catalogue order.

List of plates

Colour

1 The buckle, 1

2 The Triton spoon, 50; the Panther spoon, 66

3 The jewellery

4 Gems: 39, 40, 41

Black and white

1 Gold jewellery: the twenty-two rings.
3, 2, 4, 7, 6, 9, 5, 8, 13, 14, 15, 20, 22, 16, 23, 18, 21, 17, 19, 12, 10, 11.

2 Gold jewellery: the buckle, 1, pendants 28 and 29, gems 40, 41 and 39, amulet case, 30, necklace-clasps 37 and 38, and the beads, 42, 43, 44 and 45/46.

3 Gold jewellery: four necklaces, 31, 35/36, 33 and 32.

4 Gold jewellery: a) the matching bracelets 24 and 25, b) bracelets 26 and 27, and c) necklace 34.

5 Silver strainers: 48, 47 and 49.

6 Silver spoons: the parcel-gilt Triton spoon, 50, and Panther spoon, 66, and the Fish spoon, 67.

7 Silver spoons: duck-handled spoons 51, 52, 53, 54, 55.

8 Silver spoons: duck-handled spoons 56, 57, 58, 59, 60.

9 Silver spoons: duck-handled spoons 61, 62, 63, 64, 65.

10 Silver spoons: long-handled spoons 68, 69, 70, 71, 72.

11 Silver spoons: long-handled spoons 73, 74, 75, 76, 77.

12 Silver spoons: long-handled spoons 78, 79, 80, 81, 82.

13 The shale box, 83.

14 Ring 7 (detail)

15 a) Ring 23 (detail)
b) Buckle, 1.

16 Enlarged details of wire construction:
a) 13; b) 17; c) 23; d) 32; e) 33; f) 35.

Foreword

It is the fate of most spectacular finds of gold and silver that their discovery has been a matter of chance and that vital information regarding the circumstances of their deposition has been lost or destroyed before those able to observe these niceties could reach the site. So, alas, it has been with the Thetford Treasure. Little in the way of contextual evidence could be verified. Yet the richness of the find and the self-consistencies inherent in the items recovered have enabled an interpretation to be put forward which carries much conviction. One thing was certain, however, from the moment of discovery. The importance, not to say the magnificence, of the Thetford Treasure clearly called for prompt publication. It is a tribute to the authors of this monograph and to all those who have assisted in its preparation, not least our draughts-men Philip Compton and Robert Pengelly, and Victor Bowley, who undertook the photography, that from acquisition to submission of text a bare thirteen months have elapsed. For this it is a pleasure to record our congratulations and grateful thanks.

IAN H. LONGWORTH
*Keeper of Prehistoric and
Romano-British Antiquities*

19 August 1982

Preface

This monograph comprises what we intend to be the definitive publication of the magnificent hoard of late-Roman gold and silver found in 1979 at Gallows Hill, Thetford, and now known as the Thetford Treasure. Acquired by the British Museum in July 1981, after the due processes of the Treasure Trove law had been completed, it will soon be most spectacular new exhibit in the remodelled display of antiquities from the Roman era in Britain.

In publishing this find we have been mindful from the outset of four principal objectives: (1) to describe as fully as possible the archaeological context of the treasure; (2) to provide a comprehensive self-contained catalogue of the objects; (3) to make clear by means of large-scale drawings, supplemented by photographs, all details of the form, decoration and construction of every item in the hoard; and (4) to give such scientific and technical analyses as seem necessary and desirable. In addition, we have tried to compose an appropriate level of commentary and discussion, in the course of which we have developed a number of hypotheses concerning the date, composition, origin and interpretation of the treasure. Naturally, we are all too aware that this can be nothing like the last word on this remarkable find, and look forward in particular to the publication of other comparable material which, we feel, may well lie unnoticed in various museum collections. Nevertheless, if it can be said that we have made available as fully as possible the *primary* data for the Thetford Treasure, then we shall have achieved our main aim.

To this end we have been fortunate to have enlisted the aid of a distinguished group of specialists. First word must go to our draughtsmen: to Philip Compton, who drew the jewellery and to Robert Pengelly, who drew the silver. A glance at their superb illustrations, which set, we believe, quite new standards for this sort of work, will immediately show how theirs is as original a contribution to this volume as any other; to them, we proffer our warmest gratitude. Equally, we would like to thank our photographer, Victor Bowley, who has laboured patiently and to great effect upon the enormously difficult task of portraying the objects both analytically and yet aesthetically — the result of very long hours and repeated experiment in the studio. We have also been fortunate to have had available the immense resources of the Research Laboratory and of the Conservation Department of the British Museum. It is now widely appreciated how valuable scientific aids can be in the study of ancient artefacts, a point that is underlined by the way in which we have relied upon our colleagues' expertise and knowledge in many sections of this book. Their detailed reports are gathered together into a single chapter on the scientific examination of the treasure; but it cannot go unrecorded how unsparing they have

been with their time and skill, so that even our most obtuse and problematical questions have never gone unanswered. Our particular thanks are due to the Keeper of the Research Laboratory, Dr Michael Tite, who has guided the enquiry along most profitable lines; and to the keeper of the Conservation Department, Mr W. A. Oddy; but we would also like to make special mention of Bob Holmes, a former silversmith and now of the Conservation Department who, amongst other things, performed the delicate task of opening the amulet case. It was a memorable occasion to watch this highly skilled operation; and it has been equally memorable to talk over the objects with him and his colleagues and to see how important practical knowledge can be in interpreting them. Craftsmen like Bob Holmes are heirs to an immensely long tradition of metal-working, a *collegium* that has come down through time. Thus it was that, in restoring the Hockwold Roman silver cups, he was able to recognise the original silversmith's notation and fit the correct handles to the right body — an instruction from an ancient silversmith to a modern one that seems almost uncanny. Just how valuable the observations of these craftsmen can be will be seen in Chapter 9; here, we would stress that, in our view, the archaeologist who ignores such sources of evidence does so unwisely. How fortunate we have been to have had such expertise at hand!

It has not been the aim in this volume to embark upon a large-scale, general discussion of late-Roman jewellery or of silver spoons and strainers, nor to provide any illustrative matter of the parallels that we cite. Our book is large enough and our objective clear-cut: to publish the treasure. However, we cannot leave unmentioned our deep gratitude to the many scholars to whom we have shown the objects and who have shared with us their knowledge and deep insight into late-antique art. It would be otiose to provide a list but it is one that would include many of the acknowledged specialists in this field. In particular, it has been fascinating to see how quickly they formed their conclusions; and it has been encouraging that their observations very largely tally with our own. To this general debt of gratitude, it is a pleasure to acknowledge those who have read and commented upon sections of the volume, amongst them Kenneth Painter, David Sherlock and George Boon. Whilst we may not always have followed their advice, it has been of the utmost value to have had their perceptive and stimulating comments. In addition, we would both like to pay special tribute to Martin Henig who, his own chapter apart, has been a wonderful mine of freely given information and ideas; to Professor Kenneth Jackson and to Mark Hassall for their authorative comments upon the inscriptions; and to our colleague, Don Bailey, whose encouragement, quiet and thoughtful learning, and dedication to classical scholarship, has been especially influential in the preparation of this book. We shall always think of the gestation of this volume as a time of provocative debate and of a warming exchange of ideas and information.

Others have helped us in more practical ways. We shall retain affectionate memories of the superlative contribution of Norfolk archaeologists, particularly Tony Gregory, who did so much to ensure that the treasure was declared; of those in the Thetford Constabulary who helped to investigate the find; and of dealers, collectors and journalists who clarified many of the issues about the discovery of the hoard. We are also indebted to Dr Nacera Benseddik of the Algerian Antiquities Service, who arranged a memorable opportunity for us to see the closely guarded Ténès Treasure (Thetford's best parallel) in the Bardo Museum, Algiers; to our colleagues in the Department of Coins and Medals; and to our own colleagues in the Department of Prehistoric and Romano-British Antiquities, whose enthusiasm about the find was in no way diminished by the sometimes unsavoury publicity that it attracted, and by the overwhelming *presence* of the treasure. In particular, to our Keeper, Dr Ian Longworth and to our Director, Dr David Wilson, very special thanks are due both for their forbearance and for their skilful guidance in all phases of the recent history of the treasure and its publication. We also owe a considerable debt of gratitude to our Museum assistants for all manner of help, particularly to Ray Waters and Bob Walls (amongst whose tasks was a two-hour confinement in a Thetford prison cell, guarding the treasure!); while to our typist, Mary Fox, we would like to pay tribute for her patience as she worked her way through drafts of a complicated manuscript. Equally, we are glad to acknowledge the efforts of our friends in British Museum Publications, especially Celia Clear and Jenny Chattington, without whose enthusiastic help our efforts could well have foundered.

It remains to add a final point. Readers may well wonder why this preface is composed not by the joint authors of this book, but by one alone. This is for a single reason. Whilst I came to the Thetford Treasure as a neophyte in studies of late-antique art, Catherine Johns is, as is well known, an established specialist in this field. That she has been more than thoughtful and kind in guiding me down the right paths deserves full recognition. As far as possible, we have tried to divide responsibilities, so that she has written the chapters on the jewellery and the cult of Faunus as well as the catalogue (and has also supervised the work of the draughtsmen and the photographer), while I have composed the sections on the silver and the shale box and the introductory and concluding chapters; but each has read and tinkered with the other's sections, so that we proffer conclusions which are shared. But this must not mask the fact that, essentially, this is much more her book than mine and, so it is, that it is to her that I offer my gratitude as a memory of an especially rewarding two years of study and reflection.

TIMOTHY POTTER
The British Museum
11 July 1982

Summary

The Thetford Treasure, found in 1979, is composed of the following objects, 81 in all.

  1 gold belt buckle
 22 gold finger rings
  4 gold bracelets, 2 a matching pair
  2 gold club-of-Hercules pendants (or ear-rings)
  2 gold-mounted pendants, one containing a cameo, the other an engraved gem
  1 unmounted gem
  5 gold necklaces and 2 pairs of gold clasps
  1 gold amulet, designed as a pendant
  4 beads, 3 of glass, one of emerald
  3 silver strainers
 33 silver spoons
  1 shale jewellery box and lid

The jewellery, manufactured from some 1½ Roman pounds of gold, is in the main typical of late-antique styles, with their love of flamboyance and a prolific use of colour. Whilst all of the engraved gems derive from other reused stock, the jewellery itself is almost entirely brand-new: only one ring stands out as a certain exception. Moreover, at least two objects remain unfinished, an observation that, in combination with the pristine condition of the soft gold, indicates that the great majority of the items can never have been worn. That this is therefore a jeweller's or merchant's stock-in-trade finds confirmation in the fact that there are numerous stylistic traits which unite the group as a whole.

The thirty-three spoons, which divide into two main types, a 'duck-handled' form ('*Schwanenhalsgriff*') and a long-handled type (*cochlearia*), also appear to comprise a homogeneous group from a simple workshop. There are two outstanding examples with parcel-gilt decoration, one showing a Triton, the other a panther, and all save two are inscribed. Twelve of these inscriptions refer directly to the old Latian god, Faunus, while some have names that may be seen as alluding to the cult. It is suggested that the spoons, together with the three silver strainers, were used in the celebration of the religious ritual, probably by some form of guild (*collegium*). Altogether, some three Roman pounds of silver are represented by the hoard.

On typological grounds, both the gold and the silver can be assigned a date in the second half of the fourth century, and it is argued that their manufacture and burial probably took place in the 380s or early 390s. Both sets of objects could have originated either in Gaul or at the hands of Gallic craftsmen. Detailed consideration is given to the question as to whether it is the cult of Faunus that unites both sets of objects or if their burial together is to be explained in some other way. In either case the collection illuminates both the artistic tastes of the late-Roman period and sheds new light upon a hitherto obscure pagan tradition.

Note: The collection is registered as P. 1981. 2-1. 1–83. The necklace **35/36** was registered as two objects, and the beads **42–46** as five, making a total of eighty-three items.

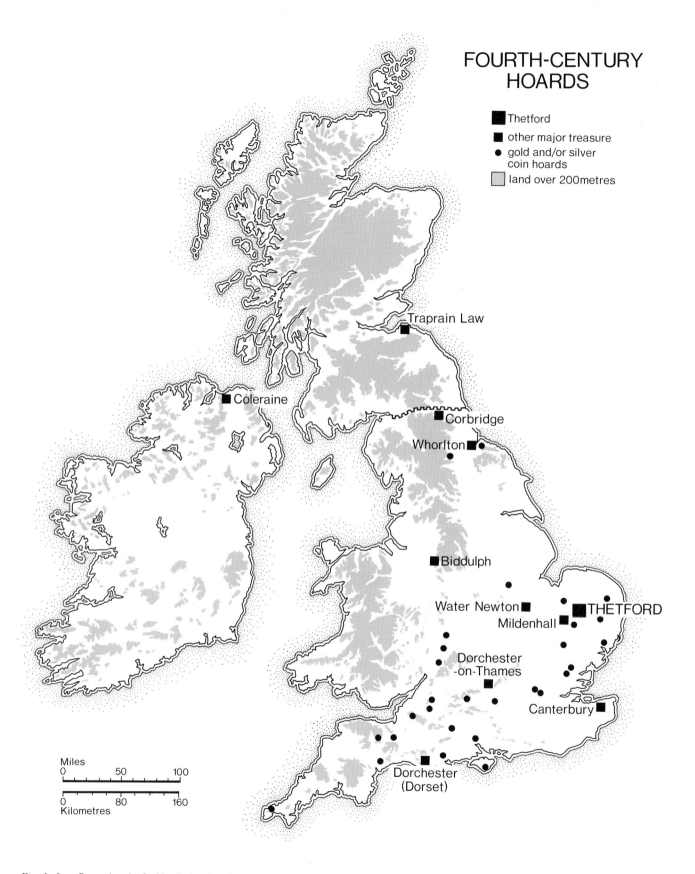

FOURTH-CENTURY
HOARDS

■ Thetford
■ other major treasure
● gold and/or silver coin hoards
land over 200metres

Traprain Law

Coleraine

Corbridge

Whorlton

Biddulph

Water Newton

THETFORD
Mildenhall

Dorchester
-on-Thames

Canterbury

Dorchester
(Dorset)

Miles
0   50   100

Kilometres
0   80   160

Fig. 1. Late–Roman hoards of gold and silver from Britain

1

The Discovery of the Treasure and its Site

Over the last decade or so East Anglia has continued to yield a remarkable series of ancient gold and silver objects. To the Mildenhall, Water Newton, Snettisham, Ipswich and Sutton Hoo Treasures can be added an extensive list of coin-hoards and other items that have recently come to light. Mirroring a long tradition in the accumulation and concealment of portable wealth, it is a trend that is discernible from before the Roman period and persists well into medieval times. Whether or not this concentration of finds is solely a reflection of the heavy degree of present-day cultivation and building activity in this region, there can be no doubt that the remarkable discovery in 1979 of Roman gold and silver from Gallows Hill, Thetford, fits into a well-defined pattern. East Anglia is above all conspicuous for the wealth of gold and silver that was buried in its soil in antiquity.

All too often, however, these finds have been made by chance, and can seldom be fitted into any sort of archaeological context. It must, therefore, be a matter for deep regret that some of the circumstances surrounding the recovery of the Thetford Treasure remain similarly obscure and that there was no opportunity to investigate the spot where it had been buried. Instead, the case has become the subject of conjecture and speculation, whose effect is to render it extremely difficult to produce any definitive account of the discovery of the finds at Gallows Hill. Here, we can only describe what we believe to be established fact, and provide some comment upon the more puzzling features of the case, with the aim of clarifying as much as possible of the archaeological background. Fortunately, we were able to talk by telephone with the finder, the late Mr Arthur Brooks of Norwich, on more than one occasion, and also with many other people involved in the events that followed the discovery of the treasure. There are also two published accounts of the background to the find,[1] as well as a detailed report, presented below, of the archaeological investigations carried out by Mr A K Gregory of the Norfolk Archaeological Unit. In sum, therefore, a considerable body of evidence is available to us, which we shall try here to summarise as objectively as possible.

Gallows Hill itself, described in detail by Gregory below, is now the focus of an expanding industrial complex on the north side of Thetford. Overlooking the valleys of the Thet and the Little Ouse, not far from the eastern edge of the southern Fenland, this sand-and-gravel capped eminence was the site of an extensive late-Iron Age/early Roman settlement, currently under excavation.[2] A later Roman timber building has also been identified close to the burial place of the treasure (Fig. 4) and, a short distance to the south, a barrow-like mound has been shown to have been heightened in the later Roman or sub-Roman periods (cf. *infra*). Not surprisingly,

this area had been a target for treasure-seekers for some little time with, Gregory suggests (*infra*), no small measure of success.[3] Numerous metal objects and coins have apparently come to light, indicating that Gallows Hill remained a centre of some importance for much of the Roman period. Indeed, the earth-moving operations involved in the construction of the factories must have considerably facilitated these clandestine investigations; above all, they were to play a vital role in the discovery of the Thetford Treasure.

Our information is that it was in the middle of October 1979 that work began on a warehouse for the Travenol group, on the most northerly side of the industrial complex.[4] Initially, a level surface had to be created, involving the strippage of between four inches and two feet of overburden. On the northeast corner of the site, some eighteen inches were to be removed, leaving a shallow incline between the building platform and the surrounding ground surface. Here, as our inspection, in June 1980, of a nearby pit showed, the subsoil comprises an acid reddish glacial sand, mixed with many nodules of flint derived from the underlying chalk. There was only a thin cover of humus, so it is clear that the factory foundations must have penetrated well into the subsoil at this point. It was into this area that, late one afternoon in 1979, Mr Arthur Brooks, together with his wife Mrs Greta Brooks, took a metal detector. At the base of the incline, close to the fence dividing the building-site from the adjoining field to the north (Fig. 3), the machine gave a positive reading. Mr Brooks then dug down through what he described as loose, sandy soil and, at a depth of about six inches below the surface, came across the shale box (83). Around it were a number of items of gold jewellery — which it is impossible to be certain — together with the silver spoons and strainers. The spikes of the long-handled spoons were sticking up more or less vertically in the ground, suggesting that they may have been tied up as a bundle or held up together in some other way. Otherwise the finds clustered around the box in an area of some two square feet, except for some items of jewellery placed within the shale box. It is not completely certain which objects they may have been, but our list includes the necklaces, some loose beads, the buckle, the heavy twisted bracelet (26) and some of the rings. In a conversation with Mr Brooks we asked him whether he had noticed any trace of a container for the other objects and he told us that there was none.

From this description it is quite clear that the objects were buried in a pit or gulley which must have extended to a depth of some 2 to 2½ feet below the present-day ground level. Gregory discusses below the remains of a nearby later Roman timber building and concludes that its demolition may have taken place in the fourth century; however, there is no good reason necessarily to associate this structure with the burial of the treasure and it is probably safer to assume that the building had been abandoned by the time the hoard was interred in the ground. On the other hand, it should be emphasised that this has not — and now cannot — be demonstrated since, by the time the treasure had been declared, the site of its burial had long since been destroyed by the construction of the Travenol warehouse.

Following the discovery of the treasure, Mr and Mrs Brooks took the objects home and washed them. The gold was cleaned with cold water and the silver in warm water and baby shampoo. Shortly afterwards the contents of the hoard were taken to Doncaster where they were placed in a bank safe-deposit box, belonging to Mrs Brooks. In the months that followed, protracted negotiations took place, involving amongst others the landowners (the Breckland District Council) and a dealer in antiquities.[5] Shortly after Easter 1980, word of the discovery permeated to some official archaeological bodies and, largely due to the good offices of Tony Gregory of the Norfolk Archaeological Unit, the negotiations were brought to a conclusion. On the 29 May 1980, the treasure was declared and taken to the Castle Museum, Norwich. The following day we collected the objects and transferred them to the British Museum, so as to prepare a report for the Treasure Trove inquest. The exception to this was the shale box. Being made neither of gold nor of silver, it was not a legal requirement that it should be part of the declaration,[6] and Mr Brooks had in fact given it to a friend who claimed that he could have it restored. Believing it to be of wood, it was subsequently soaked both in water and in linseed oil and, after passing through more than one hand, eventually arrived in London. Fortunately, Mr Brooks telephoned us about the box and enquiries eventually revealed its whereabouts.[7] Although by the time we gained possession of if, the shale had disintegrated into a number of pieces, covered with yellow blobs of wax residue, prompt first-aid stabilised its condition and saved this remarkable object.[8]

By this time Mr Brooks had become seriously ill and, in the first part of July 1980, he died. Unfortunately, he had been unable to make any very detailed statement about the finding of the treasure, which might have settled some of the areas of uncertainty, since he had been suffering from a serious disease for some considerable time.

It was not until 3 February 1981 that the Coroner's inquest was held at Thetford. At the conclusion of the evidence, the jury decided that all but the unmounted cornelian gem, the five beads and the shale box[9] comprised a Treasure Trove, and the Coroner took possession of the objects on behalf the Crown. They were immediately returned to the British Museum and the following day full reports of the treasure appeared in *The Times* and elsewhere.

In the months that ensued we presented our initial findings in a lecture at the Society of Antiquaries of London and in an article in the *Illustrated London News*.[10] Then, on 5 May 1981, the Treasure Trove Reviewing Committee met to consider the question of the reward. The valuation of the hoard of £261,540 was agreed but the question of the reward was referred to the Treasury. On 16 July 1981 the Treasury issued the following statement.[11]

THETFORD TREASURE TROVE

The Chief Secretary to the Treasury, the Rt Hon. Leon Brittan QC MP has decided that an ex gratia reward of £87,180 should be paid to the personal representatives of the late Mr Arthur Brooks the finder of the Thetford hoard.

The hoard was discovered by Mr Brooks, using a metal detector, in November 1979. It is one of the most important hoards of Roman treasure yet found. An inquest decided that the hoard was treasure trove and, as such, the property of the Crown.

To encourage prompt declaration of treasure trove and enable the archaeological significance of sites to be examined, finders of treasure trove who declare their finds promptly can expect to receive an ex gratia reward equivalent to the full market valuation (or the return of the treasure).

In the case of the Thetford hoard there was a *six month delay* before Mr Brooks declared the find. During that period the site was built on and the opportunity of examining important archaeological evidence was lost. The presumption must be that under such circumstances no reward would be payable. However, Mr Brooks was suffering at the time from a serious illness and subsequently died. The Chief Secretary to the Treasury accordingly decided that an ex gratia reward equivalent to one-third of the full market value should be paid. Had the find been declared straight away a reward of £261,540 would have been paid. Only four previous instances of deliberate concealment of treasure trove finds have come to light in the past 50 years. In two of these cases no rewards were paid. In the other two cases rewards equivalent to 10% of the full market valuation of the treasure were paid.

The Chief Secretary has emphasised that a very strict line will be taken in respect of any future instances of deliberate concealment of treasure trove.

Shortly after this statement had been released, the Trustees of the British Museum agreed to acquire the find by paying the reward, and the Thetford Treasure soon afterwards became part of the national collections.

This rather dismal history of the events following the discovery of the treasure raises a series of issues. In particular, we need to consider what might have been learnt had the site of the hoard been investigated. Three points seem to us to be of special importance:

1 There was no opportunity either to establish the nature of the pit in which the treasure had been buried, nor to explore its relationship with any other Roman features or buildings in the area. We have already referred above to a later Roman timber structure in the vicinity of the hoard; but there is no way of knowing whether this building was in existence when the treasure was buried. The lack of an archaeological context for so many major finds such as the Thetford treasure must be regarded as seriously detrimental to our understanding of the reasons behind their interment.

2 We have no guarantee at all that the hoard was dug up in its entirety. We know that the light was failing when the objects were found and, while Mr and Mrs Brooks obviously tried to recover everything, there is some evidence to

suggest that they may not have completely succeeded. In the first place, the tip of one of the spoon handles (70) is missing, as is part of the bowl of strainer **49**; in both cases the breaks appear to be recent. Secondly, the tongue and the hinge-pin are no longer present with the gold buckle (**1**), although traces of wear on the bow of the buckle establish that they did once exist. Was the buckle buried in this condition (which seems on the face of it unlikely) or did these pieces become detached and lost when the hoard was salvaged? Thirdly, there are some loose beads, which ought to belong to a necklace; however, there is no obvious candidate in the assemblage, leaving the feeling that it *could* have been missed. Fourthly, many of the cells in the jewellery contain no gems. Given that this is a jeweller's hoard, one would like to have been able to establish with certainty whether the gems had fallen out into the pit or if, as is possible, they had never been set. Only full excavation, combined with sieving, could have given an answer to this question.

3 The third problem with the hoard concerns the nature of the container for the objects. There can be no doubt that so valuable and fragile a collection must have been buried with some sort of protective cover. Possibly this took the form of a bag of cloth or leather but this seems on the whole unlikely. In the first place, this would not have prevented distortion and crushing of the objects from the pressure and weight of the earth; yet the objects are remarkable for their undamaged state. Secondly, the completely uncorroded condition of the silver is a clear pointer towards the presence of some more robust form of container which would have inhibited chemical activity from the very acid surrounding soil-matrix and protected the objects from the crushing weight of the pit's backfill. Conceivably there is some special explanation for the exceptional condition of the hoard; but a container such as a pot seems the likeliest answer to this otherwise puzzling problem.

These points clearly show that there are a good many areas of uncertainty about the deposition of the Thetford Treasure. Unfortunately, Mr and Mrs Brooks neither sought expert archaeological help — which would have solved at least some of these questions — nor did they salvage the find under the best conditions. As a result, we shall never know the answers to these problems. However, in this context, it is proper to mention one persistent rumour about the Thetford Treasure, if only to make our position on it clear. This rumour has been summarised in print by Mr Jack Ogden,[12] who played a considerable role in the declaration of the Treasure.[13] Ogden writes as follows:

> The exact facts will never be known for certain but the following is suggested as an alternative account of the rediscovery of the jewellery hoard at Thetford.
> . . . [Arthur Brooks'] find consisted of the gold jewellery and silverware and also gold and silver coins. The items were contained in a shale box (thought by Brooks to be wood) and two pots which have seemingly disappeared. The coins were gold solidii (about 10?) and a quantity of silver siliquii. The solidii were of Magnus Maximus which fixes the date of the burial to after 383 AD. [*sic*]

The report of coins of Magnus Maximus being found at Thetford is of particular interest since they would fit our suggested date both for the jewellery and for the silver very well; moreover, we already know of at least two other hoards of *siliquae* of similar date from this area (see Gregory, *infra*).[14] *However, we are aware of absolutely no evidence whatsoever for suggesting either that there were coins associated with the jewellery and silver or that the Brooks were involved in the discovery of any coins.*

This does not of course mean that coins were not found by other people, for we do know that the site was extensively explored with metal detectors. Indeed, it is by no means unknown for a hoard to be buried at several different points.[15] However, we have no proof that such coins (or, for that matter, pots) ever existed and, unless new evidence comes to light, it would be quite unscholarly to allow the alleged existence of such coins to bear upon the interpretation of the Thetford Treasure. Rather, while stressing the academic necessity of referring to such reports, we must nevertheless let the find stand on its own, only recognising that there are matters concerning its discovery which are now incapable of full clarification.

The site of Gallows Hill, Thetford
by A. K. Gregory (*Norfolk Archaeological Unit*)

Physical background (Fig. 2)

The Saxon and medieval nuclei of Thetford stand on either side of the confluence of the Thet with the Little Ouse, in the south-western part of the East Anglian Breckland, some 15 km east of the Fens. To the north, south-west and south-east the confluence is overlooked by three low hills, respectively Gallows Hill, Barrow Hill and Snarehill. All three are part of the great chalk ridge which runs into Norfolk from the south-west and here turns to head into north-west Norfolk, but are capped by considerable depths of glacial sands and gravels. Like its two fellows, Gallows Hill is flat-topped, at about 50 m O.D., and falls away gradually to the west, south and east at gradients varying between one in ten and one in twenty. To the north it is separated from the main chalk ridge by a stream valley no higher than 30 m O.D.

Archaeological background (Fig. 2)

Iron-Age and Romano-British occupation abounds in the Thetford region. The area is dominated by a route of long standing, the Icknield Way, which reaches the edge of the chalk from the south-west at the head of a small dry valley which marks the southern limits of Barrow Hill. There is considerable uncertainty about the exact route of the trackway across the valley; in fact, it is almost certainly too simplistic to expect a single crossing-point, and a network of tracks leading from the edge of the chalk to a series of fords, with a comparable network climbing Gallows Hill, is more likely.

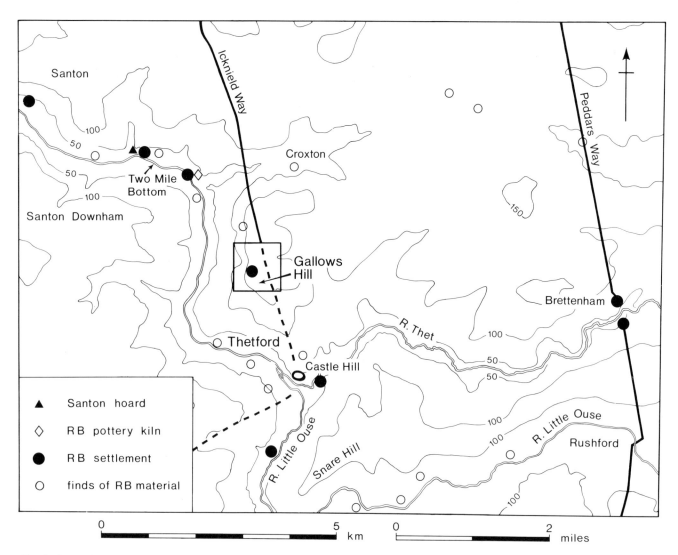

Fig. 2. Sites in the Thetford area

At any rate, the course of the Icknield Way seems to pick up again on Gallows Hill, and thence runs due north. Doubt has been cast on the prehistoric date of this route,[16] since the concentration of sites and finds, particularly in the Iron Age, lies well to the west of this line, along the Fen edge. Such a line, however, would involve considerable problems with river-crossings, and while in use as an alternative is not likely to have been the sole south-north route along the chalk.

Early settlement on Gallows Hill (Fig. 3)

The early evidence, in the form of prehistoric worked flint, has emerged from two Norfolk Archaeological Unit excavations but it is not clear what sort of settlement or land-use is implied. Late in the first millennium BC occupation of the hill top is attested by the remains of pits and ditched enclosures. These appear to have continued in use until the middle of the first century AD when a large triple-ditched enclosure, covering a total of 4½ hectares, was constructed on the apparent projection of the line of the Icknield Way. In its earliest

phase this enclosure may have been a single-ditched area of 0.5 hectare, containing three large timber round-houses. This was then modified by the addition of an inner and outer ditch, and the 30 metre berm between the new outer ditch and the original, now middle, ditch filled by an array of timbers, set in seven or eight parallel slots. This modified enclosure post-dates groups of Claudio-Neronian pottery but is highly unlikely, on historical as well as archaeological grounds, to date any later than AD 61.[17]

Occupation of Gallows Hill then apparently falls off until perhaps the third century AD, with the bulk of the evidence for the late-Roman occupation coming from metal-detector finds on the site being cleared for the new Travenol warehouse in the autumn of 1979, as well as from a controlled metal-detector survey conducted on the field north of the Travenol site in the summer of 1980, under the writer's supervision. Without a doubt, huge quantities of material recovered from this site have not been recorded archaeologically, and of the hundreds of coins which must have been found during the construction of the warehouse, only a handful were ever listed; these, together with the finds from the 1980 metal-detector survey, total 64; their dates are as follows:

Pre-Roman:	3	AD 275–94:	6
AD 41–54:	1	AD 317–30:	2
AD 69–96:	2	AD 330–48:	10
AD 117–38:	1	AD 348–64:	3
AD 161–80:	1	AD 364–78:	25
AD 259–75:	7	AD 388–402:	1

Of these, the earliest Roman coin is an irregular Claudian Minerva *as* and the latest a VICTORIA AVGG issue of Honorius,

dated AD 395–402. It would appear that the pre-Roman and Claudian coins all belong to the first-century AD occupation described above, while the Flavian to Antonine issues are likely to be residual to the main occupation, starting around the middle of the third century AD. The main peak would certainly appear to be in the third quarter of the fourth century AD, particularly in view of the scarcity of Constantinian issues; but the virtual absence of coins of the last quarter is surprising given the silver hoards and the Thetford Treasure itself.

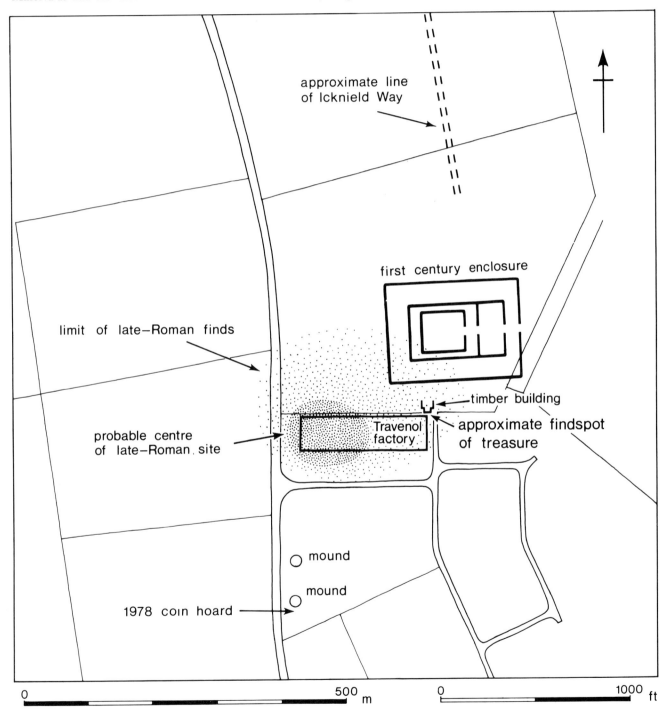

Fig. 3. Map showing the main archaeological features on Gallows Hill, Thetford

An archaeological context for these finds is not easy to define. Traces of scrappy flint and brick footings, together with small quantities of late-Roman pottery, were found during the construction work; and surface finds recorded in the early 1960s also suggest the presence of buildings, although not of any great substance. The treasure itself appears to have been found 150 m east of the main concentration of late-Roman finds; and, in order to fit the discovery into what was already known, a small area was stripped immediately north of the findspot in the summer of 1980 by the Norfolk Archaeological Unit. This was at a time after the actual findspot of the hoard had been totally obliterated by earth-moving and by the installation of water-mains. This area revealed the existence of a series of late-Roman features, tentatively identified as the remains of a substantial timber building (Fig. 4). Two post-holes, 7½ m apart, lay 1½ m north of an east-west gully which could have contained a sill; 2½ m to the north, and 5½ m apart, lay a second pair of post-holes, more or less central to the line defined by the northernmost posts and the gully. A

can be very tentatively inferred is that the building was probably taken down after *c.* AD 300. Similarly, the interpretation of the structure itself poses certain difficulties, not least its large aisle-span of 7½ m. All that can safely be said at this stage is that its form and function must remain an open question, just as its relationship with the pit or gulley containing the treasure cannot be demonstrated.

To the south of the Travenol site lie the most puzzling features of all: two mounds, traditionally identified as round barrows, within the area disturbed by the construction of the Howson-Algraphy factory in 1978–9. Excavation of one of these, under exceptionally difficult circumstances, by Andrew Lawson of the Norfolk Archaeological Unit, revealed a turf-stack sealing an old soil-line. This contained some sherds of probable Iron-Age date, together with a deposit of charred organic material on the side of the turf stack. This was sealed by the sand capping of the mound and gave a radio-carbon date of a.d. 350 ± 170 (HAR-2905); it also provided evidence for heathland vegetation. The function of this pair of

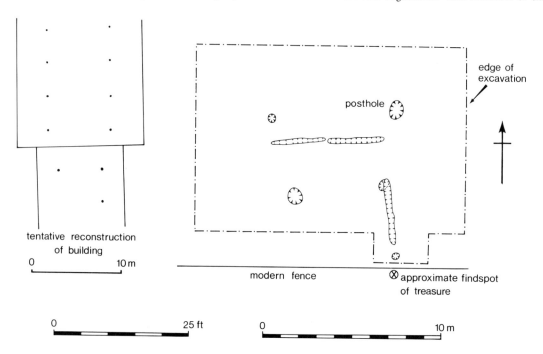

edge of excavation

posthole

tentative reconstruction of building

0   10 m

modern fence   ⊗ approximate findspot of treasure

0   25 ft   0   10 m

Fig. 4. Plan of the excavated late-Roman features near to the approximate findspot of the treasure

fifth but smaller post-hole continued the line of posts to the south, less than a metre north of the alleged findspot of the treasure. One of these post-holes, however, was truncated by a later gully running along the 'aisle-line' suggested by the post-holes so, while it is attractive to suggest that the treasure was buried in a standing building on the line of aisle-posts, concealment in a continuation of the north-south gully is also possible.

The dating evidence for the structure was meagre. In one of the post-holes was a rim sherd of a Nene-Valley colour-coated dish, probably of the fourth century, while in the gulley that cut it was a body sherd from a grey-ware jar. All that

mounds is unknown, but the southernmost apparently served as a landmark in the late fourth-century AD, when a hoard or hoards of silver *siliquae* were concealed nearby. Information about the hoards is patchy; forty-seven *siliquae*, ranging in date from AD 355–61 to AD 385 were found close to the southern edge of the mound in December 1978, while a further twenty *siliquae* of precisely the same date-range were located around the eastern side of the mound in the summer of 1981. This latter group, however, appears to have been dispersed by the earth-moving associated with the construction of the factory in the winter of 1978–79 from an original spot somewhere on the south or east side of the mound. These two groups agree so well in emperors, date and mints that it is likely that they were part of a larger split hoard. More problematical are rumours of large numbers of *siliquae*, of which the latest is reported to have been of Eugenius (392–4), found by clandestine metal-detecting in the winter of 1979–80. Reports place the discovery of these coins variously to the north and to the south of the mound, but it seems probable that over a hundred coins were disturbed by the earth-moving, and that the twenty found in 1981 were the last remnants of this group. In this connection it is also worth noting a further group of twenty or more *siliquae* found in 1962 on the agricultural boundary of Thetford, with, amongst them, four coins of Julian and one of Magnus Maximus.

Apart from the intrinsic evidence of the treasure itself there is little clue, however, as to the nature of the Travenol site in the late-Roman period; despite the attraction of an interpretation as a temple, there is only the evidence of the treasure to support this.

NOTES

1. Raven 1981; Ogden 1981.
2. *Current Archaeology* 81 (March 1982), 294f.
3. Information via the Thetford police.
4. Either in October or November; however, since the hardcore was laid at the end of October, the former is more likely.
5. Cf. Raven 1981.
6. Other items not of gold or silver were, however, declared, including the unmounted gem (41) and five beads (42–46).
7. We are grateful to Brian Spencer of the Museum of London for help in reuniting the box with the rest of the treasure.
8. By Simon Dove of the Conservation Department of the British Museum.
9. These were subsequently purchased from Mr Brooks' widow by the British Museum. Their registration number is P.1981. 2–1. 41–46.
10. Potter and Johns 1981.
11. Reference: 112/81.
12. Ogden 1981.
13. Cf. Raven 1981, 45–6.
14. Cf. Green 1979.
15. E.g. the Icklingham, Suffolk, coin hoard which was buried in three separate deposits. Cf. Archer 1979, 45f.
16. Rivet 1970, 47.
17. A plan and a provisional summary can now be found in *Current Archaeology* 81 (March 1982). However by no means all the assertions made there would be supported by the writer.
18. Green 1979.

2

The Jewellery

The jewellery from the Thetford Treasure consists of forty-four objects. Twenty-two of these are finger-rings, forming by far the largest and most important associated group of late-Roman rings yet discovered. In addition, there are five necklaces, five pendants, four bracelets, two necklace-clasps, an unmounted engraved gem, four beads and a magnificent gold belt-buckle. There are no brooches. Though one of the rings was probably designed for a man, and the belt-buckle might also have been intended for masculine use, the assemblage as a whole is essentially one of feminine ornaments. However, for a number of reasons which will become apparent, the group does not constitute the personal jewellery of one owner or even of a family: whatever the significance of the hoard may be, it cannot be explained simply as the contents of a rich woman's jewellery box buried in times of danger.

Taste and materials

Before we embark on a detailed study of the jewellery, it is worth commenting in general terms on the overall impression made by the group, and in particular by the remarkable collection of rings. The impression is one of great richness and elaboration, of a taste which tends towards the baroque and even the ostentatious. While it is easy to find examples of highly elaborate goldwork throughout antiquity (some Hellenistic jewellery is immensely intricate and richly embellished), there is a tendency in the earlier Roman Imperial period to favour simpler styles, and to allow plain polished gold and finely engraved gems to speak for themselves. From the third century onwards, however, fashions in jewellery again increasingly favoured colourful and richly textured surfaces: filigree, granulation, piercing and decoration in relief were used to enrich the gold, and settings were chosen for their brilliant colour, often in very vivid combinations, rather than for delicate engraving.[1] Some of the objects in the Thetford Treasure, such as the necklaces, belong to types which had been current for many generations and even centuries, but others, above all the rings, perfectly exemplify the florid tendencies of late-antique taste.

To take some specific examples, rings 10, 11, 12 and 14 all display very elaborate filigree and granulation work, combined in 10 and 12 with further texturing of the hoop of the ring, and in 14 with a triple setting for coloured glass. Chased designs are found on several of the rings, and in 2 and 3 this type of ornamentation is combined with excessive size of the rings and with large engraved gems. The internal diameters of both these rings are not great; they are almost certainly designed for a woman's hand, and would have been inconveniently large in use, even though the weight of the gold

has been reduced by making the hoops and shoulders hollow. Perhaps the acme of complexity is reached in ring no. 5: like two others (6 and 7) it possesses the rare feature of zoomorphic shoulders modelled completely in the round, with details of the animals' eyes and limbs added in chasing or engraving, but this already highly elaborate design is completed by a huge flat bezel set with stones in three colours, mauve (amethyst), blood-red (garnet) and vivid green (emerald).

The importance of colour in this jewellery is underlined by the fact that glass is freely used. Our modern distinctions between precious stones such as beryl (emerald), semi-precious quartzes like amethyst and onyx, and 'imitation' or 'paste' gems, i.e. glass, were clearly of little importance to jewellers in the late-Roman period. The consciousness of colour is well shown by a design feature of ring 4, which is set with a very fine, small engraved chalcedony belonging to a much earlier period. This stone appears black by reflected light, but when held up to the light it becomes a translucent yellow. This property has been noted and exploited by piercing the gold in the underside of the setting in a decorative openwork motif, enabling the stone to be observed by transmitted light.

All the engraved gems in the Thetford Treasure are reused stones of earlier date, a custom which was usual in fourth-century jewellery since the art of gem-engraving was in decline at this period. The largest and finest of the gems, the orange-red cornelian engraved with Venus and Cupid (41), has been removed from its old setting but not yet placed in a new one, a significant point to which we shall return. The black chalcedony in 4, engraved with a figure of the Tyche of Antioch, is probably the earliest stone in the group, its style indicating a date in the first century AD.

Gold used on its own without complex surface decoration was also still appreciated, as we can see from the massive bracelet, 26: even in this case, though, there is an element of ostentation, as the object weighs 108 g and is thus the largest and heaviest example of its type known. All the gold is of the vivid yellow favoured in antiquity, and like nearly all Roman gold, is very pure. The analyses are discussed in scientific terms in Chapter 9. Most of the objects contain well over 90% gold, and several have over 95%. This compares with modern 18-carat gold which contains 75% gold, and the now rare 22-carat with 91.6%. The analyses of the individual items support the stylistic evidence, which we shall examine shortly, that there are links within the group: certain items, for instance the rings 10 and 12 and the bracelets 24 and 25, were probably made from the same mix of metal. The metal itself could, of course, be reused from earlier pieces of jewellery, just as the settings were, and for this reason and others, analyses can give no information about the geographical source of the gold.

One technical feature of the jewellery which deserves special attention is the presence in many of the pieces of sulphur. This is evidently used in three ways: as an adhesive and backing material in gem-settings, as a packing in hollow areas of gold, probably to give the object greater strength and stability, and in the case of the amulet, 30, probably primarily as a material with magical properties. The stones and the cells into which they are set are often rather carelessly matched, so that a backing material was necessary to hold the stone firmly. This is very different from the practice in earlier Roman times, when gems were carefully matched to their settings, and fitted precisely without further support. Sulphur continued occasionally to be used in this way after the Roman period, and is found in some Dark-Age and Byzantine work.

Condition

The condition of the jewellery is one of its most noteworthy features. As we have noted above, the gold is in all cases of high purity, and is therefore soft and easily marked. Rings are particularly subject to slight damage in wear, as they can easily be knocked against each other or against hard objects, and the contact with clothing causes a different type of surface abrasion, burnishing and smoothing any projecting features of the design. Under a microscope, a ring which has been used will display small scratches and dents as well as polished areas where the detail of engraved or relief ornament has been blurred or lost. The first impression made by the Thetford jewellery is that, apart from the loss of some of the gems, it is in pristine condition. This impression was tested by microscopic examination of the surfaces and comparison, under the microscope, with other pieces of Roman jewellery from a variety of provenances and contexts. The results are noted in Chapter 9 and individually in the catalogue entries for each object, and they confirm the initial impression: it appears that most of the rings are indeed in absolutely fresh and unused condition, and there is very little trace of wear on the other items. The fine detail of surface decoration which is found on many of the rings would rapidly display the traces of use described above, and these traces are absent. One ring, 15, stands out as well used, the wear being obvious even without the aid of a microscope; it was possibly intended for melting down and reuse of the metal. Of the other rings, 13, which is set with the inscribed Abraxas gem, appears to have some wear, and 18 and 11 also show a little trace of use. There seems also to be very slight trace of wear on 12, a more puzzling feature, since this ring belongs to the clear stylistic group which includes the bracelets 24 and 25, themselves undoubtedly untouched by any use.

The signs of wear on the buckle, 1, are confined to the centre of the bow, where the tongue would have rested. The tongue itself is now missing, but the slight flattening and smoothing of the chased design on the oval field between the jaws of the confronted horses clearly demonstrates that it had been fitted. However, there is no sign of wear on the studs behind the buckle-plate which would have served to attach the plate to a belt, nor is there any wear at all on the hinge (the

hinge-pin is also lost). It seems right to conclude that the buckle was completely assembled, but not yet attached to a belt, or if it was, that the belt had not actually been worn. The implied former presence of the buckle-tongue, which is quite certain, raises interesting questions about the discovery of the hoard. Though it is possible that the buckle was partly dismantled before burial, it is highly unlikely, especially as it was a brand-new object. The explanation therefore must be that the hinge-pin and the tongue were missed during the recovery of the treasure, and left in the ground.

All the necklace-chains show some wear on the wire which forms the links, but like the wear on the buckle, this is caused by the different elements of the object rubbing against each other, which can be a result of handling as well as of actual use as jewellery. The chains are flexible, and the wire links move against each other every time they are picked up or moved. To some extent, this is also true of the necklace-clasps, though it is difficult to say whether handling alone would create visible wear on these small objects. The surface dents and scratches on the pendants, 28 and 29, and on the amulet pendant, 30, cannot be explained by handling alone, and we must therefore take it that these items had seen some use. The same may be true of the heavy twisted bracelet, 26, but the other three bracelets and two pendants are as pristine as are most of the finger-rings.

Stylistic links within the assemblage and their implications

Before we consider the implications of the new and unused condition of the majority of the Thetford gold items, we should go on to look at the other very striking feature of the group as a whole, namely the complex and intricate pattern of stylistic and design affinities between them. It has already been pointed out that the group as a whole illustrates the preference for elaborate design in jewellery characteristic of the late-Roman period, but the internal parallels between various pieces are far closer than can be accounted for by general fashion trends alone. The traits are summarised in Table 1, and the frequency with which many of them occur, together with the complex cross-linking of different pieces in the hoard, suggest strongly that many of the items must be the products of a single craftsman or workshop.

The use of gold wire applied in patterns (filigree) and small attached globules of gold (a coarse form of granulation) occurs in some form on thirteen of the objects, but the term is given a narrower definition for the purposes of the table, referring only to intricately curved wire combined with granulation. This type of surface treatment, even in the more intricate form, is typical of the period, and we should therefore not attach too much importance to it as an indicator of a single workshop. Some other techniques are far rarer and consequently more significant for our purpose.

For example, three of the rings have the shoulders modelled in the round in the form of animals, dolphins on 5 and 6, and birds on 7. This feature is exceptionally rare, making its occurrence three times in the Thetford hoard particularly striking; furthermore, the dolphins on rings 5 and 6 are virtually identical to each other, and there can be no reasonable doubt that they are the work of the same designer or craftsman. Almost as rare as the zoomorphic shoulders are the chased leaf patterns on rings 2, 3 and 4: a few general parallels can be found for all-over chased ornament on the hoops of rings at this date and later, but there are no really close parallels except between the pieces in the Thetford group itself, where the similarities are such that we must again postulate the work of the same jeweller. The dolphin ring 5 shares with ring 8 another exceptional characteristic, the large flat multicelled bezel intended for setting with several stones to produce a bright polychrome effect. In its turn, ring 8 reminds one of bracelet 27 in its use of gem-settings all around the hoop. Parallels for all these features from outside the Thetford Treasure are either rare or completely absent.

Two of the rings include human faces in their design (9 and 23), yet another idiosyncratic feature which cannot satisfactorily be paralleled. The extent of the internal link within the treasure is more difficult to assess in this case than in those cited above, since the faces on the two rings are stylistically very different from each other, those on ring 9 being 'Celtic' faces set on the shoulders of the ring, and 23 having a Pan-like head used on the bezel.

gold, silver and copper content (see Chapter 9), but there is one group of four objects which cannot be linked stylistically by visual examination, but which are made of very similar metal. These are the buckle, 1, two chains, 32 and 33, and probably also the ring, 23: all have low proportions of gold and high proportions of silver compared with the other material in the Thetford assemblage.

The exact values are as follows:

Cat no.	Gold	Silver	Copper
1	87.1%	10.3%	2.6%
23	90%	9.7%	0.7%
32	89%	10.2%	0.6%
33	89%	10.5%	0.5%

Another internal link which is based on a technical rather than a stylistic judgement concerns the use of a small ring-ended punch in the surface ornamentation of several of the items, namely the rings 2, 4, 7 and 9, and the pendants 28 and 29. Though a tool of this type would probably be in every goldworker's toolkit, microscopic examination and practical experiment strongly suggest that the identical punch was

Table 1 The distribution of the principal decorative features in the jewellery

1 2 3 4 5 6 7 8 9 10 11 12 13 14 15 16 17 18 19 20 21 22 23 24 25 26 27 28 29 30

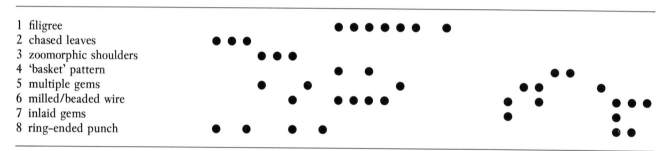

1 filigree
2 chased leaves
3 zoomorphic shoulders
4 'basket' pattern
5 multiple gems
6 milled/beaded wire
7 inlaid gems
8 ring-ended punch

Another major trait which is shared by four of the articles in the treasure is a distinctive treatment of gold strip to produce an effect reminiscent of basket-work. This is found on the hoops of the closely matching rings 10 and 12, and in the identical pair of bracelets, 24 and 25. The gold, in fairly thin sheet form, is grooved longitudinally and then crimped into latitudinal undulations. Only two parallels have been found for this effect, discussed in the section below and in the individual catalogue entries, and the technique must therefore be regarded as an extremely rare one: a link between these rings and bracelets in the treasure is certain. The one stumbling-block is the fact that ring 12 appears to show some signs of wear, all the more surprising as it lacks a setting in the bezel, and there is no trace of adhesive or backing material to suggest that a stone was ever present. Ring 10 and the bracelets are completely new and unused. The metal analyses of this group confirm the stylistic judgement: the quantitative analyses of ring 12 and bracelet 24 are respectively: gold, 96% and 96.1%; silver, 3.7% and 3.1%; copper 0.3% and 0.8%, a correspondence so close that we can state with some confidence that the same batch of gold was used for these pieces.

Several other items in the hoard have similar values for the

used on these articles. While the relationship between rings 2 and 4, for example, is obvious for other reasons, it is important to note that this separate criterion demonstrates the fact that the stylistically unique ring, 9 and the two pendants can be related to them. The slight wear on the pendants again poses a problem of interpretation, but whatever its significance, we must regard this group as the work of one workshop.

It has already been noted that the engraved gems used in the jewellery are in a secondary context. This can be inferred because the styles of engraving are datable (see Chapter 3), because the use of old gems was a common practice in the fourth century, and also, of course, because the signs of reuse are actually visible in some cases. It is obvious that the lion cameo, 39, and the unmounted cornelian, 41, have been trimmed down from their original shape. There are some general points about the gems which are probably best noted at this juncture. The amethysts in rings 2 and 3 are sufficiently alike in several respects (colour, size and style of engraving) to suggest that they might originally have come from the same source, and other settings also fall into related groups, though when they are not decorated with engraved designs, it is more difficult to judge whether they come from older pieces of jewellery or have been used for the first time in the Thetford jewels.

The most obvious relationship is between the two gold-inlaid glass settings which are found in the pendant, 28, and the ring, 21. The technique of making these highly unusual objects is described in Chapter 9. They are almost unparalleled, but the actual design of the gold inlay is very similar in the two pieces, and these facts, taken together with the point that the technique of making them is a skilled and delicate one, must indicate that they emanate from the same source. There is no indication of whether they belong to an earlier period, like the engraved gems, or whether they are contemporary with the Thetford jewellery. Other glass settings, and the plain gems (garnets and emeralds) are likely to be contemporary: the square blue-green gems found in the ring, 7 and the bracelet, 27 (and possibly also ring 17), are similar to each other. So too are the green-and-yellow marbled glass beads incorporated in the necklace, 31, and the three found separately (43–46). Only one bead is missing from necklace 31, so there are more of these matching beads than can be accounted for by the surviving pieces of jewellery. The beads could have been removed from an earlier chain for reuse, but they could also be part of a stock of such beads, new and awaiting use for the first time. In either case, their presence is further confirmation of a group of jewellery which is still in the hands of the manufacturer or trader rather than one which has reached its ultimate customer.

Many of the internal stylistic affinities discussed above are difficult to interpret precisely, but it is impossible to deny that some of the objects fall into design groups that must imply manufacture at the same place and time. It is also noteworthy that the links cut across the different categories of object, and are not found only amongst the rings: a glance at Table 1 will illustrate this. We have touched on the general nature of the assemblage and on the typology and the very fresh condition of the majority of the pieces, but have so far made only oblique references to the possibility that some of the objects are not yet even finished and ready for use. This, obviously, would provide additional support for the theory that the group constitutes a jeweller's stock, but there are problems in dealing with the evidence. Probably the strongest element in the case is the presence of the unmounted cornelian engraved with Venus and Cupid (41). There is no doubt at all that this stone has been removed from an earlier ring or pendant and has been retrimmed to fit a new setting. The upper and lower edges of the rectangular form barely skim the head and feet of the main engraved figure; the engraver of this fine-quality piece would not have designed it thus. It is suggested in Chapter 3 that the gem would originally have been an elongated oval. It seems very unlikely that a separate stone, not only removed from its old setting, but already cut to fit its new one, would be found in any hands except those of a jeweller. In its present state, the gem would be a useless item in any woman's jewellery box, as it cannot be worn or even conveniently used as a seal (a function which, by the fourth century, was subordinate to the purely decorative one for engraved gems).

Necklace 32 also appears to be unfinished. The slight wear which it has suffered is probably simply from handling; its condition is far too good to support the view that it is gold

scrap, intended for remodelling. Instead of being attached to a clasp, the ends of the chain are held by a rough twist of gold wire, as though the necklace awaits the fitting of a suitable fastener. Like the cornelian gem, this necklace cannot be worn in its present state. There are two separate necklace-clasps in the hoard, and it is tempting to theorise that these were intended to provide some choice in the completion of a necklace such as 32.

The incomplete state of the buckle, 1, is due to damage and loss which has occurred since the object was buried, but several of the other items have elements missing which are only probably, not certainly, due to the circumstances in which the treasure was found. The many empty settings for gems are most likely to reflect the difficulty of recovering such minute objects except under controlled professional excavation conditions, but some of them could be further evidence of unfinished articles in the group. While the ring, 8, and the bracelet, 27, retain a few of their settings, and also the sulphur backing in many of the cells, demonstrating that they were probably perfect and complete when buried, rings 11 and 12 seem to have no trace at all of the stone or metal ornament which should be set in the bezel, almost as though they had not yet been placed in position. Skilled examination of the site where the treasure was buried might have enabled us to be more certain on these points, but we can state that there are unfinished pieces in the hoard, though the exact number remains doubtful.

The presence of unfinished objects provides additional support for the theory that the hoard was unsold, and was not a normal domestic assemblage. It is extremely difficult to imagine a personal set of jewellery in which virtually all the pieces had been made at the same time and in the same style by one manufacturer, and which had all remained virtually or completely unused. Certainly a large matching suite of jewellery might be acquired by a rich woman at one time, but a person in a position to buy or be presented with a valuable possession of this sort would almost certainly already own older jewellery. There are great problems in interpreting the extraordinary group of jewellery from Thetford, but any explanation has to be based on the assumption that the material, whatever its ultimate purpose, had not yet entered the retail market for jewellery, let alone been acquired by a customer.

We have dealt with the internal parallels in the treasure which are such a noteworthy and significant feature, but the dating of the group naturally depends upon external parallels, and it is to these that we must now turn our attention. Parallels are cited in the individual catalogue entries under the heading *Discussion*, but we shall select here those which are of particular importance in setting the hoard in its chronological context.

External parallels and dating

The buckle, 1, which is perhaps the most outstanding single item in the whole treasure, belongs to a known group of late-Roman belt-buckles which has been extensively discussed,[2] but examples of the type in gold are extremely rare. Probably the closest parallel for the Thetford buckle is an unprovenanced one with duck- or swan-heads decorating the bow, now in Berlin,[3] but as the piece has no history, it is of little help to us. More relevant is the larger of two gold buckles in the hoard from Ténès, Algeria.[4] The Ténès Treasure appears to have been deposited in the fifth century, and in spite of the widely distant findspots, contains several parallels with the Thetford material. The Ténès buckle, also decorated with ducks' heads, rather than the horses of our piece, is exceptionally large and heavy, but is still recognisably of the same general type as ours.

Bronze zoomorphic belt-buckles of the late-Roman period occur quite frequently in fourth- to fifth-century cemeteries in northern France and occasionally in Britain, but the animal ornament in the bows of these buckles is generally very much more stylised than that of the Thetford buckle or of the other known gold examples. One of these bronze buckles is very similar to ours, however; an incomplete example from Richborough, of which only the bow survives, is decorated with confronted horse-heads quite like those from Thetford.[5] The majority of the bronze buckles bear highly stylised creatures which are of no known species, and combine elements of horse, boar and dolphin in their shape. The late-Roman date of the type as a whole is beyond doubt.

The general style and the Bacchic theme of the Thetford buckle are also echoed in fourth-century silverware; making due allowance for the different scale and technique, the dancing satyr on our buckle is very reminiscent of the satyrs on the Mildenhall great dish. Though at first sight, therefore, the Thetford buckle may seem distinctive almost to the point of uniqueness, it can in fact be placed within a known category of late-Roman artefact. It is interesting to speculate what other items may have been intended to form a set with the buckle: the metal embellishments on belts of this period were not usually confined to the buckle loop and plate alone, but included a decorative strap-end and frequently additional plaques and mounts. The large Ténès buckle was accompanied by matching items of this kind, but there is no evidence that such pieces formed part of the Thetford hoard. The buckle was presumably buried as a single gold object, not yet attached to a belt, and certainly not used.

Amongst the rings in the treasure, there are several highly distinctive types which we have to regard as designs exclusive to the 'Thetford jeweller', and for which true parallels from other sites are absent. The closely related group, 2, 3 and 4, for example, can be paralleled only in the most general terms. Their most striking feature is the pattern of leaves chased on the hoop, and no ring has been found which has a similar chased design. There are examples of other rings with chased or engraved decoration covering the hoop, notably three very similar rings with an engraved vine-scroll and birds, one of which is from Italy, and two from Italian collections, though unprovenanced;[6] they are dated to the sixth century AD, though the evidence is not conclusive. The style is bolder than the leaf-pattern on our rings, and may be engraved rather than chased.[7]

Rings 5 and 6, with their stylised dolphin shoulders, are again more like each other than they are like any ring from outside the Thetford Treasure. Taking them together with 7, its shoulders in the form of birds, it is possible to cite only one or two parallels, of which the most important is a ring in the British Museum collections with rabbits modelled on the shoulders and the bezel set with a coin of Marcian (AD 450–7).[8] Though the parallel is not a very close one, this ring is important because of the *terminus post quem* provided by the coin setting, and because it is a provenanced piece, found in the Seine at Rouen. It is also related to Thetford in that the animals which form the shoulders are a hollow shell of gold, like our rings 2 and 3. The dolphins of rings 5 and 6 provide in themselves further chronological evidence. They are strange beasts, with long beak-like jaws and a bristling crest like a boar. Stylistically, they are very similar indeed to the boar-crested dolphins modelled on the bows of many of the zoomorphic late-Roman bronze buckles which we have already mentioned above.

Rings 8 and 9, the first with a large multi-gem bezel like that of 5, are further examples of the 'Thetford jeweller's' distinctive style. Numerous parallels could be quoted for the 'Celtic' characteristics of the faces on the shoulders of ring 9, but it is doubtful whether this would serve any purpose. The features conventionally regarded as Celtic, and clearly displayed in these tiny reliefs, are the elliptical eyes, the up-swept hair and the straight, slit mouths: if they are genuinely indicative of some Celtic artistic element, then they should strengthen the case for a British or Gaulish origin for the jewellery, but that is all.

Not all the rings are difficult to parallel, however; 10 and 12 have already been mentioned in connection with their important internal relationships within the hoard, but they, together with 11 and 14, and to some extent all the other rings which are decorated with applied wire and/or tiny globules of gold, i.e. 13, 15, 16 and 17, can be compared with many late-Roman rings from the northern provinces with more or less intricate filigree decoration. The closest parallel for 10 is a fourth-century ring from Richborough[9] which shares every feature except the 'basket' pattern with ours. The rings from New Grange in Ireland are also important parallels, because they are associated with bracelets of the same type as Thetford 26, and therefore confirm the contemporaneity of this type of bracelet with late rings decorated with spiral volutes in filigree work.[10] Filigree in spirals and other fancy patterns, such as a plaited effect, is to be found on several rings which form part of coin hoards, and in all cases, these hoards belong to the late-fourth or early fifth century AD. Filigree volutes, plaited pattern, and a roped surround to the bezel occur on two rings found at Terling, Essex, associated with gold and silver coins (*solidi* and *siliquae*) up to Honorius (AD 394–423).[11] The plaited pattern in the hoop is seen in its most typical form on 15, and this ring is in every respect an excellent parallel to the square-bezelled ring from the Canterbury Treasure, dated to the end of the fourth century or the beginning of the fifth.[12] Yet another ring of similar type, though this time in silver, was found in a coin hoard from Whorlton, Yorkshire, containing coins up to Honorius,[13] and the Bentley Priory coin hoard, once more with a date-range culminating in the same emperor, also included a ring with filigree volutes.[14]

No. 16 stands out as the one ring, and probably the one item of jewellery altogether in the Thetford Treasure, which was almost certainly intended for a man's use. It is much larger internally than any of the other rings.

The style is very plain, applied decoration being confined to a row of gold globules at each side of the bezel; yet again, a close parallel can be found in a coin hoard deposited in Britain in the fifth century. A ring of exactly the same form is associated with a hoard of *siliquae* ranging in date from Constantius II to Honorius found at Tuddenham in Suffolk.[15]

The remaining rings vary in style from extremely basic and simple ones, such as **19** and **20**, to the unusual and decorative **23**, but none of them can be paralleled in such a way as to cast further light on date and origin. But as we have seen above, a number of the rings in the impressive group of twenty-two from Thetford can be compared closely with examples from other sites in Britain, and wherever these parallels occur in dated contexts or associations, the date-range is consistently in the late-fourth to early fifth century. There is no ring in the Thetford Treasure which belongs to a known type current before the fourth century.

The same cannot be said for the bracelets. There is only one parallel known to us for the superb matching pair of bracelets, **24** and **25**. The 'basket' pattern which is shared by **24** and **25** and by the rings **10** and **12**, appears on a pair of bracelets from a hoard found in the 1840s in Lyon.[16] This hoard is substantially earlier than the Thetford Treasure, apparently belonging to the early third century, and therefore no direct connection can be proposed. In view of the occasional hints of Gaulish connections in the treasure as a whole, it is perhaps tempting to see the parallel as geographically significant, and to speculate on the Lyon area as a possible source for the jewellery. A technique as distinctive as the 'basket' pattern could have been passed down within a local jewellery tradition, and Lyon, as a mint and the most important town in Roman France would surely have supported a local market in expensive jewellery. There is one other parallel for the 'basket' pattern, a double ring said to be from Amrit in Syria.[17] There is no dating evidence for it, but its design suggests that it is nearer in date to the Thetford Treasure than to the third-century Lyon hoard.

The bracelet, **26**, is a representative of a well-known Roman type, formed of thick wire or rod twisted together and provided with a stud and loop fastening. We have already mentioned the association in the New Grange find of two bracelets of this kind with rings which have spiral filigree on the shoulders.[18] Another important occurrence of the type is in the Ténès Treasure, which has two twisted bracelets, one complete and one fragmentary.[19] Further unprovenanced examples are known in gold, at least two allegedly from Britain,[20] and the type also occurs in bronze. Bronze specimens are known from graves in a late-Roman cemetery in Hungary,[21] and with the other finds coming from sites as far apart as Ireland and Algeria demonstrate that this type of bracelet was very widespread in its distribution. The Thetford bracelet is the largest and heaviest of all the known examples.

The fourth bracelet, **27**, is a hoop consisting entirely of settings for stones, alternately circular and lozenge-shaped. The latter cells contained blue-green glass. None of the stones in the circular cells has survived, but it can be assumed that they were of a contrasting colour, perhaps red. The only satisfactory parallel for this bracelet is yet once more from the Ténès Treasure.[22] It is set with garnets and emeralds, but all the cells are circular, and they are placed alternately on either side of an undulating gold wire. Though this bracelet is not a perfect parallel, its general appearance is fairly close to our **27**, and it adds additional weight to the many general similarities between these two late-Roman hoards.

With the pendants and chains, we move into a class of jewellery which on the whole presents greater dating problems than do the rings and bracelets. Some of the styles and techniques used in their manufacture had an extremely long currency in antiquity, and parallels can range in date from Hellenistic to Byzantine or even more widely. Inevitably, therefore, we find some good parallels in hoards or other contexts which are not very close chronologically to the late fourth-century range we are proposing for Thetford.

The two large pendants in the form of a stylised club of Hercules, **28** and **29**, are immediately reminiscent of ear-rings of this form which are known from at least the later first century AD. The motif was a surprisingly common and popular one, widespread in the Roman Empire, with examples known from Britain, France, the Rhineland, Romania and no doubt other areas, including the Mediterranean provinces: there are more than a dozen unprovenanced pendants of this form in the British Museum collections, some of which are likely to be from the latter area. The British examples are from the Walbrook, Birdoswald and Ashtead, Surrey.[23] Most of the complete pendants in this form are ear-rings, furnished with simple wire hooks. The two Thetford pendants, which are not a matching pair, could also have had ear-ring fittings, but it seems more likely that they were separate necklace pendants. They are considerably larger and heavier than most of the ear-rings of this shape, which are usually made of quite thin sheet gold. The fact that they are not a pair also supports the theory that they are necklace pendants. Of the many parallels, there are two which are, like ours, unusually large: one was in the Beaurains Treasure, and is now unfortunately lost,[24] and another, described as an amulet-pendant, is from a Romanian hoard.[25] We know of no example which is positively dated by association later than the ear-ring from a late third-century woman's grave in Bonn,[26] but in view of the popularity and persistence of the type, its continuing presence in the fourth century is no surprise. Many of the slighter, earlier examples worn as ear-rings have plain glass settings in the base; the fine cabochon garnet of **29** and the exceptional gold-inlaid glass setting of **28** are far more magnificent.

The amulet-pendant, **30**, a hexagonal-sectioned tube made to be hung horizontally, is a type which is found over an even longer period and broader geographical range than the club-of-Hercules pendants: the span is from Middle Kingdom Egypt at one extreme to medieval Persia at the other, and Jewish amulets of similar type continue in use into the post-medieval period.[27] The Ténès Treasure includes two examples, one of which, like ours, was found to be filled with sulphur.[28] There are some variations in form: some, including the larger Ténès piece, have flared and decorated end-plates, but it is doubtful whether there is any chronological significance in this. The pendants were intended to be apotropaic, and were designed as containers for some object or substance which had magical properties. Some have been found to contain slips of gold with gnostic inscriptions. The sulphur, too, must have been credited with magical qualities, perhaps linked with the physical properties of the material, with its connection with volcanoes, or the medicinal and healing properties of sulphurous waters: Pliny remarks on the use of sulphur to purify by fumigation.[29] It follows that the undoubtedly practical use of sulphur as an adhesive and filling in many of the other Thetford items is probably only part of the reason for its presence. Its use may be dual-purpose, magical and utilitarian, and we should note the siting of the oracle of Faunus in a region of sulphur springs, discussed in Chapter 7.

The chain necklaces, 31, 32, 33 and 35/36 likewise belong to a very long-lived type. Greek and Hellenistic chains are frequently formed of 'plaited' or loop-in-loop gold cord, and are often astonishingly fine and delicate. The technique was also familiar to ancient Egyptian goldsmiths; the method of manufacture is clearly described and illustrated in an article by Reynold Higgins.[30] Necklaces such as those in the Thetford group were probably intended to be worn with pendants, though we do not have any evidence to enable use to match pendants and chains to each other in the treasure. The probably incomplete state of 32 has already been commented upon, but the other chains are all finished. Necklace 31 would not have required a pendant; it is decorated with green beads, one an emerald, three imitation emeralds in green-and-yellow glass, and one missing. This type of necklace is so common throughout the Empire that there is little purpose in dicussing parallels here. We are unable to cite one from a dated late fourth-century group.

Chains 31–33 have very plain clasps, but 35/36 is distinguished by a handsome snake-head fastener. The clasp and chain were separate when found, but there is no doubt that they belong together, the ends of the chain fitting neatly into the collars of the clasp, and the holes for the small gold pins which held them in place lining up perfectly. The best parallel for this necklace is an unprovenanced one, which is moreover dated (probably on little or no evidence) far earlier than ours.[31] Snakes as decorative motifs in rings, bracelets and other items of jewellery have been common from antiquity to the present day, and there is nothing intrinsically datable about the clasp of this chain. A stylistic judgement of the modelling of the snake-heads is probably less helpful than the likelihood of a fourth-century date based simply on the presence of the object in the Thetford assemblage, but it may be worth noting that the simple and stylised form of the snakes in this fastener is very different from the highly detailed and realistic treatment of the subject in many Roman pieces of the first and second centuries.

While the loop-in-loop gold cord necklaces are virtually undatable because they are so common, necklace 34 is difficult to place because it is extremely unusual. There is no close parallel for the small biconical interlocking gold beads; the only objects which bear some resemblance to them are the larger gold 'beads' from the third-century hoard found at Wincle, Cheshire.[32] It seems very likely that the major factor in the rarity of necklaces like 34 is simply that of survival potential. Even in the Thetford Treasure, and allowing for the fact that these gold beads were said to have been found in the shale box, one must presume that only a proportion of the full number was recovered, since there are too few to complete

a necklace unless numerous other beads (of gold, emerald or glass) were incorporated. Once the thread of organic material on which the beads were strung had broken or decayed, the individual gold beads, tiny and fragile, would have been very easily scattered and lost. It is unlikely that many necklaces of this type could have been found if buried in hoards. The necklace as a whole takes its date from the parallels for the three larger beads, which are quite closely related to examples found in graves of the late fourth and early fifth century in Belgium.

The two separate necklace-clasps, 37 and 38, are of importance mainly for their possible implications about the unfinished state of some pieces in the treasure. There are, however, some noteworthy parallels for the distinctive decoration of 37, which consists of a narrow gold ribbon applied so as to form a raised zig-zag line. This technique is used in the decoration of some amulet cases of the same general type as our 30, notably those from the fourth-century hoard from Planche,[33] and some of the gold tubes or collars used as spacers in the multi-medallion necklaces like those from Beaurains, Naix and L'Houmeau.[34] A third- to fourth-century Gaulish background seems therefore to be indicated for this design feature, a conclusion which fits well with much of the other evidence.

The final items in the Thetford assemblage of jewellery are three gem pendants, 39, 40 and 41, two newly mounted in gold frames with suspension rings, the other removed from its previous setting and trimmed down ready for remounting in the same way. In the case of the blue and grey onyx with a cameo lion, the gold frame is a completely plain one: the chalcedony engraved with Diana and a hound is a little more elaborate, but its frame merely has a roped effect similar to the flanges surrounding the bezels of our rings 10, 12, 13 and 15. This design occurs in the Beaurains Treasure.[35] The intricate lobed, toothed or petalled ornaments found in the mounts of some late-Roman medallion or gem pendants do not occur at Thetford.

In summary, the search for external parallels for the Thetford jewellery is in some ways a frustrating one. On the one hand, there are unique types totally unparalleled elsewhere, and on the other, there are some types of Roman jewellery so standard that they can be matched in contexts of widely varying dates. There are a few types, however, most notably the rings with filigree decoration, which are not only in typically late-antique taste (a judgement which applies just as strongly to many of the unique pieces), but which can be matched in dated contexts. These contexts are all of the late fourth to early fifth centuries, and most are in Britain. We can feel confident that a ring such as 12 or 15 must belong to the second half, and more probably the last quarter, of the fourth century. The internal workshop links within the treasure carry the other pieces along with this date. There is a dearth of well-dated groups of jewellery of this period, but those which do exist, above all the Ténès Treasure, provide very satisfactory parallels for our assemblage.

The evidence for the place of manufacture is practically non-existent, and the pointers towards Gaul are tenuous in the extreme. Many of the parallels are from Britain, though we cannot say whether these pieces originated in Britain itself or in an adjacent province such as Gaul. It seems reasonable to assume that the Thetford jewellery, like the silver objects in the treasure, are from the northern, Celtic provinces. Whether the gold objects were made in the same area as the silver depends on how closely associated one believes the two groups to have been before burial, a matter of interpretation which is examined elsewhere.

Weights

It remains to discuss one more general subject, and then to bring together the main points which have been covered in this survey of the jewellery. The individual weights of all the objects have been recorded in the catalogue descriptions, and the study of the spoons (see Chapter 5) indicates that it is worthwhile to study these in some detail, even though there is as yet too little evidence to support any firm conclusions. Above all, the precise weight of the Roman pound is a matter of debate, which lends a certain flexibility, if not unreality, to all arguments about the weights of gold and silver objects at that period. In the case of the jewellery from Thetford, it must be stressed that many of the pieces contain settings in the form of glass or gems, and many, as we have noted, also contain sulphur in small quantities. Precise weights *of metal* are therefore impossible to record in many cases; the values noted include the settings (see Table 2).

With all these provisos in mind, we may nevertheless draw attention to one or two points which, though they may prove little in the present state of knowledge, should still provide food for thought and useful basic data for future research. The total surviving weight of the gold objects from the hoard, expressed in terms of contemporary gold coinage and Roman pounds, enables us to gain some idea of the actual wealth enshrined in the gold part of the hoard. The problems of different theories and standards of Roman pounds is discussed in connection with the silver in Chapter 5, but when considering the total weight, with all the inaccuracies due to incompleteness and non-metallic components, this problem can be ignored. More precise and meaningful measurements can be made of the few items in the group which are complete, perfect, and made of gold alone. Other calculations can be made, which may or may not be significant: the important fact is that weights should be recorded wherever possible so that this branch of study can become more broadly based than it is at present.

If we add together the weights of the gold objects from Thetford complete with their settings, sulphur, etc., but exclude the two pendants, **39** and **40**, in which the gold would be a relatively small proportion of the total weight, we have a total of just under 505 g (504.9, but tenths of a gram are not significant in this approximate type of calculation). Taking the assumed Constantinian standard of a 4.45 g *solidus* (= 320.4 g to the pound), this represents 113–114 *solidi*, or about 1½ Roman pounds. Discussions of the purchasing power of currency in antiquity are necessarily complex,[36] but we might quote the estimate that, in the fourth century, a year's ration allowance for a soldier was only four to five *solidi*. Comparison with coin hoards of this period in Britain is also of interest: there are inadequate records of a very large

hoard of '450 to 600 *solidi*' from Cleeve Prior, Worcestershire, but otherwise, hoards such as Water Newton, with 30, and Corbridge with 48 *solidi* rank as large.[37] In purely monetary terms, therefore, the gold in the Thetford Treasure is worth nearly four times as much as that in the 1974 Water Newton coin hoard. The wealth represented by these rings, necklaces and bracelets is very considerable indeed.

The points made in the preceding paragraph are very general. If we turn to the objects in the hoard which are suitable for more precise weighing, conclusions emerge which are of interest on a more detailed level. Three of the Thetford bracelets are perfect, complete, and made only of metal, and therefore lend themselves to this approach; they are the matching pair, **24** and **25**, and the heavy twisted bracelet, **26**. In all cases, their weights when related to Roman ounces and pounds do appear to be meaningful. The pair of 'basket' pattern bracelets, **24** and **25**, weight 26.8 and 25.9 g respectively. They are intended to be a matching pair, and the 0.9 g difference may well be an indication of the degree of accuracy in weighing which was considered acceptable or necessary in the manufacture of fine jewellery at this period, at least when producing a perfect pair of ornaments. These weights are surely intended to represent a Roman ounce, a twelfth of a Roman pound, for each bracelet. The weights of the Thetford duck-handled spoons, clustering around a standard of 26–27 g, support this (see Chapter 5), and further confirmation comes from the Ténès Treasure: the twisted bracelet and the pierced, openwork bracelet in that group weigh respectively 27.8 and 26.2 g.[38] Our other complete bracelet, **26**, weighs 108.1 g; divided by four, this would give us a 27 g ounce (27.025). These values cannot be fortuitous.

A rather more contentious calculation may be made with the group of four items (**1**, **23**, **32** and **33**) which were picked out in a section above as being related by their metal analyses, with a lower gold and higher silver content than the other material. Bearing in mind that the buckle lacks its tongue, the

Table 2 The weights, in g, of the jewellery

Cat. No		Cat. No	
1	39.8	21	2.3
2	15.5	22	2.2
3	8.8	23	2.8
4	6.0	24	26.8
5	11.3	25	25.9
6	6.8	26	108.1
7	8.4	27	17.8
8	8.6	28	10.5
9	9.2	29	10.6
10	6.6	30	13.3
11	6.5	31	18.4
12	4.9	32	19.5
13	8.7	33	17.2
14	6.4	34	9.8
15	7.4	35/36	28.6
16	19.7	37	4.4
17	2.6	38	3.8
18	2.0	39	3.9
19	2.5	40	3.3
20	1.2		

combined weights of these articles add up to 79.3 g of this distinctive mix of gold. This is close to three ounces, or a quarter of a pound, and could possibly be significant.

Some further general observations are that several of the rings (17–19, 21–23) weigh an average of 2.2 g, while another group clusters around a value of 6.5 g, about a quarter of an ounce; these are 6, 10, 11 and 14. Rings 2, 3 and 4, with their close stylistic affinities, weigh together a total of 30.3 g including settings; this could hint at an ounce of metal originally being used for the group. However, it would be most unwise to attach too much significance to such figures until we know far more about this aspect of ancient jewellery manufacture. The weights may be significant in some cases, and perhaps future carefully recorded hoards may provide evidence which will take us further.

For ease of reference, the weights of the individual objects are listed in Table 2.

Conclusions

The jewellery component of the Thetford Treasure is unparalleled as a group. It is outstanding in terms of sheer size: two hoards which we have frequently mentioned as comparisons are those of Ténès and Beaurains, and the former contains seventeen gold objects, the latter about twenty-five, compared with forty from Thetford (though the total weight of gold in the Ténès Treasure is greater — just over two Roman pounds; several of the pieces are exceptionally large and heavy).[39] The group of twenty-two rings is by far the largest from a late-Roman hoard. More important than the size of the assemblage, though, is that the evidence proves beyond reasonable doubt that it represents the work of one atelier. In this it appears to be unique so far amongst hoards of Roman jewellery. The evidence for a date late in the fourth century is secure.

The arguments against the Thetford jewellery being a personal collection have already been stated. The range of style and date, and above all the state of wear of the objects would certainly be far more variable in a personal collection. It is far more difficult to assess what the group does represent. If the material had not yet been sold to the ultimate customers, it must still have been in the hands of the manufacturer or of a middleman, a merchant. If the objects were made in another province, for what purpose were they brought to Britain?

One possible explanation is that the jewellery was associated with the spoons before the immediate occasion of burial for safety, and was thus in some way connected with the Faunus cult which is indicated by the inscriptions on the silver. This does not necessarily imply that the gold objects were votive in the strict sense of the word. Rings and other jewellery, being items of high intrinsic value, are indeed found as votive offerings to deities (the New Grange jewellery may well be a case in point), but in the case of the Thetford Treasure as a whole, the spoons appear to be practical objects to be used during the rituals of worship, precisely as Christian church plate is used, rather than gifts to the god. Before we consider whether or not it is possible to envisage some such role for the jewellery, it is necessary to review any evidence which would support or undermine the theory that the jewellery and the spoons are related.

There is no specific reference to Faunus in the form of an inscription on any item of jewellery. It is not easy to judge what purely pictorial references might be relevant, as the visual iconography specifically referring to Faunus is so scarce. But if we accept, as argued in Chapter 7, that by the fourth century the worship of Faunus was an aspect of the more general Bacchic cult which constituted the main antithesis to Christianity, and that Faunus himself was not sharply distinguished from other deities such as Pan and Silvanus, the picture may become a little clearer.

The two possibly specific Faunus references in the jewellery are to be found in rings 7 and 23: the birds supporting a vase as the bezel of the first can convincingly be identified as woodpeckers; the Latin name for the woodpecker is *picus*, and some (not all) versions of the pedigree of Faunus name his father as Picus.[40] Ring 23 is decorated on the bezel with a face modelled in relief which has long, goat-like features and small horns. This may be Pan, or even Faunus himself, since the distinction is far from clear.

More general Bacchic themes also occur, and it is worth drawing attention to the Bacchic elements on the two parcel-gilt spoons, 50 and 66; the panther on the latter is of course the Bacchic animal *par excellence*, the constant companion of the god himself, but the Triton also has Bacchic connections, as can be seen in the marine thiasos which forms one frieze of the Mildenhall great dish.[41] Returning to the jewellery, the satyr on the buckle is a purely Bacchic figure, and may also be compared with figures on the Mildenhall dish. Other animals which occur in the jewellery, dolphins and snakes, can certainly be connected with Bacchic imagery, but they are far too widespread as decorative motifs in Roman art for us to argue that they have been selected here with any religious purpose. They are likely to be purely decorative.

The selection of engraved gems produces the following list of deities: Cupid riding a lion, Mercury, the Tyche of Antioch, Mars, Diana, Venus and Cupid, and the deity called Iao or Abrasax. Again, it is possible to quote Bacchic significance for some of these, but this would probably be misusing the evidence. The selection of the gems is far more likely to have been made primarily on the basis of their colour and quality, if not on that of simple availability, rather than the subject-matter of the decoration. The Abrasax gem is probably an exception, as it is certainly amuletic in itself. What is stressed is the overall non-Christian nature of the group.

Nevertheless, we are left with at least some evidence that there could be a connection between the gold objects and the Faunus cult of the spoons. If this is so, we have to consider what function the jewellery might have had in a pagan cult of this kind. It is extremely difficult to see how it could have been used in any ritual function without exhibiting precisely the same signs of use and wear as a private set of jewellery, signs which we have established are absent. It is also difficult to envisage a cult image of a deity like Faunus being decked out with rings, necklaces and bracelets. This leaves us with the obvious explanation that the jewellery is votive, and was presented to the shrine of the cult simply as a valuable gift from a worshipper. But once more, the very qualities which make it highly unlikely that the Thetford jewellery was a personal set also make it at the very least unusual as a votive one:

because we have inferred that the material was still in the hands of a manufacturer or merchant, the group as a whole must be a single gift from one person, a votive offering of rare magnificence.

Yet another explanation is that our jewellery merchant was personally connected with the Bacchic cult, and that he therefore favoured designs which were appropriate to this religious affiliation, but that the spoons and the gold were not directly linked in themselves. Other suggestions, considered in our final chapter, are that the jewellery was a special order executed for somebody involved in the cult, but not yet completed, or that the juxtaposition of these two groups, the spoons and the jewels, is fortuitous, and the apparent Faunus references in the latter are not significant.

We can only place on record what evidence we have, regretting that the circumstances of discovery have further clouded an already mysterious matter. In spite of the difficulties of interpretation, there are many positive results from the study of the jewellery so far. In particular, the recognition of a specific atelier with a highly distinctive style in the design of rings, at least, is an important step forward in the study of late-Roman jewellery, and will provide a basis for the assessment of future discoveries of jewellery of this date. Scholars in the future may well be able to assign the Thetford jewellery to a definite place of origin and to an even more precise date than we can do at present.[42]

NOTES

1. See Henig 1981 for a useful discussion of the stylistic developments in jewellery from the third century AD.
2. Heurgon 1958, 31–35; Hawkes and Dunning 1961; Bullinger 1969; Clarke 1979, 264–91.
3. Greifenhagen 1975, Abb. 34, 13.
4. Heurgon 1958, pl. 3, 1.
5. Bushe-Fox 1949, pl. XXXII, 69.
6. Peroni 1967, no. 75, from Torriano; Battke 1953, no. 45, said to be from a Roman collection; Dalton 1901, no. 44, from the Castellani collection.
7. The distinction between chasing, in which a groove is made in the gold without removing any metal, and engraving, in which the tool cuts away some of the gold, is described and illustrated in Ward 1981, 12, fig. 3.
8. Dalton 1901, no. 210.
9. Bushe-Fox 1949, pl. XXV, no. 93; the ring is also illustrated in Catalogue 1976, no. 434.
10. Kent and Painter 1977, nos 231 and 232.
11. Arch. Journ 3 (1841), 162–3.
12. Painter 1965; the ring is his no. 15.
13. Burnett and Johns 1979, no. 9.
14. Gough 1789, vol. 1, pl. II (facing p. lxxii), vol. II, 30–31.
15. Henig 1978, no. 581.
16. Comarmond 1844, nos 3 and 4.
17. Catalogue 1911, no. 2105.
18. Kent and Painter 1977, nos 234 and 235.
19. Heurgon 1958, pl. v, 3 and 4.
20. Two examples in the British Museum which were acquired with the Payne Knight bequest in 1824 are said to be from Suffolk.
21. Sági 1981, e.g. Grave 97.
22. Heurgon 1958, pl. v, 2.
23. Charlesworth 1977.
24. Bastien and Metzger 1977, B.20.
25. Simion 1977, pl. x, 7.
26. Haberey 1960.
27. We are indebted to Dr Henig for drawing attention to the latest types.
28. Heurgon 1958, pl. v, 5 and 6; Heurgon also has a general discussion of the type, pp. 57–9.
29. Pliny, Nat. Hist. 35, 174–7.
30. Higgins 1976, 56–9.
31. Greifenhagen 1970, Taf. 26, 5; the date given is 1st century BC to 1st AD.
32. Johns et al. 1980, fig. 4.
33. Poncet 1889.
34. Bastien and Metzger 1977, B.23 and pl. B; Flouret, Nicolini and Metzger 1981, 93, 3.
35. Bastien and Metzger 1977, B.17.
36. Evidence for the costs of various items in solidi etc. is discussed in Kent and Painter 1977, 18 and 160.
37. For details of these hoards, see Carson 1976 and Carson 1979 (Water Newton), and also Chapter 9.
38. Heurgon 1958, 47–8.
39. The total weight of gold in the Ténès Treasure comes to 681.6 g or the equivalent of about 153 solidi: the large buckle alone weighs 152.7 g.
40. Virgil, Aeneid 7, 48.
41. Painter 1977a, pl. I.
42. For further discussion of the date of the hoard, cf. Chapter 10.

3

The Gemstones

by Martin Henig

The engraved gemstones are very probably the earliest objects in the treasure, for although some signet-stones were still cut in late antiquity for important officials and especially the Imperial Court, they are exceptionally rare in archaeological contexts.[1] The true situation in the late-Roman period is given by the non-appearance of signet-rings in the Ténès Treasure and the reuse of second- or early third-century gems in the Beaurains Treasure and, as will be shown, at Thetford.[2] The only reasonably common fourth- and fifth-century intaglio rings in antiquity are entirely of metal and have raised rectangular, circular or polygonal bezels.[3] The reason for this apparently drastic shift in fashion and custom lies back in the second century and stems from an increasing interest in colour and display at the expense of intricacy of carving. The great number of coloured stones and pastes of all sorts set against great expanses of gold at Thetford marks an accentuation of the aesthetic first observed in, for instance, the Severan Treasure from Lyon.[4] It is a far cry from the beautifully cut gems in simple gold rings from the House of the Menander at Pompeii, dating from the early Principate.[5]

Direct evidence of the reuse of the gems is shown by the manner in which a number of them are now set. The cameo, **39**, has been cut away on the right side thus removing part of the tail and rear left leg of the lion. This shaving down is not at all necessary for the present pendant-setting and must belong to an earlier one. The whip carried by the Cupid on one of the large amethysts (**2**) comes up too close to the bezel for it to register properly in an impression. The chip on the front face of the other amethyst showing Mercury (**3**) seems to belong to a time prior to the manufacture of the rings, for the goldwork is not damaged at this point. The dark chalcedony depicting Antioch-on-the-Orontes (**4**), apart from the fact that this is certainly an early Imperial gem, is too small to fit the bezel without an over-wide frame or collet around it; it is loose in its settings, implying that some adhesive — now gone — had to be used to hold it in place. The bloodstone, **13**, showing the Anguipede (Abrasax), though later in date, is also loose in its setting. Well-made rings do not require such secondary adhesive. The use of pendant-settings for intaglios implies that they are not being used as functional seal-stones but as jewels. The chalcedony showing Diana Venatrix (**40**) is surrounded by a pendant-setting used, incidentally, for two intaglios at Beaurains, one of them set sideways.[6] Signs of wear on some of the gems, contrasting with the pristine condition of the goldwork are also significant evidence, but the key object here is the one gem which is not set in a ring or pendant, the cornelian intaglio portraying Venus Victrix and Cupid (**41**). It is now virtually rectangular with slightly bowed sides, but whereas the longer edges display the same high pol-

ish as the engraved face and the underside, the top and bottom have been ground down, so that Venus's head now touches the very edge of the gem. This can hardly have been the designer's intention in any case, for the devices of Roman gems usually stand in the centre of the field, and the present very narrow bridge between the crown of the head and the edge is both a point of weakness and an obstacle in mounting the gem as a signet in a satisfactory manner. Surely the gem was originally oval like most Roman gems — even an elongated oval as favoured in Severan times — before the fourth-century *anularius* wished to change the shape. We may note in passing that amongst the uncarved gems in the Thetford Treasure there are others of rectangular form.

As implied, these gems were selected for brilliance or colour — the cut gems, amethyst, chalcedony, cornelian, onyx, bloodstone, nicolo are found with unengraved amethyst, emerald, garnet and coloured glass. So, too, at Beaurains, aquamarine, amethyst, topaz and green glass, etc. were surely no less valued than the cut sardonyx, amethyst, onyx and nicolo, and were probably chosen for their colour. Heliodorus wrote a magnificent passage on the colouristic qualities of amethyst in the early third century AD.[7]

The subjects and the styles of cutting employed for the gems help to establish an origin and possible date for the stones to have been assembled. The chalcedony, **4**, is certainly the earliest gem in the group, neatly cut on the small, convex face in the Hellenistic tradition which the Dutch scholar Dr Marianne Maaskant-Kleibrink designates as the 'wheel style'; it probably dates from the earlier first century AD.[8] The delicate, careful cutting of the Thetford gem is well paralleled by that of a plasma intaglio in the British Museum, also showing the Tyche of Antioch from the side, with a small Nike holding a wreath behind her.[9] The Thetford gem bears a Greek inscription ΓΝΔ (as read in impression) which, coupled with the particular relevance of the type to the Levantine/Syrian city, makes an eastern origin very likely.

The heliotrope, **13**, is similarly cut with an Oriental device; here the motif on the obverse is a figure with the head of a cock, a tunic, and snaky legs. He brandishes a whip and holds a shield on which is inscribed the name ΙΑΩ (Iao), the Hellenised form of the name of the Hebrew God. The reverse is inscribed AB/PACA/ΣCAB/AΩΘ (Abrasax Sabaoth). Amulets showing the Anguipede have been found in Britain at Silchester and also in the third-century hoard from Aesica where the intaglio was likewise set in a ring.[10] Mrs Mary Whiting writes that:

Sabaoth is more often invoked in amulets with Iao.[11] Apart from regular use in Greek Magical Papyri, the names of these magical deities also occur in the more theological gnostic writings.[12] Sabaoth, for example, is given a specific role as guide for the ascending soul in the so-called 'Untitled Writings',[13] and in this capacity occupies a similar position for the benefit of man as the figure of the anguipede Abrasax on the obverse of this amulet: the solar, cock-headed creature with its chthonic, serpentine legs straddles the celestial and terrestrial worlds while the mediator Sabaoth offers access to the heavenly spheres for earth-bound man.

It may be added that the name *Abrasax* has an isopsephic value, the letters rendered numerically adding up to 365, the number of days in the solar year ($\alpha = 1$; $\beta = 2$; $\rho = 100$; $\alpha = 1$; $\sigma = 200$; $\alpha = 1$; $\xi = 60$) — and it thus expressed infinity and eternity.

The coarser style of cutting on our gem is associated with an interest in pattern and texture, for instance in the use of parallel grooves on the legs, and this is a feature of late second and early third century glyptics.[15] A similar 'patterned' treatment is to be seen on the amethysts, 2 and 3; these are large gems and the bold cuttings of the devices at first recalls the glyptic of Augustan times; but further examination reveals that the cutting is much debased and simplified. Both have a rich colour; perhaps they have the same (?eastern) source.

On 2, Cupid rides a leaping lion. The motif of Cupid on a lion which belongs to the repertory of the Bacchic thiasos is to be seen on Protarchos's splendid cameo of the first century BC,[17] where the lion is shown walking sedately, but leaping lions are known on gems as well, including one on an amethyst intaglio from Richborough set in a gold ring of first-century AD form.[18] On the Thetford gem, the use of rather coarse and disorganised grooves on the mane and the absence of detailing on the body of the Cupid recall such pieces as the Cybele and lion in the Hague, dated to the end of the second or the third century AD.[19]

The seated Mercury, 3, is a common type, especially on amethyst — perhaps because the god was connected with feasting and his representation on a stone which was a specific against inebriation might prevent hangovers.[20] For the same reason, Bacchus and Methe often appear on amethysts. Again the grooving is coarse, but the gem-cutter has obtained a pleasing patterned effect in the striations of the hair and the ovoid wheel-cuts comprising the rock. The head is fairly large and attached to the shoulders by a long rather tubular neck, an idiosyncrasy also seen on a plasma intaglio from Silchester showing Caracalla (wearing the corn-measure of Serapis) in the persona of the *Genius Populi Romani*.[21] The elongation of this stone is, as we have said, a third-century feature probably consequent on the use of rings with expanded shoulders and long flat bezels. It is of some interest that Dr Marie-Louise Vollenweider assigned the Beaurains amethyst showing a sphinx attacking a man to the Severan age.[22] It is an elongated stone and the heads of both the warrior and the sphinx which it portrays are not unlike the head of Mercury. The body modelling is altogether softer, however, and recalls that of the unset cornelian, 41.

The composition of this gem is a fine one. Venus holds a transverse spear and leans upon a shield. In one hand she holds a sword. In front of her is a Cupid holding a helmet.

The theme is found on early Imperial gems and pastes,[23] but the misunderstood spear twice repeated, the scarcely understood shield and the coarsely executed figure of Cupid (which recalls the lion-riding Cupid of 2) belong with the degeneration of glyptic art in the early third century. The body of Venus is boldly and deeply cut but the rather flabby and soft treatment of the flesh goes with that of the Beaurains amethyst.[24] The head is not far removed in style from that of Mercury, 3, but its large size in proportion to the body is especially reminiscent of the treatment of the cutting of a rock crystal which, like the Silchester gem, portrays Caracalla as the Genius of the Roman people.[25] Prior to being trimmed, the gem was probably fairly elongated.

The figure of Mars on a nicolo (16) is much more spindly in character, but this too can be ascribed to the late second or third century: the highly 'patterned' cutting of some Severan gems and the exaggerated depth of carving in others represent two well-attested contemporary styles; the third is, however, more familiar to numismatists, though it is recorded on both gems and sealings.[26] Thus, although hardly in the same class as the gems already discussed, it is likely to be of the same date.

The chalcedony showing Diana Venatrix (40) is of a fairly common type.[27] It has prototypes at least as early as the Augustan age, but the disorganised grooving of the drapery looks later. There is a certain similarity between the head and that of Mercury (3). It, too, could be of Severan date, but it would be unwise to insist on this.

Much more certainly of this period is the lion on a cameo (39) whose coarsely cut mane recalls the treatment of the coat of a well-known Severan animal study from Britain, the bear-cameo on Indian sardonyx from South Shields.[28] The best parallel to the lion on the gem is an almost identical cameo in the collection of HM The Queen at Windsor Castle.[29] Indeed in cameo-cutting, Severan glyptic art sometimes achieved a certain originality of style.[30] Cameo-cutting seems in general to have been practised in the late-Roman period more frequently and with greater confidence than the production of the intaglios for signets — perhaps because it was essentially a decorative craft.

Only one gem, 4, can be ascribed with certainty to the pre-Antonine period; 2, 3, 16, 39, 41 are Severan; 13 and 40 could well be of this time or are not much earlier.

Two gems, 4 and 13 are eastern; and the others may well come from the eastern Empire. The amethysts, 2 and 3, look so similar that I suspect they come from the same place and were carved in the same studio. In colour they recall Heliodorus's remark on the superiority of amethysts from Ethiopia and India which has been mentioned above. It may be suggested that the jewels are a group belonging to one person; apart perhaps from 4 all were set in jewellery in the early third century, from which they were removed by the 'Thetford jeweller'. Perhaps he even refashioned the gold, if they were set in gold, though he had not yet got down to fixing 41 into a ring or pendant. While the old rings were broken up as useless, the gems were still relevant to the new age.

In the light of what we have said about colour replacing interest in gem-cutting it is perhaps too much to expect any direct reference to the god Faunus in the group (unless it was realised that Diana, in the pendant, alludes to hunting activities or that in some accounts Mars was Faunus's father.)

In a wider sense the gems may help us to understand something of the theosophical background to the Faunus cult. For although Faunus was indeed a Latin deity, the revival of his worship belongs in the context of a sophisticated Graeco-Roman culture adapted by the late-Roman aristocracy whose enthusiasm, epitomised by the themes of mosaic floors such as those at Littlecote and Brading (one of which apparently shows Abrasax-Iao), may have been fired by speculations from the Orient.[31] Perhaps at least one member of the 'Faunus con-gregation' had eastern ancestry and this is revealed by her jewels.

One final point may be made. There are all sorts of rings from Thetford and two have representational devices in relief on their bezels, one a mask and the other clasped hands.[32] But none employs the popular square bezel, mentioned at the beginning of this section. This in itself suggests deliberate choice; what was created by the Thetford *anularius* was not a collection of signet rings but a very special order of gold-work, sometimes employing gems to superb, but purely decorative — or amuletic — effect.

NOTES

1. This rarity is masked by the fact that some late-Roman gems in museum collections, such as the splendid amethyst in the British Museum portraying the Emperor Constantius II (Walters 1926, no. 2032 = Richter 1971, no. 605) are well known and frequently published.
2. Heurgon 1958; Bastien and Metzger 1977, 159–86, now mainly in the British Museum.
3. Henig 1978, nos 789–803.
4. Henig 1981, 127–43.
5. R. Siviero, *Gli Ori e le Ambre del Museo Nazionale di Napoli* Florence, 1954, pp. 84ff., especially nos 343, 352, 355.
6. Bastien and Metzger 1977, 172–3, B.13, B.14.
7. *Aethiopica* v, 14.
8. Maaskant-Kleibrink, 1978, 195–7.
9. Walters 1926, no. 1759, pl. XXIII. The device copies the famous statue by Eutychides of Sikyon: Richter 1970, 231–2, citing Pausanias VI, 2.7; T Gesztelyi, 'Die Tyche von Antiochia auf einer Gemme von Debrecen, *Živa Antika* 25., pp. 274–84.
10. Henig 1978, nos 366, 367. See also Henig, *Arch. Ael.* 50, 4th series, 1972, pp. 282–7 and D. Charlesworth, *Arch. Ael.* 1, 5th series, 1973, p. 233.
11. Bonner 1950, 12; on the Palestinian rider-saint amulets where Iao and Sabaoth are listed with angels, namely Michael, Gabriel and Ouriel: cf. Bonner 1950, 211–14, nos 298–300 and 309–11. But see Krug 1980, 180–1, no. 47 (from Xanten) inscribed IAΩ on Anguipede's shield and ΑΒΡΑΣΑΣΑΒΩ below. Le Glay 1981, 2–7 comments: 'Abrasas est donc. . . un nom propre, un des noms (avec Iaô, Adonai, Sabaoth) par lesquels on invoquait le dieu suprême pour capter sa puissance ou du moins obtenir sa protection.'
12. K. Preisendanz, *Papyri Graeci Magicae* Berlin-Leipzig, 1928–31, *passim*.
13. M. Tardieu, *Trois Mythes Gnostiques. Adam, Éros et les animaux d'Égypte dans un écrit de Nag Hammadi (II, 5).* Paris, 1974.
14. On the use of Abrasax in magical formulae see particularly A. A. Barb, 'Abraxas-Studien', in *Hommages à W. Deonna, Coll. Latomus* 28. Brussels, 1957, pp.67–86. Other important references to the Anguipede are Bonner 1950, 123–39; Maaskant-Kleibrink 1978, 350–2, nos 1097–1104; le Glay 1981, 2–7 and A. Delatte and Ph. Derchain, *Les Intailles Magiques Gréco-Égyptiennes.* Bibliothèque Nationale, Paris, 1964, pp. 23–42.
15. Henig 1978, 34.
16. R. Stuveras, *Le putto dans l'art romain. Coll. Latomus XCIX.* Brussels, 1969, pp. 23, pl. XLIX, fig. 112.
17. M. L. Vollenweider, *Die Steinschneidekunst und Ihre Künstler in Spätrepublikanischer und Augusteischer Zeit.* Baden-Baden, 1966, p. 23 and pl. 12, no. 1.
18. Henig 1978, no. 639.
19. Maaskant-Kleibrink 1978, no. 1018 (incoherent grooves style).
20. M. Henig in Cunliffe 1971, 83–88 especially p. 87. For seated figures of Mercury on amethyst see *Britannia* 11. 1980, 264 from Lympne (gem may be later than stated there); P. Zazoff (ed.), *Antike Gemmen in Deutschen Sammlungen IV Hannover, Kestner-Museum.* Wiesbaden, 1975, no. 1444; Maaskant-Kleibrink 1978, no. 668; Krug 1981, 172–3, no. 5.
21. Henig 1978, no. 103.
22. Bastien and Metzger 1977, 172, B.13.20.
23. A. Furtwängler, *Königliche Museen zu Berlin. Beschreibung der Geschnittenen Steine.* Berlin, 1896, no. 2393. Maaskant-Kleibrink 1978, no. 525; and especially pastes, E. Simon, *Die Portlandvase.* Mainz, 1957, p. 71 and pl. 38, 1; E. Schmidt in *Antike Gemmen in Deutschen Sammlungen I. Staatliche Münzsammlung, München Teil 3. Gemmen and Glaspasten der römischen Kaiserzeit.* Munich, 1972, no. 3182.
24. Compare the even deeper cuttings of the figure of Sarapis on an amethyst: Weitzmann 1979, 192, no. 171.
25. Richter 1971, no. 583.
26. Toynbee 1962, 185, no. 139, pl. 158 = Henig 1978, no. 250, cited as Severan by Cornelius Vermeule in *The Goddess Roma in the Art of the Roman Empire.* Cambridge, Mass., 1959, pp. 72–3, pl. 111, 5; also Henig, *Ant. J* 60. 1980, pp. 331–2, pl. LXb.
27. Henig 1978, nos 254, 255, App. 35. Note especially E. Zwierlein-Diehl, *Die Antiken Gemmen des Kunsthistorischen Museums in Wien.* 1 Munich, 1973, no. 415. Similar, holding same shape of bow, but far more regularly cut; Augustan date.
28. Henig 1978, no. 735.
29. Fortnum 1880, 11, no. 250 (I am grateful to Professor John Boardman for showing me a photograph).
30. H. Mobius, *Rev. Arch* NS, 1968, 315–26 for the best Severan gem in the Museum. Julia Domna as Luna in a chariot drawn by two plunging bulls, the fronts of their bodies boldly patterned with the same gusto as the South Shields bear and the Thetford lion.
31. Toynbee 1962, 202, no. 197 pl. 231.
32. As Henig 1978, nos 775–8.

The rings

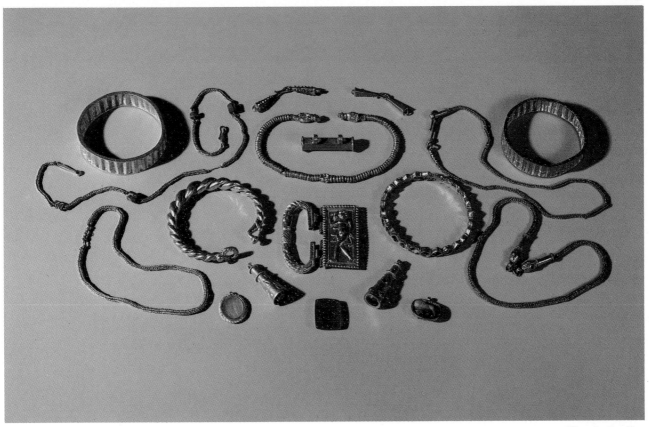

The other jewellery

41

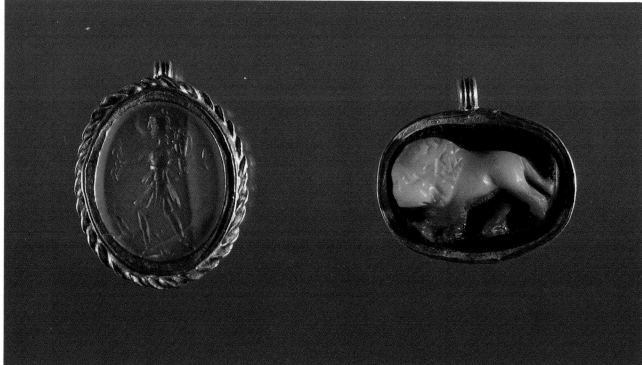

Left: **40**; *right:* **39**

4

The Shale Jewellery Box

The shale jewellery box, together with its lid (83), comprise in themselves objects of no little interest and importance. Apparently more or less complete when found, they had a chequered career before finding their way to the British Museum. By the time they had arrived there, both the box and the lid had collapsed into a number of pieces, and were covered with a yellow waxy deposit: this appears to have been the result of treatment with linseed oil, preceded by washing in water, under the mistaken impression that the objects were made of wood. They have now been consolidated with polyethylene glycol wax and rendered relatively stable.

One fragment from the side of the box was certainly lost due to its cavalier treatment before it received proper attention, and some of the lip of the container may also have suffered damage. A section of the rim of the lid comprises a further piece that is now missing. It is therefore difficult to establish with any precision the degree of damage or wear that may have taken place in antiquity as opposed to recent times. Nevertheless, their condition apart, the box and lid provide excellent examples of the sort of lathe-turned vessels made particularly at Kimmeridge,[1] but also at centres such as Hengistbury Head,[2] during the Iron-Age and Roman periods.[3] That their manufacture was maintained into the fourth century is evident from sites exclusively occupied in the late-Roman period: for instance at Portchester, where there appears to have been little or no activity prior to *c.* AD 280, objects of shale were particularly common, including spindle-whorls, bracelets, beads and the remains of a number of vessels.[4]

However, we know of no exact parallel to our piece. Whilst vessels with foot-rings are common enough,[5] there is none which matches the precise form of the Thetford box (although such simple shapes cannot in reality have been especially rare). Perhaps the nearest analogy is provided by a vessel recovered from an early Saxon level on the site at Dorchester-on-Thames and recently published:[6] but this is a much smaller box and its shape only approximates to that of the example from Thetford. Moreover, it also lacks a lid, although covers made in shale are attested. Hengistbury, for instance, has yielded an example of Iron-Age date (although its form is quite different from ours)[7] and many bowls must have been manufactured together with matching lids.[8] The closest parallel for our example comes, in fact, from Verulamium.[9] Although interpreted in the report as the base and foot-ring of a vessel, the piece is probably best regarded as a fragment of a lid of very much the same type as our one from Thetford. Indeed, it may not entirely be coincidence that both derive from late-Roman contexts, ours belonging to the later fourth century and that from Verulamium coming from deposits dated *c.* AD 350–410+.

How old the Thetford piece may have been when buried is a matter for conjecture. Whilst there are no obvious signs of wear (e.g. on the underside of the base), it is not easy to affirm this with confidence, given the damage that took place after it was salvaged from the ground. Nor can the original purpose of the box and lid be ascertained. We call it a jewellery box since this was obviously its purpose when buried; indeed, the bright lustrous polished surfaces that it must once have possessed would have rendered it an attractive and suitable container for rings, necklaces and the like. Whether it was designed with this in mind is, on the other hand, entirely a matter for speculation.

The fossil

On the underside of the shale box is a fossil incorporated in the fabric of the shale. We are grateful to the Department of Palaeontology of the British Museum (Natural History) for examining a photograph of the fossil. They tell us that the fossil is an ammonite, probably of the genus *Pectinatites*. This would be entirely consistent with an origin in the Kimmeridge area of Dorset.

NOTES
1. Davies 1936.
2. Bushe-Fox 1915, 63–4.
3. Lawson 1976.
4. Webster 1975.
5. Numerous examples cited by Webster 1975, Lawson 1976 and Cunliffe 1964, 92 and fig. 25, no. 2.
6. Cf. *Oxoniensa* 46. 1981, fig. 22, no. 19.
7. Bushe-Fox 1915, pl. xxx, no. 17.
8. Sometimes, however, it would be easy to mistake flanges used to join different sections of a large vessel together for lid-seatings. A vessel from Warden (Beds) provides a good instance: BM registration number PRB 1855. 7–10. 1.
9. Frere 1972, fig. 57, no. 228.

5

The Silver Spoons

The thirty-three spoons in the Thetford Treasure comprise a remarkable collection. This is not simply a comment upon their fine artistic qualities nor upon the wealth of unique epigraphical material. Equally exceptional are both the excellent and undamaged condition of the objects and the very large size of the group. These matters, together with a detailed typological analysis, will be considered in the sections that follow. It will be suggested that the group of spoons comprise a homogeneous set, quite probably the product of a single workshop. Furthermore, where close dated parallels for individual spoon-forms can be found, they consistently fall within a bracket of AD 350 to 400, with a bias towards the later part of that period. It is plausible, therefore, to see them as a group that is not only more or less contemporary with much of the jewellery but also, in its own way, as homogeneous an assemblage.

The size of the collection

A catalogue of finds of silver spoons (and strainers) of the late-Roman and Merovingian periods has been assembled by Milojčić, and his lists have been revised by Sherlock (although he includes some spoons that are neither of silver nor exclusively of late-antique date).[1] Many of these objects occur either in graves or as casual or poorly recorded discoveries; but Milojčić does describe twenty-nine hoards with spoons, to which at least five more can be added from Sherlock's catalogue. Although these hoards occur as far apart as Traprain in Scotland and Hama in Syria, the great majority derive from Italy (with nine instances) and the northern provinces — a comment, perhaps, more upon the nature and availability of the published evidence than upon a meaningful distribution.

The number of spoons found in these hoards varies very considerably. Using Milojčić's figures only two hoards have yielded more than twenty spoons, namely Kaiseraugst in Switzerland (thirty-six)[2] and 'Kerynia' in Cyprus — i.e. the 'First Cyprus Treasure'.[3] This latter hoard was found towards the end of the nineteenth century and is said by Dalton to have consisted originally of three vessels and 'about 36 spoons', of which twenty-five survive. However, this treasure is much later in date than Thetford or Kaiseraugst, with objects bearing control-stamps of AD 641–51. Of the other hoards, eight contain between ten and twenty spoons, ten between five and ten spoons and nine fewer than five spoons. This overall distribution is not significantly altered by Sherwood's supplementary catalogue, except to increase by four the number of hoards with fewer than five spoons.

Whilst making due allowance for all the vagaries of retrieval (which seem particularly to affect the recovery of hoards of precious metal), there seems little doubt that the Thetford group of spoons is exceptional on account of its size alone. There is probably a good chance that it represents the greater part or the entirety of an ancient collection which, as will be shown, is likely to have formed some of the plate of a sanctuary where the Latian deity, Faunus, was worshipped.

The condition of the spoons

Three questions seem here to be of particular importance: in the first place, to try to make an assessment of the degree of wear that had occurred by the time that the spoons were buried; secondly, to decide what damage had occurred by the time of burial and, thirdly, to establish whether anything happened to affect the condition of the spoons when they were lifted out from the ground.

We shall consider these questions in reverse order. To deal first with the recovery of the silver from the pit that housed them, this seems to have occasioned little damage. There is a small recent hole in the bowl of 76, and the bowl of one of the strainers (49) is missing a fragment; but none of the spoons is otherwise affected.[4] Moreover, the silver is in remarkable condition. We know that the objects were washed by the finders in baby shampoo so as to free the soil that adhered to them, but there was said to have been no other form of treatment. Yet the silver surfaces are completely unpitted or uncorroded and, while a little tarnished when first seen in late May 1980, there were no deposits either of silver chloride or of silver sulphide.[5] The high purity of the silver (generally 96–98%) might to some extent account for this, but their overall excellent condition is not easily explained: generally speaking, without some sort of protective matrix, the sand and gravel subsoil of the sort encountered at Gallows Hill could be expected to yield a marked level of corrosion products. Something such as a pottery vessel as a container for the spoons might account for their fine condition; but no evidence for such a vessel was reported. It is an exasperating reminder of the fact that excavation on the site of the find could have resolved questions of this sort.

Nevertheless, we can be certain that the silver objects were buried in a pristine and undamaged state. Clearly, the Thetford group cannot be considered as another of the well-known class of *Hacksilber* hoards, which are typified by fragments of silver, sometimes carefully folded up, which are so characteristic of the late-Roman period.[6] Indeed, we must recognise the possibility that the spoons were interred not just for their value as a quantity of precious metal but also because they were thought to have a certain importance as objects. This matter will be discussed further in the final section of this monograph.

The final point to be considered is the degree of wear that had taken place between their manufacture and the moment of burial. This is not an easy problem to resolve. Even with the help of microscopic aids, such an assessment involves a considerable degree of subjectivity but it is a question that does need to be posed. As it happens, wear-traces on spoons can take a distinctive form, brought about mainly by the process of scraping them across the abrasive surface of a vessel. Under certain conditions — for instance, if the vessel is made of a material such as pottery or bronze — this can result in a gradual lipping at the right- or left-hand corner of the bowl of the spoon. One needs to look, therefore, both for traces of smoothing at this point and for actual thinning of the metal. With this specific question in mind the Thetford spoons, as well as other Roman examples from Britain, were examined by several people noting down their impressions independently. That these observations proved remarkably consistent does not necessarily make them any more valid: but they are worthy of record. Of the thirty-three spoons, no less than fifteen were thought to be without any trace of wear; the metal is of a consistent thickness around the whole of the bowl, no signs were seen of rubbing beneath the lip and, where prominent, the keel beneath the bowl is sharply defined throughout its length. On the other hand, a further fifteen of the spoons appeared to demonstrate what is best described as 'slight' signs of use. Occasionally this takes the form of a rather softened profile at the front part of the keel and an abraded tip to the underside of the spoon; but, much more commonly, there is a definite thinning on either the left or the right side of the front part of the bowl, combined with some signs of abrasion in this area. Thus in these cases we can be certain that the spoons had seen some degree of use, although over what period of time it is impossible to guess. Finally, there is a group of three spoons — all of the duck-handled class — which could be defined to be 'quite worn' or 'worn' (61, 62, 65). Here, the metal has been thinned down in a quite pronounced fashion, as though they might have been used for some particular purpose or are older than the rest. However, since we believe that the spoons were manufactured as a single group, it would appear that some special explanation must here apply. Possibly they served some particular function in the religious ceremonies, but there is no way of knowing what that could have been.

Another feature that emerged from study of the wear-marks is that many of the more worn spoons had been primarily used either by right-handed or by left-handed people but rarely by both. On eleven of the spoons there were fairly unambiguous indications of wear caused by movements from right to left, while five showed signs of left-handed use. Only on two (64, 80) were there any hints of rubbing on both sides of the bowl although in neither case can this be more than a tentative conclusion. Given, however, that the spoons were used in some arcane ritual, it is impossible to draw any very meaningful conclusions from these observations. What is important is the demonstration that the group as a whole consists neither of pieces that are completely unused and unabraded nor of spoons that were obviously old when buried. With this point in mind, it is interesting to compare the Thetford assemblage with some other more or less contemporary groups of spoons.

For example, the Mildenhall set, which comprises three spoons with foliate motifs in pear-shaped bowls and five, all with inscriptions, with pear-shaped bowls, shows noticeably more wear than the Thetford spoons.[7] The wear is most pronounced on the foliate specimens (although here the metal is overall much thinner), but is equally conspicuous on all but two of the others. The area of wear implies that all were used by right-handed people. It is perhaps worth adding, also, that the surface of the Mildenhall silver is generally much smoother and more polished than that of Thetford or, indeed, the group from Dorchester-on-Thames.[8]

These five Dorchester spoons, which date to the latter part of the fourth century, also display conspicuous evidence of use. The signs of wear are, however, not confined to the tip and side of the bowl (although this is their most obvious feature); in addition, under the binocular microscope traces of rubbing and abrasion can also be detected at several points on the handle. This is not the case on any of the Thetford spoons, so far as we can judge. Thus the evidence of both the Dorchester-on-Thames and the Mildenhall spoons should imply that, unless the Thetford spoons were used in such as a way as to minimise most traces of wear, they must be regarded as comparatively new when they were interred in the ground. Given that the hoard seems to have been buried towards *c.* AD 400, we might expect them to have been made not much earlier than the last decades of the fourth century. Indeed, they may not have been much more than a few years old when they were concealed, a conclusion which, if speculative, does have important implications for the absolute chronology of the group.

Typological considerations

The thirty-three spoons divide into two major groups, one that we shall term the 'duck-handled' spoons ('swan-handled' would be an acceptable alternative) and the other the 'long-handled' spoons. Each group can be subdivided in various ways but, as we shall see, there is every reason to suppose that they are all the product of a single workshop.

THE DUCK-HANDLED SPOONS (50–65)

There are sixteen spoons in this group, which takes its name from the bird-head terminals on the handle, which are variously identified as representing swans or ducks. As a whole the collection is remarkable for its homogeneity, and the differences are generally ones of detail; however, a stylistic analysis does provide a basis for some interesting conclusions.

The outstanding piece is unquestionably the Triton spoon (50). It is decorated with motifs which are rendered in an idiom that is entirely classical, drawn in a skilful and accomplished manner. Whilst not perhaps the work of a master craftsman, some of the detail, such as the pecking on the Triton's tail and on the dolphin, does recall some of the decorative infilling on vessels in the Mildenhall Treasure and on the Corbridge Lanx.[9] Both in theme and, to a lesser degree, in style, Mildenhall and this piece from Thetford clearly belong to a similar genre. Extra detail is also lavished upon the parcel-gilt duck's head and includes some indication of the nostrils and a set of vicious-looking teeth — one of only two pieces in the group where the teeth are shown.[10]

Although parcel-gilding is by no means uncommon upon silver objects of the later Roman period (e.g. the Traprain Treasure or the third-century Helpston spoon),[11] our Triton spoon finds its best parallel with the Thetford Panther spoon, **66**, the finest of the *cochleare*. They have several features in common, amongst them the parcel-gilt decoration, the classicising motifs, the gilt rim around the bowl, the pointed and keeled form of the bowl and the overall quality and finish of the two pieces. Their weights are also not dissimilar, 25.4 and 22.3 g, and, perhaps significantly, their inscriptions are closely comparable: namely DEINARI on the Triton spoon and DEIFAVNINARI on the Panther spoon. The way in which the letters are drawn does differ — one is engraved with double lines while the other has been filled with niello — but the style of individual letters does suggest a close comparability between the inscriptions. This is particularly noticeable with the letters D, E and A, but is also true of the R and the N. Such conclusions must necessarily be tentative but it would be our feeling that the two inscriptions may well be by the same hand. If so, it is an inference of some importance. Given the other typological features that the two spoons share, it is difficult to resist the suggestion that both spoons were made within the same workshop or, more probably, by the same craftsman. Only in this way can we properly explain the idiosyncratic treatment of the two objects. More significantly, however, it also allows us to propose a link between the duck-handled and the long-handled spoons, groups which typologically are otherwise quite diverse. Given the assumption that (1) the two sets of spoons were the product of single workshops — a matter considered in detail below — and (2) that the Triton and Panther spoons are merely exceptionally elaborate items which also come from the workshop that manufactured the other spoons, then we are in a position to suggest that the whole assemblage may well have been made by the same group of artisans.

To sustain this conclusion, it is of course necessary to demonstrate some typological affinity between the Triton spoon and the other duck-handled forms. This is best provided by spoons **50** and **51**, both of which have an overall similarity of bowl-shape to the Triton spoon. Otherwise, the bowls of this group are somewhat different. Generally oval in form, and with a fairly deep profile, the tip is normally rounded rather than pointed, while, on the underside of the bowl, many of the spoons show a marked keel line. More variable is the length of the bowl which ranges between 6.3 and 8.3 cm, with an average of 7.5 cm. Nevertheless, as a group they present the impression of being more or less the same size — i.e. of being a set rather than a haphazardly assembled collection.

A greater range of variability is to be found in the weights of the spoons, which may be set out as follows:

25–30 g		30–40 g	40 + g
50	57	60	51
52	58	65	59
53	61		62
54	63		
55	64		
56			

Despite a range from 25 to more than 40 g, the great majority of the spoons nevertheless fall within the 25–30 g bracket, and it is thus worthwhile breaking down these figures in more detail:

25 g	26 g	27 g	28 g
50	54	52	57
58	56	53	
	61	55	
		63	
		64	

It follows from these lists that half of the sample is made up of spoons weighing 26–27 g and a further three lie almost within the same range. It is therefore necessary to ask whether this fits any known module. This is, of course, a notoriously difficult area of study since we must recognise that orders of precision in weight in the ancient world were by no means very accurate. The point is underlined by late-Roman silver ingots which, it would appear, were intended to weigh one Roman pound and were used for Imperial donatives or other forms of payment.[12] Taking the eleven complete examples known from Britain, catalogued by Painter,[13] we find that their actual weight varies from 301 to 342 g, a range that is well matched by a new find from near Reculver which contains 317 g of silver.[14]

The variation in the weights of these supposed one-pound ingots emphasises, however, the difficulty in interpreting data of this sort. A one-pound weight could, in practice, differ quite widely, despite fourth-century legislation on tax collection.[15] Nevertheless, it is probably significant that the average weight of the twelve ingots — 318.9 g — is fairly close to some estimates based on coin studies, e.g. 324.25 g and 327.45 g,[16] so that an ounce of silver — a twelfth of a pound — could therefore amount to 26.57 g. That said, it is undoubtedly more correct to assume that an ounce of silver was as approximate a measurement as that of the pound, so that, in effect, an ounce could vary from just over 25 g to as much as 28.5 g.

With these figures in mind, we should compare them with the weights of the Thetford duck-handled spoons in the tables above. This will immediately show that there is a close correlation. When due allowance is made for some variation in the balances of the silversmiths, it seems clear that they intended all but five of the sixteen duck-handled spoons to weigh one Roman ounce. What, then, of the others? Here, we enter into a speculative field, but there are some clues. Two have weights which amount to just over 41 g, that is to say about $1\frac{1}{2}$ Roman ounces, a coincidence that seems unlikely to be fortuitous. On the other hand, the remaining three spoons fit no obvious module which might seem to invalidate this inference. There is, however, another approach. If we make a calculation of the *total* weight of silver contained in the duck-handled spoons, we find that it comes to 497.5 g, namely 1.56 Roman pounds. This could also be dismissed as coincidence but that seems improbable. On this assumption, we might reconstruct events as follows.

The silversmiths were commissioned to make sixteen spoons with duck-handles, one embellished with gold. The instructions were that eleven should weigh one ounce, and two should be 1½ ounces. This left about four ounces of silver for the remaining three spoons, **51, 60** and **65**, and it was therefore decided to produce one exceptionally large spoon (**51**), and two smaller spoons but of much the same size and type. We cannot overemphasise the degree of conjecture in these speculations; but there is a certain symmetry in the figures which fits fairly neatly with what we understand of mensuration in this period — and with the importance that is known to have been attached to it.[17]

We must now consider the typology of the handles. We may first note that they were made as an integral part of the spoon so that, when the object was cut out from a piece of silver, a long strip was retained for the handle. This was then coiled round and the tip made into a bird's head, resembling a duck or a swan. Two main variants in this form of handle are known.[18] On one type, known from Hof Iben (Germany), Kaiseraugst (Switzerland), Canoscio (Italy), and probably from Vermand (France) and from Traprain Law (Scotland),[19] the bird's head is bent sideways so that the beak touches the side of the bowl. This form is however not represented in the Thetford group. The other main type consists either of a simple s-form or of a more elaborate coil of silver wire that rises straight up from the bowl. In the Thetford group there is just one example of a simple s-shaped handle (**56**), but all of the others belong to the more complex double-coil form — a reflection, perhaps, of the high overall quality of these pieces.[20] The modelling of the bird-head terminals, on the other hand, displays considerable variation in detail. The most obvious typological division is between those that face inwards over the bowl of the spoon and those that look outwards. The inward-looking birds constitute the rarer class with six examples. None of the heads are identical, however: some, for instance, have straight beaks, some have beaks that curve upwards and one shows a finely portrayed creature, lunging malevolently downwards. The outward-facing birds, while including a number of individually modelled heads, nevertheless separate more clearly into two distinct subgroups. The principal feature that divides these handles is the fact that five (**52–56**) have small round cakes or pieces of fruit in their mouths.[21] In all but one of these spoons this type of head occurs in combination with a square, decorated moulding at the base of the handle and a v-shaped incision beneath (a combination that is not found on any other spoon). Indeed, when allowance is made for the fact that the duck's head of **53** may be bent out of its true position, then **52, 53** and **55** can be regarded as being in more or less every respect identical. This even applies to the dimensions and the weights, which differ by only 0.1 g, and it seems likely that all three were made by a single craftsman, working to precisely framed instructions.

The other outward-looking duck-spoons comprise a more miscellaneous collection, with no instances either of identical or of very similar pieces. Indeed, taking all sixteen duck-handled spoons as a group, it is the degree of individuality that is the striking feature. For example there are at least six main variants in the treatment of the eyes: amongst them are are simple circles (**50, 51, 58**); ovals with a single side comma

(**57, 62, 63**); ovals with a comma on either side (**52–55, 64**); a circle with a stalk and commas on one side (**59**); and two different types of motif indicating plumage behind the eye (**56, 65** and **60, 61**). Yet, despite these individual touches, the balance of the evidence is nevertheless to suggest that the assemblage as a whole represents the products of a small group of craftsmen, working in a single workshop.

This subjectively based hypothesis can, however, be tested by statistical means, namely by a matrix (see Table 3).[22] This is a simple mathematical device which compares the frequencies of typological traits shared by the artefacts. The primary aim is to see whether certain subgroups manifest themselves or if there is a broad cohesion across the assemblage. In fact, as the matrix clearly shows, it is the latter that is the case. The absence of any numerical clusters and the even distribution of the frequencies across the matrix substantiates in full measure the conclusions reached upon more subjective grounds: namely that there is nothing to indicate that this group of spoons contains either items that are of different dates or pieces that derived from more than a single source.

The dating of the duck-handled spoons
It will have become obvious from the parallels cited in the course of this discussion that duck-handled spoons are a type that appears in the fourth century and becomes increasingly common after *c.* AD 350–60. The earliest dated occurrence is the Kaiseraugst Treasure, buried *c.* AD 351,[23] but it is possible that this shape of spoon may not have become especially popular for some time since it is not represented in the Mildenhall Treasure (*c.* AD 360).[24] Unfortunately, however, we still have too few well-dated contexts to trace in detail the evolution of the form. It could be that the type with a sideways handle — as in the Kaiseraugst Treasure — is an early form, which then developed into the Thetford shape of handle. This is hinted at by the Canterbury duck-handled spoons which belong in an assemblage best dated to the late fourth century.[25] Alternatively, there may be two separate but contemporary workshop traditions. All that we can safely conclude at this stage is that the duck-handled spoons become an important element in some sets of silver plate from the middle of the fourth century and, as the Traprain hoard demonstrates,[26] appear still to have been current in the early fifth century.

THE LONG-HANDLED SPOONS (*cochlearia*)
The second major set of spoons in the Thetford assemblage comprises seventeen examples of long-handled *cochleare*. A general association of duck-handled with long-handled spoons is of course well-attested in late-Roman hoards of silver, with as instances the Kaiseraugst, Traprain and Canterbury Treasures.[27] However, as we have seen, in the case of the Thetford Treasure we can also establish a typological link between the two groups of spoons, by means of the parcel-gilt Triton and Panther spoons. Here, the close resemblances between these two pieces allow us to suggest that both were made by the same craftsman. Thus, if we can establish that the Panther spoon also shares areas of similarity with the other *cochlearia*, then the case for positing a single workshop assemblage becomes still stronger.

Table 3 Frequency matrix for the duck-handled spoons

	parcel-gilding	single-coil handle	outward-looking duck	cake in mouth	V-shaped decoration below handle	simple eye	double-coil handle	bowl inscription	elaborate eye	inward-looking duck
parcel-gilding	1	1		1		1	1	1		
single-coil handle		1	1	1				1	1	
outward-looking duck			10	5	6	7	9	9	3	
cake in mouth				5	4	4	4	5	1	
V-shaped decoration below handle					9	5	8	8	4	3
simple eye						10	10	10		3
double-coil handle							15	13	5	6
bowl inscription								14	4	5
elaborate eye									6	3
inward-looking duck										6

Two general points relating to this question can usefully be made here. One concerns the *appearance* of the two groups of spoons, both of which demonstrate a relatively thick use of metal and a fairly rough surface with, in some cases, pronounced faceting. This technique finds a close degree of comparability with the Canterbury spoons and, equally, is in strong contrast with the much smoother finish manifested by the spoons from Mildenhall and Dorchester-on-Thames.[28] Secondly, we must note the evidence of the metallurgical analyses, considered in detail elsewhere. We have, of course, to recognise that many late-Roman silver objects must have been made from older melted-down objects which recycled the silver supply.[29] Nevertheless, it is striking that the metallurgical variation from one object to another is, in a statistical sense, minimal, and that there are no grounds in the results of the XRF studies for separating the duck-handled group from the long-handled types. This provides an additional reason for regarding the two sets of spoons as a single assemblage and is a working hypothesis that now needs to be examined from a typological standpoint. We shall approach the question by defining the main subgroups amongst the long-handled forms.

1. The spoons with zoomorphic offsets (68–72, 75) There are six spoons of this type, all of similar size and weight except for 70, which has lost — probably in recent times — the end of the handle. The most characteristic feature of the group is the presence of a feline or horse-like animal-head (also sometimes described as a griffin) on the offset between the bowl and the handle; but this is just one of several distinctive characteristics which are worth enumerating in detail.

All of the handles are decorated, five in a very similar way. The arrangement of these decorative elements is as follows. The tip is plain and consists of a long tapering piece of wire, which is essentially circular in cross-section but has a slightly faceted appearance. On all five examples, the tip is about 4 cm in length. There is then a baluster-type moulding, beyond which is a length of square rod. This is placed diagonally to the main plane of the spoon, and is decorated on all four sides with a form of chip-carving, giving a lattice-like or zig-zag effect. There is then a second baluster moulding separating the chip-carving from the zoomorphic offset.

The length of the chip-carved rod is almost precisely the same on all five examples, namely 6 cm, ± 0.2. This measurement is repeated both on one other Thetford spoon, 73, and also on the Papittedo spoon from the Mildenhall Treasure;[30] the latter also has the same form of baluster mouldings. Decorated handles of this sort are, however, comparatively uncommon in late-Roman hoards and we know of no other example of a spoon handle with this type of chip-carved decoration; instead, the normal preference is for a length of twisted rod, as on the Mildenhall Papittedo spoon. This, indeed, is precisely the type of embellishment used on the sixth spoon of the group, no. 69, although the baluster mouldings are similar but not identical to those of the other spoons.

The creatures that form the offset between the bowl and the handle are modelled in an engaging and accomplished way, and are stylistically sufficiently close to suggest that they could have been made by the same craftsman. Two heads, 68 and 72, are in fact virtually identical, as are all other features of these two spoons except the inscriptions: they can safely be regarded as a pair. Nos 70 and 71, both of which have a horse-like creature at the offset, also share many points of similarity, except for the fact that there is an absence of engraved detail on 70; this may indicate that this head was never properly finished since the other animals are all embellished with a wealth of finely drawn lines, depicting features such as the mane, the eyes and ears. There is also some scale-like engraving on 69 resembling, albeit distantly, two of the Canterbury zoomorphic spoons.[31]

Turning to the overall form of the zoomorphic offset, we may begin by noting a general morphological division between the three-dimensional modelling of 68, 69 and 72 and the way in which 70, 71 and 75 have been represented as extensions of the handle.[32] This is a feature that is by no means restricted to the Thetford spoons, however; for instance the spoons with zoomorphic offsets in both the Canterbury and the Dorchester, Dorset hoards demonstrate a similar separation of forms.[33] On the other hand, there are a number of other aspects of the design of the Thetford offsets that are not readily paralleled on other zoomorphic spoons and which may indicate a diverse workshop tradition. For example, on two of the Thetford spoons there is a gap between the animal heads and the rim of the bowl, a stylistic trait that recalls the type of offset sometimes employed on second- and third-century designs.[34] It is also used on the non-zoomorphic offset of the Fish spoon (67) in the Thetford group, but is not a feature of other known zoomorphic spoons. Equally uncommon are the Thetford zoomorphic pieces where a tongue-like projection joins the mouth of the animal with the bowl, a morphological quirk that recalls the otherwise plain design of the Mildenhall Papittedo spoon.[35] This is in marked contrast to the zoomorphic spoons found at Little Horwood (Bucks),[36] Canterbury,[37] Dorchester (Dorset)[38] and Dorchester-on-Thames,[39] where the animal-head and the bowl represent a much more closely integrated design. Our tentative suggestion, therefore, is that we could perhaps regard the Thetford zoomorphic spoons, with their strong modelling and individual style, as representative of a related but nevertheless distinct tradition in this area of silverwork. Indeed, one might legitimately take the point further and wonder if we can separate these finds into, on the one hand, a British group and on the other, a Continental school, with the Thetford set as an example of the latter. It is a speculation upon which further discoveries will surely cast some light.[40]

The bowls of this group are exclusively of oval form, a shape which is quite distinct from the other main type, those spoons with a pear-shaped bowl. Otherwise, the morphological differences are more ones of detail than of form. Both the degree of keeling and the length of the 'rat-tail' on the underside of the bowl vary, but there is no correlation between these features and the other traits listed above. Nor is there any obvious relationship between the inscriptions and the forms. For instance, the pair 68 and 72 have quite different inscriptions, SILVIOLAVIVAS and AGRESTEVIVAS, just as the two SILVIOLA inscriptions occur on different sorts of spoon (68 and 69, the spoon with a twisted handle). More interestingly, the style of the lettering on the pair 68 and 72 is so close that we can be fairly certain that they were done by the same person. The lettering of 70 could also be in that hand, although those of 69 (a second SILVIOLAVIVAS, with a +) and 71 seem not to be. Our overall conclusions about the number of hands and the lettering are discussed in a subsequent section but it does seem likely that the work of making and inscribing this class of spoons was undertaken by more than one person. However, one further point of importance should be mentioned here. It concerns the one inscription in this group that is placed on the handle, namely the letters BLO which are cut on the part of the handle nearest the bowl on spoon 75. Close examination of this handle shows that it was tapered *after* the inscription had been made. Moreover, other long-handled spoons, including 76, 77, 78 and 79, demonstrate a similar pattern. On this evidence, then, we can probably assume that the inscriptions are not a secondary feature on the Thetford spoons, but were made *before* the final finishing touches had been applied to the objects.

Parallels have been discussed recently by Painter and others.[41] They are by no means numerous but include examples from Canterbury, Dorchester-on-Thames, Dorchester (Dorset) and Little Horwood (Bucks) in Britain;[42] one from a burial at Saint-Quentin in northern France;[43] and more distant parallels from Kertch in the Crimea and from Rome.[44] Few of these contexts are dated; but there were coins with the Dorchester (Dorset) spoons which show that its date of deposition was after AD 395;[45] there was a coin of Gratian (AD 367–83) with the Saint-Quentin burial; and coins of Julian, Valentinian I, Gratian, Theodosius I, Arcadius and Honorius were found at the time of the recovery of the Canterbury hoard, although unfortunately there was no evidence what-

soever of association. Further to this, we can note that animal-head spoons are not present in great hoards such as Kaiseraugst (*c.* AD 351) or Mildenhall (probably buried in *c.* AD 360); and that zoomorphic decoration on other types of object, such as buckles, strap-ends and bone combs, appears to have become widely prevalent only in the later fourth century. It is fair to conclude, therefore, that the zoomorphic style of spoon offset, whilst, as Painter has stressed,[47] belonging to the mainstream of classical art rather than to some specifically Teutonic tradition, nevertheless is a late-Roman development. However, since the highly individual genre represented by the spoons from Thetford occurs only on spoons from northern Europe (the offsets on the Rome and the Kertch spoons are in an analogous but distinct style), we would prefer to think of them as the product of a Gallic or British workshop. This conclusion is supported by the evidence, mentioned above, that suggests that some at least of the inscriptions were made before the spoons were completed. Whilst we do not know if the Celtic names are Gallic or British, they nevertheless point to a general north-European provenance for the workshop. To this comment, we should also add our cautious inference, advanced earlier, that the workshop is more likely to have been located in Gaul than in Britain. Overall, then, the weight of the evidence *may* be to suggest that the Thetford spoons were imports rather than indigenously manufactured items.

2. Spoons with pear-shaped bowls and twisted handles (73, 74, 81) The remaining spoons with handles made of twisted rod can most usefully be considered together. Indeed, two of the three, 73 and 74, are so very similar that, despite minor differences, they can probably be regarded as a pair. The features in common include a long pear-shaped bowl, with a well-defined keel and a 'rat-tail' beneath; an open foliate offset where the scroll takes a form approaching that of the letter S; baluster mouldings of the type found on the zoomorphic spoons discussed above; and a section of twisted rod between the mouldings with a length of 6.0 and 6.2 cm respectively, measurements that are identical to those of the decorated section of handle on spoons of the zoomorphic group. The principal differences between the two spoons are that the rod is twisted in opposite directions and that the foliate scrolls, although close, are not identical. Nevertheless, these would seem to be minor variations which do not seriously weaken the argument for regarding them as a pair. The third spoon, 81, is allied with the other two by its twisted handle (6.4 cm in length) and its baluster mouldings, as well as by its keeled, pear-shaped bowl. Its offset is however quite different — a single comma-like form, — and, unlike the other two, its inscription is to be found at the offset-end of the handle, not within the bowl. It is one of the abbreviated inscriptions, AN, whereas the other two have both dedications referring to Faunus.

The simple offset employed on no. 81 is a common late-Roman design. There are analogous examples from Mildenhall, Traprain, Canterbury and Köln-Müngersdorf, *inter alia*.[48] The more elaborate S-scroll foliate offset of the other two spoons is less easily paralleled, although there are points of similarity with the Pascentia spoon from Mildenhall,[49] as well as with other examples within the Thetford group, especially **78** and **82**. These offsets presented great opportunities for experiment with designs and no doubt there were many variants upon the foliate theme.

3. *Spoons with a long plain handle* (**76–80, 82**). Typologically, this is a rather unsatisfactory class, since the degree of variation within the group is quite considerable. However, there is justification for regarding four of the spoons as comprising two sets of pairs and the remaining two as being closely similar, while there are some morphological traits which run through the group as a whole, providing a broad degree of typological unity.

The one certain pair is made up by spoons **76** and **77**. Both have oval bowls with a sharply defined keel and a 'rat-tail'; a simple open offset in the form of a comma-like scroll (closely paralleling the shape of the offset of no. **81**, discussed above); a long plain tapered handle; and identical inscriptions, RESTITVTI. These were almost certainly done by the same hand, and, significantly, must have been engraved *before* the handle was tapered off to a point.

Spoons **79** and **80** also probably constitute a pair. Although they have different inscriptions, namely BLO and MED, and are of slightly different lengths and weights, their design is more or less identical. Both have elongated pear-shaped bowls and long tapering handles, as well as simple open scroll offsets. Indeed, the design of the offset is very close to that of the two RESTITVTI spoons, described above, and also akin to that of **81**. Thus it is clear that very similar types of offset can occur on spoons with quite different shapes of bowl. The last two spoons in this group, **78** and **82**, also demonstrate this point: both have long tapering handles and a similar design of open scroll offset, but very different bowl-forms. One, **78**, is broadly pear-shaped while the other, **82**, is more oval in form. Nevertheless, the two shapes do not strike one visually as being particularly different (even though, on strict typological grounds, they should be placed in two different classes), a point that underlines the dangers of too rigid an approach to classification with this sort of material.

4. *Spoon with an engraved fish and plant* (**67**). From both a typological and a decorative standpoint, this spoon is amongst the most unusual examples in the Thetford collection. In the first place, while it has the conventional long tapered handle, it is provided with a bowl that is circular rather than oval in shape and is very shallow in profile. There is no other bowl of this form in the Thetford assemblage, although there is a not dissimilar example amongst the zoomorphic spoons from Dorchester-on-Thames.[50] Secondly, the offset is also unusual in that it is designed so that there is a gap between the lip of the bowl and the scroll. This is a feature already noted with the Thetford zoomorphic pair **70** and **71**; but it would appear to be an archaic trait[51] that is by no means common on spoons of the late-Roman period. Thirdly, although there is no inscription on the spoon, it bears within the bowl an engraving of a fish, swimming towards, or nibbling at, some sort of plant. This motif, if unparalleled amongst the other Thetford spoons, nevertheless is known on spoons from other sites. Examples include a spoon in the Traprain Treasure; one from Loché near Thivars in northern France; another from Canos-

cio near Perugia in central Italy; and one from the hoard found at Dorchester, Dorset.[52] Like the Thetford fish, none of these engravings is gilded, but it is worth noting that, to judge from the published illustrations, all of these *comparanda* are drawn in a much more perfunctory and stylised manner than the fish on the Thetford spoon. Moreover, only one of these fish is shown with an additional motif, namely the example from Canoscio, where there is a palm-like design,[53] reminiscent of the plant on the Thetford spoon.

The best analogy for the Thetford fish-and-plant motif occurs, however, upon a long-handled silver *cochleare* with a pear-shaped bowl, recently acquired by the British Museum.[54] Although not closely provenanced, it is likely to have been found in south-east England. Within the bowl is the engraved drawing of fish, rather sloppily covered with parcel-gilding, and, in front, a plant-like motif, also in gilt. Both in the quality of the draughtmanship and in the engraved dashes used to infill the motifs, this new spoon and that from Thetford would seem to belong to a common genre. Indeed, it is not impossible that they derive from a closely related workshop tradition.

Further to this, it is worth observing that the Thetford fish, associated as it is with a set of spoons directly related to the worship of the pagan deity, Faunus, cannot have been intended as a symbol of Christianity. Despite the common assumption that the fish, together with VIVAS inscriptions, is a reflection of a Christian component, it is clear that, in iconographical terms, pagan and Christian themes could be closely interwoven, at any rate in the northern provinces.[55]

5. *The parcel-gilt Panther spoon* (**66**). Our earlier discussion of the Thetford Triton spoon concluded that it was almost certainly by the same hand as the remarkable *cochleare* which shows a lively, cheerful panther, leaping in front of a tree. In common are numerous features, not least the style and nature of the decoration; the distinctive, pointed shape of the bowl; and, in all probability, the hand that engraved the two inscriptions (both of which include the name Narus).

The Panther spoon has, however, various points in common with the other long-handled spoons. Apart from its elongated tapering handle, with the inscription at the bowl end (an inscription clearly made before the handle was thinned to a point), it has a plain scroll offset. This is comparable to those of the RESTITVTI pair, **76** and **77**; to those of a near-pair, **79** and **80**; and to the offset of **81**. It is one of the commonest designs on late-Roman spoons although, as we have seen, it could be elaborated into much more complex motifs. In this case, the craftsman lavished most of his attention upon giving the spoon a fine finish, a well-cut inscription and, above all, upon an elegantly drawn and highly accomplished representation of one of Bacchus' constant companions. Overall, however, the form of the spoon belongs comfortably within the general range of the long-handled *cochleare*, underlining the fact that, in a typological sense, it has close affinities with the group as a whole.

THE TYPOLOGY OF THE LONG-HANDLED SPOONS: DISCUSSION

The five groups of spoons discussed above do not form in any sense a series of types with mutually exclusive features: as Table 4 below shows, common themes can be traced through the assemblage, suggesting both a general contemporaneity and, in all probability, production in a single workshop. There are three definite pairs (66/72, 73/74, 76/77), three near pairs (70/71, 79/80, 78/82) and five spoons with quite individual characteristics. However, since only one pair has identical inscriptions, it is difficult to know what significance should be attached to this distribution of types; indeed the absence of any consistency in the pattern warns against any over-elaborate interpretation.

Nevertheless, it is worth noting the general association on the one hand between zoomorphic offset, chip-carved handles and oval bowls and, on the other, between pear-shaped bowls (which in the Thetford group are generally less narrow than for example those from Dorchester-on-Thames),[56] plain handles and scroll offsets. But we should emphasise that this is a *trend* in the distribution, not a rigid separation of traits.

is also of interest, namely 424.5 g. Taking a Roman pound of silver to be 318.9 g, this amounts to 1.33 pounds.[57] Some allowance must be made for a few grams lost by the damage to 70, and for the difficulty in assigning a value to the Roman pound (a matter discussed above); but it may be significant that the total is not far short of $1\frac{1}{2}$ Roman pounds. Indeed, the addition of three more spoons (which would make an even number for the *cochlearia*) would bring the total weight to just over $1\frac{1}{2}$ pounds, a weight which would then match that of the duck-handled spoons, and give a total overall of about three pounds of silver. On the other hand, it may be that we should regard the range of variables as sufficiently imprecise as to render invalid calculations of this sort: only by the recovery and analyses of other large hoards of this sort can such a hypothesis be tested. Meanwhile, the possibility that one spoon, or more, of the long-handled series was not included when the treasure was buried (or, alternatively, were missed when the hoard was salvaged) cannot completely be ignored.

Table 4 The distribution of the main typological characteristics of the long-handled spoons

	66	67	68	69	70	71	72	73	74	75	76	77	78	79	80	81	82
Parcel gilding/engraved design	●	●															
Oval bowl	●		●	●	●	●	●			●	●	●					●
Bowl inscription			●	●	●	●	●	●	●								
Zoomorphic offset			●	●	●	●	●			●							
Chip-carved handle			●		●	●	●			●							
Twisted handle				●				●	●							●	
Plain handle	●	●									●	●	●	●	●		●
Pear-shaped handle								●	●				●	●	●		
Scroll offset	●	●						●	●		●	●	●	●	●	●	●
Handle inscription	●									●	●	●	●	●	●	●	●

THE WEIGHTS OF THE LONG-HANDLED SPOONS

In an earlier section, we drew attention to the fact that most of the duck-handled spoons appeared to weigh about one Roman ounce of silver. Much the same conclusion applies also to the long-handled spoons. Leaving aside the damaged spoon, 70, which now weighs only 18.6 g, the figures are as follows:

22 g	23 g	24 g	25 g	26 g	27 g
66		67	68	69	73
		71	75	79	74
		72	76		77
		80	78		
		81	82		

It will be remembered from calculations made earlier that an ounce could apparently vary from about 25 to 28.5 g. In this case, all but 66, the parcel-gilt Panther spoon, would fall within this range of weights, a distribution that seems unlikely to be the result of chance. Moreover, the total weight of silver

The different 'hands' among the inscriptions (Fig. 5)

The very detailed drawings of the inscriptions present an excellent opportunity to set one alongside another in an attempt to see how many 'hands' might be represented. We should of course recognise this for what it is, namely an exercise in subjective judgement. For instance, a change in the type of punch might well result in a rather different style of lettering, just as there is no reason to assume any great degree of consistency in one person's hand. Nevertheless, whilst allowing for all these limitations, an attempt to trace groups amongst the inscriptions seems well worth making.

In fact, one group (A) became apparent very quickly. It is characterised by a careless and sloppy use of the punch so that the strokes in a letter frequently overlap each other. There is also a striking uniformity of letter-style, well illustrated, for instance, by the letters E, F, V and S. Only the inscription DEITVGI with its slightly tidier approach and lesser emphasis upon serifs seems to us at all doubtful. Nevertheless, we could conclude that all these inscriptions are by the same hand.

Fig. 5. Group A: 51; 55; 57; 58; 78; 76; 77

Fig. 5. Group B: 60; 59; 61; 69; 68; 70; 72; 73

Fig. 5. Group C: 63; 54; 56; 62; 71

Fig. 5. Group D: 50; 66; 74; 52; 53

Group B is much more difficult to analyse. The neat, well-spaced letters of the first three would seem to provide a common link, as does the form of individual letters. Silviolavivas+ and avspicivivas would also seem to share some of these characteristics; on the other hand, there are a number of points of comparison with the remaining three inscriptions (e.g. the shape of the a, v and s). Our feeling, then, is that there are two hands represented here but that it is not easy to assign all of the inscriptions to one group or another.

The third group, c, seems likely to be the work of one hand, although there is a certain measure of uncertainty. The overall effect is fairly neat, with a tendency towards a rather florid style of serifs (particularly on ingenvaevivas). Moreover, some letter-forms are remarkably consistent through the group, especially in the use of a g with a comma-like curl at the bottom; this should be compared with the Gs of the other groups, all of which are quite different. Despite some minor variation through the group, therefore, we would nevertheless feel that the uniformity of approach is a more telling factor than a few discrepancies of letter type.

The last group, d, includes both the Panther (50) and the Triton (66) spoons; these inscriptions must be compared by letter-form rather than by style, since one uses a double-stroke technique of outlining the letters. However, the individual letters shows so many points of similarity that it is difficult to

resist the conclusion that they are by the same hand. Moreover, the other inscriptions also show a consistency in the shape and the arrangement of the letters and in their spacing, suggesting that these too were produced by the craftsman who lettered the Triton and Panther spoons.

The remaining abbreviated inscriptions are far too short to permit any judgement about the style of the lettering, although it is perhaps worth noting that the spoon inscribed MED (79) does have a strikingly individual character, which is not easily paralleled amongst the other inscriptions. Overall, however, we are left with the impression that there are likely to be some five different hands represented by the inscriptions. Naturally, we must recognise the strong possibility that the number could be more and, indeed, it could be less; but our conclusion that it was a small group of artisans who inscribed these spoons — in some cases *demonstrably* before they received their finishing touches — does seem to be fairly well founded. Once again, it is an area of study which could well be applied to other large groups of epigraphic material, should they come to light.

The spoons: some conclusions

It will now be useful to gather together some of the main points that have emerged in the previous discussion, and to set them in something of a wider context.

WEIGHT

The importance of measures of weight of precious metals is well attested on literary, epigraphic and archaeological grounds in the fourth century. This may in part derive from the fact that payments of gold and silver donatives, made to soldiers and civil servants, were a particular feature of late-Roman times. For example, there was a five-year donative of five gold *solidi* a person, paid by the *comes sacrarum largitionum*, probably on the emperor's birthday.[58] There were also accession donatives, as well as payments on some quinquennial, decennial or vicennial occasions. The practice began at least as early as AD 317 and became increasingly common. Ammianus Marcellinus (xx. 4.18) tells us, for instance, that upon Julian's accession in AD 361 each man was promised five gold *solidi* and a pound of silver. It may also explain why it was that so many silver objects were inscribed with their weight[59] and, equally, why packets of silver were sometimes made up to a precise weight. As examples we may take the two folded parcels of silver in the 1974 Water Newton hoard, which weigh 642 g (= two pounds) and 321 g (= one pound) respectively;[60] or an ingot from Kent, which was made up to a one-pound measure by the addition of a small knob of silver.[61]

These silver ingots, of which twelve complete examples are now known from Britain alone,[62] provide explicit archaeological confirmation of the practice of paying donatives. Despite some variation in weight, it seems clear that each was intended to amount to one Roman pound; moreover, they are also remarkably standard in design. Many were in fact stamped with the name of the workshop that produced them, a further indication of the degree of official control that was exercised over the supply of precious metals.

In the light of these remarks, it is clearly legitimate to examine the weights of the silver in the Thetford assemblage to see if there is any evidence for conformity with known standards of weight. The relevant figures are as follows:

	duck-handled spoons	long-handled spoons	strainers	total
	497.5 g	424.5 g	56.3 g	978.3 g
pound at 318.9 g[63]	1.56 pounds	1.33 pounds	0.17 pounds	3.07 pounds
pound at 325 g	1.53 pounds	1.31 pounds	0.17 pounds	3.01 pounds

We have already discussed the difficulty of assigning a precise value to the Roman pound of silver; it was evidently a figure that could in practice vary quite widely. Nevertheless, we felt able earlier to suggest that all but six of the thirty-three spoons were each intended to weigh an ounce and to draw attention to the measurement of just about 1½ pounds for the total weight of silver in the duck-handled spoons. As far as the rest of the silver is concerned, there seem to be two possible hypotheses. The first hypothesis would assume that we should take the *total* weight of silver, including the strainers, and convert it into Roman pounds. This would amount to just over three pounds, a figure that might well justify the suggestion that the strainers were intended to bring the total weight of silver to a whole figure. On the other hand, the strainers could be excluded from the calculations and the spoons considered on their own. This leads us to observe that, were another three long-handled spoons added to the assemblage, making it an even-numbered set of the same size as that from Kaiseraugst, this would also bring the total weight of silver to just over three Roman pounds.

In reality, it is of course impossible to choose between these alternatives, based as they are upon such vague numerical premises. We can do no more than draw attention to a range of possibilities, some of which might usefully be tested by work on other assemblages of late-Roman silver. Eventually, one suspects, a good deal of light could be shed on the whole question of weights and measures — and the way in which they were controlled — in this period.

PRODUCTION CENTRES

We must now turn to the notoriously difficult question of workshops and production centres. Silver was of course both extracted and worked in Britain. There are ingots stamped EX ARG. BRIT., and cupellation furnaces have been identified at Wroxeter and Silchester.[64] Indeed, the Water Newton Christian silver, which is an assemblage of fairly second-rate artistic quality, could well have been produced within the province.[65] The main centres are, however, extremely difficult to identify.

Many of the capital cities such as Rome, Constantinople, Alexandria, Antioch, Carthage, Milan, Ravenna, Trier and Lyon must have possessed workshops that made sets of fine-quality silver vessels, such as the Mildenhall and Kaiseraugst Treasures, for the top echelons of society. In fact, some pieces were stamped by government officials and may, in due course, eventually provide a firm basis for identifying these centres. The few stamps that are known show that some objects — probably including the great dish and platters from Mildenhall and also items in the Carthage Treasure — were certainly made in Constantinople, while two stamps in the Kaiseraugst Treasure indicate that one vessel was made by Euticius of Naissus (= Niš in Yugoslavia, Constantine's birthplace) and another by Pausylypos of Thessalonike. Inscriptions on the so-called 'Munich Treasure' are also helpful, in that they establish the existence of two workshops at Nicomedia in Bithynia, a workshop at Antioch, and that a piece in this group was made at Naissus. A large treasure could therefore be composed of objects from a number of sources although stylistic considerations do not necessarily separate one centre from another.[66]

Painter has, however, attempted to distinguish the general provenance of one set of objects on stylistic grounds. The case rests upon a technique of engraving with a double-stroke as exemplified by a silver spoon from Biddulph and by spoons from Hof Iben (Mainz) and from Carthage, as well as by various vessels including the Proiecta casket in the Esquiline Treasure.[67] Painter compares this technique with inscriptions upon a series of glass goblets, flasks and bowls, most of which appear to have been made in the east Mediterranean, and concludes that these silver objects with double-stroke inscriptions very likely derive from workshops in the eastern part of the Empire. 'Conversely,' he adds, 'the spoons stamped with single-line inscriptions may well have a western origin, particularly in view of the common use and occurrence of such objects'.[68] Shelton, on the other hand, argues that the Esquiline Treasure was the product of a workshop in Rome, and would count the Parabiago patera, the fluted dish from Mildenhall and the Traprain fluted bowl and flagon amongst the items made in this workshop.[69]

This contention is a matter that is to a certain extent illuminated by one of the Thetford inscriptions, that on the Triton spoon (50). Whilst the letters are practically sanserif and are crudely drawn in comparison with those on the Biddulph spoon, they are rendered with an engraved double-line. There is no trace of niello infilling and the intention, we presume, was to design an inscription whose visual effect was relatively bland, and did not detract from the figures in parcel gilding. What is significant about the inscription, however, is the fact that it contains — like so many of the spoons — a Celtic element, in this case Narus. This, we take it, should imply production in a Celtic-speaking area, namely Gaul or Britain since, as we have already demonstrated, many of the inscriptions were engraved before the spoons were finished.

Unfortunately, we know next to nothing about the centres that may have manufactured these smaller items of silverwork. Even so, it seems reasonable to assume that they were often produced in the major cities. There are, in fact, some useful clues from the Mildenhall, Traprain and Esquiline Treasures. We have already noted the links, as suggested by Shelton, between items in the groups. What has received less emphasis are the parallels between the three Mildenhall spoons with fluted decoration in their bowls and the strikingly similar arrangement of alternate straight and sinuous fluted decoration on the Mildenhall 'scallop' bowl — a vessel thought by Shelton to be a product of the 'Esquiline' workshop. There is also a very similar spoon, no. 100, in the Traprain Treasure, as well as an Esquiline-type fluted bowl, and a series of other fluted spoons, from Great Horwood, Vermand and elsewhere, which appear to belong to a similar tradition.[70]

Our conjecture might be, therefore, that some of these spoons, together with the Mildenhall and Traprain fluted bowls, were all products of the 'Esquiline' workshop, most convincingly located in Rome itself. If so, it establishes the existence within the western empire of a strong tradition of silversmithing at the highest standard in the mid to late fourth century. Many of the Thetford spoons would fit comfortably within this category but, on the evidence of the primary inscriptions, are most likely to have been manufactured within the Celtic-speaking world. Where, then, were they made?

Naturally, we can do no more than make a reasoned guess, working on the premise that the spoons do derive from a single workshop. The choice is essentially between Gaul and Britain (although Cisalpine Gaul could also be a possibility), and there are a number of reasons which prompt us to suggest Gaul as the likeliest place. In the first place, the parcel-gilt spoons with their accomplished and refined classical designs seem much more appropriate to a Gallic milieu than to a provincial British workshop. Secondly, while many of the typological features are quite close to those of other spoons found in Britain, exact parallels are mostly lacking; it is as if there were divergent trends, developing from common prototypes, as with the zoomorphic spoons. Indeed, it may well be significant that we have been able to draw quite close analogies with the Papittedo and Pascentia spoons from the Mildenhall treasure.

Thirdly, we might wonder if the revival of an old Latian cult, best known from writers of five hundred years earlier, is not more likely to have originated in Gaul than in Britain. The qualities that Faunus symbolises had, of course, not been forgotten (as the homily of Arnobius[71] reminds us), and some villa-owners in Britain opted for antique mythological allusions in the decoration of their mosaic pavements.[72] Even so, it seems altogether more plausible to see the adoption of Faunus as a cult deity, with its conscious harking-back to Virgil, Ovid and others, as a Gallic rather than British phenomenon, that subsequently shifted to rural East Anglia. It is unfortunate that the Celtic names cannot be assigned on linguistic grounds either to a Gallic or to a British tradition, for this would probably clinch the case. Meanwhile, we can only make our necessary subjective assessment that the spoons were both manufactured and inscribed in Gaul.

THE DATE OF THE THETFORD SPOONS

We have been able to cite a good many parallels for the Thetford spoons in contexts dated between *c.* AD 350 and 400. It seems certain, therefore, that the spoons must have been manufactured at some point in the second half of the fourth century. The question must be to decide how late in that century we should assign these types. Unfortunately, too few dated hoards are so far available to us to establish this with any certainty. Due weight might be given to the presence of long-handled spoons with zoomorphic offsets, a form attested *inter alia* in the late-fourth/early fifth century treasures of Dorchester (Dorset) and Canterbury,[73] but it is not yet clear how early in the fourth century this style of decoration became prevalent. Other considerations, such as the style of the jewellery, point to a late fourth-century date for the Thetford assemblage as a whole; however, viewed on its own, it would be incautious to regard the Thetford silver as diagnostic of that period without further corroborative evidence.

NOTES
1. Milojčić 1968; Sherlock 1973.
2. Laur-Belart 1963; Kent and Painter 1977, 40.
3. Dalton 1900; Kent and Painter 1977, 102.
4. The tip of one spoon, 70, is missing and could have been broken when it was excavated. There is also slight damage to the duck's beak of 62.
5. H. J. Plenderleith and A. C. Werner, *The conservation of antiquities and works of art.* 1977, p. 220f., discuss this question.
6. *Hacksilber* hoards are considered by Burnett and Johns 1979 and by Grünhagen 1954, 58f.
7. For the spoons, cf. Painter 1977a. The date of the Mildenhall group is much debated, but Painter (1977a, 22–3) has argued that it could have been buried in AD 360.
8. Dorchester-on-Thames: Kent and Painter 1977, 57; Clutterbuck 1870–3. On the other hand, the Canterbury spoons (Painter 1965), which like the Thetford set, probably date to the closing decades of the fourth century, have a very similar type of finish. We are grateful to Mr K. Reedie, curator of Canterbury Museum, for a chance to examine the Canterbury spoons and to carry out metallurgical analyses.
9. Cf. Painter 1977a.
10. The other is spoon 60, a piece of very high quality.
11. Traprain: Curle 1923; Helpston: *Britannia* 12, 1981, p. 340 and C. M. Johns, 1982. An unprovenanced fourth-century spoon, probably from Britain, has a fish in parcel-gilt upon it (Potter, *forthcoming*).
12. Painter in Kent and Painter 1977, 26; cf. also an unprovenanced spoon in the Cleveland Museum of Art (Weitzman 1979, no. 316) and two inscribed spoons with gilt scenes from near Aquileia (*CIL* 5 8122.10).
13. Painter 1972.

14. Now in the collections of the British Museum, to be published by Kenneth Painter.
15. Usefully summarised by Painter 1965, 5; cf. also Kent 1956.
16. On weights generally cf. H. Chantraine *Pauly-Wissowa Real. Encycl.* 1961, pp. 617f.; F. G. Skinner, *Weights and Measures.* Science Museum 1967, p. 65: 'it is useless to speak of any pound weight measure as *the* Roman pound'. J. P. C. Kent, *Roman Coins.* 1978, p. 358, notes for coins 'it is possible that a standard 1/50 pound was aimed at (6.50 g) though rarely achieved.' On this measurement one pound could be equal to 325 g. Cf. also F. Hultsch, *Griechische und Römische Metrologie,* Berlin, 1882. Weights were of course sometimes inscribed upon a vessel: e.g. the monogram plate in the Esquiline Treasure, one of a set of four, with an inscription reading *Scut [ellae] IIII P [ondo] V* — 'four small dishes [with a total weight of] five pounds' (Shelton 1981, 80). We are grateful to Dr Mansel Spratling both for a copy of his paper on the subject, to which the reader is referred (Spratling 1980), and for referring us to the important discussion of Grierson 1964.
17. A point underlined by the well-established Imperial practice of presenting pounds of silver as donatives or accession gifts.
18. Painter 1965, 7; Strong 1966, 205.
19. Ibener Hof: Cabrol and Leclerq 1914, 3175–6 and Painter 1965, pl. VI; Kaiseraugst: Laur-Belart 1963, Kent and Painter 1977, no. 82; Canoscio: Giovagnoli 1935, 325; Vermand: Eck 1891, pl. XX; Traprain: Curle 1923, 67–8.
20. E.g. in the Canterbury hoard (Painter 1965), both duck-handled spoons have simple handles.
21. A good many instances of this sort of motif are known. E.g., a Roman example from Tiddis, now in Constantine Museum (Algeria); Ténès, Speyer and Dijon, illustrated in Heurgon 1958, pl. XXIV; a late-Iron Age example from Milber Down, Devon (A. Ross, *Pagan Celtic Britain.* 1967, fig. 149); and an instance from Felmingham, Norfolk (*Guide to the Antiquities of Roman Britain.* London, 1964, pl. XXIV). The only other spoon that we know of where the bird has a bun in his mouth is an example in the Traprain Treasure (Curle 1923, fig. 45–7). It is interesting to see how many of these instances belong in the Celtic part of the world. For further discussion cf. Heurgon 1958, 45–6.
22. We are most grateful to Dr I. A. Kinnes for constructing the matrix.
23. Kent and Painter 1977, 40.
24. Painter 1977a, 22–3.
25. Painter 1965, 11–12. For an unprovenanced spoon that morphologically and metallurgically is identical to duck-handled spoon no. 4 in the Canterbury hoard, cf. Potter, *forthcoming.*
26. Curle 1923, nos 102, 103. Unfortunately, the handles are bent out of shape and we cannot be certain how they should be reconstructed. The dating evidence for the Traprain hoard consists of coins of Valens (AD 364–78), Valentinian (AD 375–92) and Honorius (AD 395–423).
27. Laur-Belart 1963 and Kent and Painter 1977, 40–3; Curle 1923; Painter 1965.
28. Mildenhall: Painter 1977a, 30–34; Kent and Painter 1977, 57.
29. For an interesting study of the possible consequences of the closure of the Riotinto silver mines in the later second century, cf. G. D. B. Jones, *JRS* 70. 1980, pp. 161f.
30. Painter 1977a, 31, no. 28.
31. Painter 1965, nos 12, 13.
32. Both variants can be found in other groups of zoomorphic spoons, e.g. Canterbury (Painter 1965) and Dorchester, Dorset (Dalton 1922).
33. Painter 1965; Dalton 1922.
34. Strong 1966, 177 and fig. 36.
35. Painter 1977a, 30, fig. 7.
36. Waugh 1966.

37. Painter 1965, nos 11–13.
38. Dalton 1922.
39. Kent and Painter 1977, 57, nos 109–111.
40. For a discussion of the location of workshops, cf. the concluding section to the chapter. It is worth noting the possibility that the Mildenhall Papettido spoon could be ancestral to the Thetford tradition of zoomorphic types.
41. Most recently in Kent and Painter 1977, 57; cf. also Painter 1965, 7.
42. References as *supra.*
43. Eck 1891, pl. I, no. 21.
44. Rome: Cabrol and Leclerq 1914, no. 3459 (p. 3180); Kertch: *Archäologischer Anzeiger* 23. 1908, p. 175, fig. 11.
45. Mattingly 1922.
46. Now usefully discussed in the context of the Lankhills (Winchester) cemetery (Clarke 1979).
47. In Kent and Painter 1977, 57. Strong (1966, 178) suggests on the basis of spoons from Köln-Bickendorf, dated 270–80, that 'this form of embellishment . . . was coming into fashion at the end of the third century.'
48. Mildenhall: Painter 1977a, nos 30, 31; Traprain: Curle 1923, nos 97, 99; Canterbury: Painter 1965, nos 5–8; Köln-Müngersdorf: Milojčić 1968, Abb. 9, nos 4, 6.
49. Painter 1977a, 30, fig. 7.
50. Kent and Painter 1977, 57, no. 109.
51. See note 34.
52. Conveniently illustrated together by Milojčić 1968, Abb. 9.
53. Giovagnoli 1935, 325; there is, however, the drawing of a fish on a dish in the Kaiseraugst Treasure, which shows the creature consuming a worm: Laur-Belart 1967, Abb. 18.
54. Potter, *forthcoming.* Registration number: P.1982, 5–1, 1.
55. Henig (1977, 352f.) discusses this question and also draws attention to a pewter spoon from London engraved with three fish within the bowl.
56. Kent and Painter 1977, 57.
57. Cf. note 16.
58. Cf. Painter 1965, 5f; Painter 1972; Kent and Painter 1977, 26.
59. Cf. note 16.
60. Painter 1977b, 27 and pl. 32.
61. Painter 1972.
62. Painter 1972, cf. also Salomonson 1961.
63. Cf. note 16 for discussion of the weights.
64. Cf. J. Liversidge, *Britain in the Roman Empire.* 1968, p. 206; Frere 1978, 320f.
65. Painter (1977b, 24) notes that 'What does seem clear is that the hoard belongs in the western half of the Roman Empire.'
66. For a very useful discussion of these matters, cf. particularly Kenneth Painter in Kent and Painter 1977, 19 and under his descriptions of the individual treasures; also Painter 1977a, 14f.
67. Painter 1977a, 15f. For the Biddulph spoon, Painter 1975 and Sherlock 1976.
68. Painter 1977a, 16.
69. Shelton 1981, 57f.
70. Traprain: Curle 1923; Great Horwood: Waugh 1966; Vermand: Eck 1891.
71. Arnobius, *Adversus nationes* 5, 1 *inter alia.* We use the word 'revival' but, as we shall see in Chapter 7, it is likely that the worship of Faunus had never died out; indeed, Arnobius' denunciation, *c.* AD 300, reminds us of this fact.
72. E.g., the well-known Low Ham mosaic with its scenes from Virgil's *Aeneid.*
73. Dorchester: Dalton 1922; Canterbury: Painter 1965.

6

The Inscriptions on the Silver Spoons

by Kenneth Jackson

The basic language of the inscriptions

This is Latin, not Celtic; that is, everything but the divine epithets is in Latin, including the god-name Faunus and the human personal names. This does not of itself necessarily mean that the whole context of the hoard was a purely Roman one. Certainly there must have been a Celtic background to this cult of Faunus exemplified by the inscriptions, but whether the worshippers spoke only Latin is unclear. The exclusively Latin personal names suggest they were at any rate thoroughly Romanised.

The standard of Latin used

There is very little sign of Vulgar Latin in the forms, which implies that the Roman context was a considerably educated one. The only clear example is the final -ae in the INGENVAE of 62. The sense shows that this cannot be genitive or dative of feminine *Ingenua*, but must be the vocative of masculine *Ingenuus*; and this means that the -ae is an instance of the common non-Classical confusion of *e* and *ae*, and that the form is simply a spelling for *Ingenue*. The vocative AGRESTE (72) from *Agrestis* or *Agrestius* does seem to suggest an ungrammatical confusion of declensions, unless indeed a genuine second-declension name *Agrestus* had come into existence.

There appear to be a few errors on the part of the engraver. In **51**, **56**, and **66** there is an 'ignorant' or merely mistaken spelling for DEI, or perhaps a slip due to a sort of over-correction of the alternative genitive DI. In **58**, DEO appears to be the dative, '*for* the god' (the contents of the spoon offered to the god), and this is supported by the dative SATERNIO in agreement with it, in spite of the genitive FAVNI. This last would have been a slip due to the exclusive genitive FAVNI in all the others. This seems rather more likely than that both DEO and SATERNIO were mistakes and FAVNI correct. The genitive DEI FAV(NI) of **51–57** and **74**, and the DEI TVGI in **78** mean, of course, 'of the god Faunus/Togius', i.e. 'the property of . . .' or '[spoon] belonging to the cult of . . .', or the like. The RESTITVTI of **76** and **77** seems more likely to refer to a human proprietor, Restitutus, that is, 'Restitutus's [spoon]'. The only other engraver's error is the IT in **61**, which is meaningless and must be a careless transposition of TI, which together with the preceding ligatured V gives *uti*, the variant form of Latin *ut*, 'that'. Hence, 'Persevera, [I wish] that you may live long', if the adjective *persevera* is used here as a woman's name, or 'stick to it, I wish that you may live long', which, however, seems a little unlikely in the context of the others.

Nos **61**, **62**, **63**, **68**, **69**, **70** and **72** contain the Latin personal names Ingenuus, Primigenia, Silviola, Auspicius, Agrestis/-(i)us, and perhaps *Persevera, in the vocative, followed by VIVAS (or in **61**, VTI VIVAS), literally 'may you live [long]'; that is, 'long life to you, your good health'. In **60** the phrase is made more impersonal and of wider application by substituting the vocative VIR BONE, literally 'good man'; i.e., 'my dear fellow, my good sir'.

Inscriptions of this sort are familiar on Roman domestic utensils, particularly drinking vessels, just as we use the 'your good health' type of address in toasting someone, and formulae of the kind are still found on peasant ware such as is sold to tourists. The use of definite personal names in all but **59** and **60** is, however, interesting and surely significant.

It must mean that the spoons were made, or at any rate inscribed, for the use of a definite body of people, whether for a family or some other kind of group, who in either case were worshippers of Faunus. But what were they used for? The *vivas* instances suggest that they were used in some kind of love-feast or communal (ritual?) banquet during which the diners toasted each other. Did they fill the spoons with wine and pour it down their throats? Their shape would suit that. Or was the purpose of the sharp points to scoop up (rather like scooping out a Stilton cheese) some possibly fixed and identical quantity of food or sacrificial grain offered to Faunus? But only **58** suggests this clearly, if the correct reading is really DEO FAVNO SATERNIO.

The general significance of the Celtic epithets

Double-barrelled names of deities like Apollo Grannus, of which the first is Latin and the second Celtic, are of course very familiar in Romano-Celtic religion. This, the so-called *interpretatio Romana*, arose when the Celts were Romanised and attempted to assimilate their gods to the Roman ones by prefixing to them the name of some Roman god whose attributes seemed to suit those of the Celtic one concerned. The next step was to drop the Celtic part of the name altogether. But these Faunus inscriptions are evidently not a case of *interpretatio Romana*, since it is exceedingly unlikely that a number of separate *Celtic* gods (Narus, Cranus, etc., etc.), identified independently with the Roman Faunus, would be fused into a single cult of Faunus. It is much more probable that these Celtic names represent epithets descriptive of various aspects of one and the same Faunus under which he was worshipped by these people, perhaps connected with various features of his 'myth'.

THE CELTIC EPITHETS[1]

There is no clear means of telling whether they are Gaulish or British, and the continual Gaulish parallels quoted in what follows, and the absence of British ones, is due to the fact that so much more is known about Gaulish and Gaulish religion and gods than about British. But this may none the less support the belief that the spoons are of Romano-Gaulish manufacture — indeed that perhaps they were made for a group of *Gaulish* worshippers of Faunus in the first instance, but subsequently exported for the use of a similar 'conventicle' in Britain (or even imported by emigrants from Gaul?).

1 DEI NARI (50); DEII FAVNI NARI (51 and 66): The name occurs in Gaulish *Narius*, feminine *Naria*, and there are Gaulish *Deae Nariae*.[2] If this is *Nārius*, and related to Old Irish *nár*, the meaning would be 'powerful, noble, great-hearted'.[3] If Narius, with short *a*, related to early Welsh *nar* of rather doubtful meaning, it might mean 'lord'. Therefore, 'of Faunus Narius', i.e. 'Faunus the Mighty, the Noble', or 'the Lord'. But these etymologies of *Narius* are uncertain.

2 DEI FAVNI CRANI (52 and 74): I cannot solve DEI FAVNI CRANI (see below on 82), though if this is *Crāni* it might be connected with Welsh *crawn*, 'accumulated treasure', and therefore 'of the god Faunus Cranius', i.e. 'Faunus the God of Hoards' — suitable enough!

3 DEI FAVNI ANDI CROSE (53): Nor can I solve DEI FAVNI ANDI CROSE except to say that ANDI looks like the familiar Gallo-Brittonic *andi* or *ande*, a prepositional or adverbial prefix of various meanings of which the chief are 'in, into' and 'great, much', the second being more likely here; and that if so, it should have been engraved as one word with CROSE. But a word *crose* is unknown to me; it cannot mean 'cross', and a final *-e* in this context is peculiar. Professor Evans suggests (by letter) that ANDI might be a separate name, since a Gaulish *Andius* is known, and this could be its genitive. However this causes further problems with CROSE.

4 DEI FAV[NI] MEDVGENI (54); DEII FAVNI MEDIGENI (56); and DEI FAV[NI] MEDIGENI (71); as well as the abbreviated MED (79): I have no doubt that this is the Celtic *medu*, 'mead', compounded with the verb *gen-* 'to beget, give birth to'. The two examples in MEDI- might appear to make this less likely, but since the vowel after D is an unstressed stem-vowel, the *i* may merely represent a secondary reduction from *u*. The name is already known in Gaulish, genitive *Medugeni*, as here, in, for example, an inscription from Portugal[4] (and in other examples added by Professor Evans by letter); in Primitive Irish in an Ogam inscription from Co. Cork;[5] and in Old Irish as *Midgen*, in which the *Mid-* has *-i-* under the influence of lost following *-u-*. The meaning is 'Mead-begotten', compare the Old Irish name *Fíngen*, from *wīnogenos*, 'Wine-begotten'. Both must refer to a parental episode of drunkenness, no disgrace in early Celtic society, and in the case of Faunus this epithet was presumably connected with some myth about his parentage, perhaps echoed in ritual among his worshippers. This fits in well with what seems to have been a Bacchic aspect in the cult of Faunus. Therefore, 'of the god Faunus Medugenus, the Mead-begotten'.

5 DEI FAVNI AVSECI (55); DEI FAV [NI] AVSECI (73): the only etymology I can suggest for this is the Indo-European *aus-i-* or *aus-es-* 'ear', seen in Old Irish, *au*, later *ó*, 'ear', and in the Gaulish woman's name *Suausia*, 'Having Beautiful Ears'; as well as in Latin *auris*, 'ear', and *ausculto*, 'I listen'. AVSECI probably represents the genitive of masculine *ausicos*, that is, **ausi-* with the adjectival-formative suffix *-ico-*, and therefore literally 'ear-ish'. The *-e-* for *-i-* would be an example of the occasional alternation between 'i' and 'e' in Gaulish,[6] rather than a case of the Vulgar Latin *e* for *i*, though that too might be possible. The meaning would be, then, 'of the god Faunus Ausicus, Faunus Prick-Ear, or Long-Ear', which well suits the conflation with Pan that seems to have occurred in Roman religion.

6 DEI FAV[NI] BLOTVGI (57); and abbreviated BLO (64, 75 and 80): I think the first element must be either the Gallo-Brittonic **blātu-* (or **blāto-*), 'flower, blossom', as in Welsh *blawd*, related to Latin *flos*; or perhaps **blāti-* or **blāto-*, 'flour', the source of French *blé*, as in the other Welsh *blawd*. In either case the adjectival-formative suffix *-uco-* is added. A slight difficulty here is that *ā* does not normally give *ō* in Gaulish; but there are some examples, mostly in late Gaulish, where it does seem to have become *ō*, one of them being actually another instance of *Blotu-*, that is, the name of a god *Bloturix* in an inscription from Lorraine,[7] obviously standing for *Blaturix*, 'King of the Blossom', presumably a god of Spring and Fertility.[8] Another slight difficulty might appear to be -VGI for -VCI, genitive of *-ucus*, but this is of no significance, since it is well known that Gaulish *c* was often spelt *g* and vice versa, in Latin letters, the sound in Gaulish having been very likely something between that of Latin *c* and Latin *g*.[9] Therefore, 'of the god Faunus Blatucus, the Bringer of Spring Blossom', or perhaps 'Faunus the Fosterer of Corn'. Either would suit him.

7 DEO FAVNI SATERNIO (58), 'for the god Faunus Saternius', as already suggested. SATERNIO looks at first sight like an error for SATVRNIO, derivative of Saturnus, which would be fairly appropriate since Saturn was a god of civilisation, agriculture, etc. But it hardly seems likely that the Latin Faunus would actually be identified with the Latin Saturnus in this way,[10] and in any case the form in 58 has a derivative suffix, *-ius*. In fact, Saterninus, with *-e-*, is actually recorded as a genuine Gaulish personal name, as well as Saternus as a river name[11] so that *Saternius* may be really Gaulish. It might be from the Indo-European root **sā-/sa-*, with various meanings such as 'plenty, swarm', etc. (cf. Latin *satis*), and might therefore mean 'giver of plenty' or the like. The suffix *-erno-*, common in Latin, is rather rare in Celtic, but it does exist. So, possibly 'for the god Faunus Saternius, Giver of Plenty'; again a suitable epithet.

8 DEI TVGI (78): note that it is not DEI FAVNI TVGI, but compare 50 with 51 and 66, so that 78 does no doubt stand for DEI FAVNI TVGI. There was a place-name *Tugia* in Roman Spain.[12] As regards the *u*, short *o* may be spelt *u* sometimes, in Gaulish, in which case TVGI could be the same element *togi-* or *togo-* as in the Gaulish compound name *Togimarus*, *Togirix*, etc., and British *Togodumnus*.[13] The meaning of TVGI is obscure, but if we take it as *Togi-*, this could well be a derivative of Indo-European **teg-/tog-*, 'to cover; roof, clothing', etc., and if so, DEI TVGI would be 'of the god (Faunus) Togius, Faunus the Shelterer, Protector'.

9 Nos 79 and 80, the abbreviations MED and BLO have already been dealt with. AN (81) might well be for the ANDI of 53.

GRA (82) could represent the CRANI of **52** and **74** with the confusion of *c* and *g* just mentioned under BLOTVGI and TVGI. It is not likely to be the well-known Gaulish god Grannus, as that would seem to imply an improbable case of *interpretatio Romana*, since Grannus was a sun-god, whose functions would be incompatible with those of Faunus; and such an example would be unparalleled in these Thetford inscriptions, in which all the other Celtic names are epithets.

NOTES

1. I want to acknowledge warmly here some generous help given by Professor D. Ellis Evans, of Oxford, who sent lists of further examples of some of the names and valuable comments on them.
2. See Holder 1904, 689. Professor Evans adds other examples of *Nar-* in Gaulish names.
3. Pokorny 1948, 765.
4. Holder 1904, 256.
5. Macalister 1945, 92, genitive MEDDOGENI; this is an error for MEDDUGENI (cf. Pokorny 1918, 424.)
6. Evans 1967, 392; he now draws attention, by letter, to an actual example of *Ausicus* in a potter's stamp: cf. Whatmough 1970, 805.
7. Schmidt 1957, 151.
8. On *ō* for *ā* in Gaulish, see *Révue Celtique* 50, 1933, p. 261.
9. Watkins 1955, 17f.
10. Since this article was written, I find Mr M. Hassall suggests (Hassall 1981, 392) that as FAUNUS was grandson of Saturn it would be appropriate to call him 'Saturnian', which may well be correct but does not explain the *e* for *u*.
11. Holder 1904, 1374.
12. Holder 1904, 1980, who adds others in *Tugi-*; and Professor Evans compares names in *Tuc(c)-*, suggesting that TVGI is a spelling for TVCI. But the etymology of this is obscure.
13. Schmidt 1957, 279.

Editor's note: Professor Jackson's discussion of the inscriptions and the observations made by Mr Mark Hassall in *Britannia* 12. 1981, p. 389–93 were prepared independently: for a few minor differences of interpretation, the reader is referred to that publication.

7

The Cult of Faunus

Though the name of Faunus is familiar enough, and the fact that he was a pastoral Roman deity is well known, any attempt at a detailed study of his nature and his cult quickly reveals that he is surprisingly obscure and ill documented. The literary evidence for Faunus is chiefly concentrated in writings of the late Republican and early Imperial periods, and though there are numerous references, the sum total of the information they impart is not great. Furthermore, archaeological evidence for the worship of Faunus, either at that time or during the later Empire, seems to be almost non-existent.

We find ourselves, therefore, without any sound framework of knowledge into which we might fit the Thetford assemblage, with its large group of inscriptions referring to this god. It is obviously necessary to set out what is known of the deity and his cult, and to put forward some ideas about their possible role and significance in the Romano-Celtic milieu of late-Roman Gaul or Britain in which the Thetford objects originated, but it is important to remember throughout that our sources are incomplete and arbitrarily biased, and that religious belief and practice within one cult might vary considerably over space and time. It is extremely difficult to judge how the ancient Latian deity described by writers such as Virgil and Horace relates to the one worshipped in the provincial late-Roman context of the Thetford Treasure. As we shall see, there is much scope for the identification of Faunus with other deities, including almost certainly Celtic gods of whom we have no record at all; the use of the name *Faunus* could contain an element of conscious archaising which is a known feature of pagan religion in the fourth century.

All of what follows is in some sense tentative: the inscribed spoons from Thetford have already added a new dimension to our understanding of the Faunus cult, but further work and perhaps future discoveries will be needed to fill the many gaps in our knowledge.

The characteristics of Faunus

There are several modern sources which summarise what is known of Faunus and refer to the literary sources from antiquity.[1] Faunus was originally localised as a god and/or an early king of Latium. He was an earth deity, concerned with the woods and the fields, and with the protection and fertility of flocks and herds. He therefore belongs to a deep and basic stratum of pastoral religious belief which can be paralleled in almost any ancient rural community, since the health and increase of the crops and the stock were the basis of the economy. There are other Graeco-Roman deities known to us who share some of these characteristics, but there were also undoubtedly many other local gods and spirits in Celtic as well as in Mediterranean lands who had the same areas of influence.

Though Faunus exercised a protective power over animals and promoted their health and fertility, like other deities of this kind he had a corresponding malevolent side, and if displeased could cause illness and harm to the very same creatures. Appropriate propitiation and sacrifice was therefore necessary to ensure than he remained benevolent. These two sides are perhaps reflected in his possession, on the one hand, of some goat-like characteristics and, on the other, of his connections with the wolf.

The literary evidence and one of the theoretical derivations of the name of the god indicate a further specific power: Faunus was a seer or foreteller, and his oracular skills could be placed at the disposal of human worshippers if the right approach was made. Closely linked with this was the god's connection with dreams, which can be the vehicle of prophecy or divine inspiration. Faunus could cause dreams of various kinds, including nightmares and erotic dreams, if it is correct to regard Incubus as another of his several names. Fertility deities frequently take on the role of protecting property (this is marked in the case of Silvanus and certain aspects of (Hermes), and there is also a hint of this quality in Faunus, who seems to have been concerned with guarding treasure.

A final noteworthy point is that Faunus was on occasion referred to in the plural (*fauni*), and that there also existed a female counterpart, Fauna, variously identified as the sister or spouse of Faunus, but perhaps simply a feminine manifestation of the god himself. Fauna has been equated with the Bona Dea.

It will be seen that many of the traits briefly summarised above could apply to other gods, above all to Silvanus and to the Greek god Pan. Some of the correspondences are remarkably close; for example, Pan was responsible for the irrational fear, panic, which can afflict humans in lonely country places, while Faunus very similarly was said to be the source of the mysterious and unearthly noises which sometimes frighten people in the same circumstances. The plural aspect of the god is also important. Both in antiquity and in modern times the fauns have been regarded as virtually synonymous with the satyrs, who in turn are similar in many ways to Pan himself, and form part, with him, of the Bacchic entourage or thiasos. In Greek myth, the satyrs and the sileni, though separate in origin, eventually become conflated, and the *fauni* seem to constitute the Latin counterpart to this process. Indeed, it is probably the casual use of the term 'faun' as a synonym for 'satyr' which gives us the idea that Faunus is a familiar deity, an impression which is rapidly dispelled by further investigation.

The names of Faunus and the myths

The above is a very brief survey of the characteristics which seem to mark Faunus, according to the written sources. We can turn now to more specific points. Both in antiquity and in recent times, attempts have been made to define this mysterious and elusive deity more closely by studying the possible derivations of his name, and by considering other names which, for various reasons, have been taken to refer to Faunus.[2]

The most commonly cited derivation of Faunus is from *favere,* with its sense of favouring, protecting and being well-disposed. The name would thus mean 'the kindly one' or 'propitious one'. This is an appropriate, and indeed typical kind of name for a spirit which is known on occasion to be the very reverse of kindly and protective. The Greeks called the Furies the *Eumenides* ('the kindly ones'), and later societies have used similar flattering epithets for the Fairies ('the Good People', and in Welsh, *y tylwyth teg,* 'the fair folk'); names such as these were intended to avert the ill-will of the powers concerned. Another suggested derivation for Faunus is from *fari,* which would give the meaning 'seer', 'speaker' or 'fore-teller', undoubtedly an appropriate designation for the god.

The possible link with the name *Daunus* suggested by Smits would lead back to the Greek θαυνον, and hence to a wild animal/wolf interpretation. It we accept that Faunus was the god venerated at the major Roman festival of the Lupercalia (a matter which will be discussed further below), then the wolf connection is significant, but it is difficult to share the confidence of the many authorities who assert that Faunus was the god of the Lupercalia. For the same reason, the identification of Faunus with an otherwise unknown deity, Inuus, said by Livy to be the deity of this festival, is fraught with uncertainty.[3] The name *Inuus* could be connected with mating and fertility, and would therefore be appropriate to Faunus in his guise as a god of flocks and herds. As *Incubo* or *Incubus,* Faunus's role as a causer of dreams is again stressed: according to Smits, the dream and nightmare aspect is itself tied up with the wolf identification, and the wolf is further characterised as a murderer or strangler; this animal must naturally fit into the mythology of Faunus to some extent, if only because a protector of flocks would have to deal with the threat posed by predatory wild animals, but it seems extremely doubtful whether the very close link postulated by Smits, which would make Faunus primarily a wolf-god, can be justified by the evidence.

As in the myths of so many gods, the actual pedigree of Faunus varies slightly in different sources. He is listed as one of the early kings of Latium; it is not unusual for an ancient deity of an area to be humanised as an early king (though the contrary, the deification of an actual early ruler, has also been proposed). In Virgil,[4] Faunus is the son of Picus, grandson of Saturn, and father of Latinus; another version[5] states that Faunus was the son of Mars. Picus can, however, be interpreted as a manifestation of Mars.[6] Picus is also the name for the woodpecker, sacred to Mars in many parts of ancient Italy.[7] It should be noted that wolves, too, were sacred to the same god.[8] There are even further ramifications: though Picus in the sources is treated as a king or god figure, there is

probably much actual conflation between him and Faunus himself. In particular, it should be remembered that Faunus is concerned with nightmares, and that Picus in the sense of the sacred bird, the woodpecker, had powers over nightmares and over the herbs which were said to forestall them.[9][9]

There are two myths about Faunus which, for different reasons, are of particular interest to us in our attempt to fit the fourth-century Thetford Treasure into the context of the Faunus cult. The first concerns the oracular powers of the god, and the characteristics of a site where a Faunus oracle was situated. The story, related by Virgil,[10] is an account of Latinus consulting the oracle of his father Faunus at a place called Albunea. There were no priests, no temple or shrine; the ritual required the suppliant to bring votive gifts and make sacrifices, and then to sleep at the site, where the oracle would be revealed to him in a dream. This type of ritual was well known in Greek religion, and perhaps particularly well recorded for the major shrine of the healing god Asclepius at Epidauros. The nature of the Faunus shrine, being merely a holy place rather than a built-up, man-made temple precinct, is interesting, and points to the primitive and basic nature of the god; it also provides a link with some Celtic religious practice, particularly in the pre-Roman and early Imperial period, in which sacred places were often left in their natural state, as woods and groves, hills or water sources, without the addition of man-made features. It is thought that the place where the Faunus oracle was situated may be a site called Zolforata in the Roman Campagna, an area of numerous natural sulphur deposits which have been commercially exploited at least since medieval times.[11]

Another Faunus myth is worth quoting because it was selected for ridicule by the fourth-century Christian writer Arnobius of Sicca.[12] It is an account of how Numa, wishing to discover how the evil portended by lightning might be averted, obtained the knowledge from Faunus and Picus by the simple expedient of making them drunk and having them bound fast until they gave him the information. Arnobius picked this story as an example of the absurdity of pagan beliefs, and the foolishness of the deities which were venerated. He was writing at the beginning of the fourth century, and as it is reasonable to assume that he would not have singled out a deeply obscure, almost forgotten legend, it is useful evidence of the currency of the Faunus cult at this period.

While the legends of the oracle of Faunus stress the fact that this was a rural god who could be worshipped in woods or open country places, there is mention of one formal temple to him: this was in Rome itself, on the Tiber island.[13] It was built in 196 BC, and its dedication day was 13 February, two days before the feast of the Lupercalia. No archaeological trace remains of this temple. The fact that the dedication date, which would have been celebrated annually, fell very close to the Lupercalia, has been seen by some as additional evidence that there was some connection between Faunus and that festival, though it does not seem clear why this conclusion should be drawn.

The only festival which we know of which certainly was in honour of Faunus took place on 5 December. It is not recorded in any of the calenders, but is mentioned and described in one of Horace's odes[14] as a rustic festival with sacrifices, feasting, drinking and dancing. Such events would leave no archaeological trace, and the fact that we have literary evidence for these rural Faunalia is probably quite fortuitous; it is safe to assume that there were many other such festivals in country places of which we know nothing.

While the mention of the December Faunalia may be just a lucky chance, the Lupercalia was sufficiently important to be spoken of by a number of authors.[15] We can summarise the celebration very briefly here. The ritual began at the cave called the Lupercal at the foot of the Palatine Hill, the place where Romulus and Remus were believed to have been nurtured by the Wolf; the name is connected with *lupus*, 'a wolf'. Goats and a dog were sacrificed, and two youths played an important part in the proceedings, as, clad in the skins of slaughtered goats, they ran the circuit of the Palatine, striking out with strips of goatskin at women who came forward, with the aim of curing infertility. There are elements in this both of the marking of territory, underlined by the connection with the myth of the founding of the city, and of plain fertility ritual. Both of these are areas in which Faunus could be involved; Ovid states that Faunus was the god venerated at the Lupercalia,[16] though, as we have noted, Livy gives the god the name Inuus. It looks very much as though, by the time of the late Republic and early Empire, there was considerable uncertainty about the meaning of the ritual, and one may suspect that Smits is correct in suggesting that, at least originally, there was no specific god involved at all.[17] The connection with Faunus, if any, could be a later rationalisation and tidying-up of a rite so ancient that it was almost as obscure to those who celebrated it as it is to us.

A point of great interest is the fact that the Lupercalia continued to be celebrated until the very end of the fifth century AD; it was not finally abandoned until AD 494, when Pope Gelasius I transmuted 15 February into the feast of the Purification of the Virgin Mary. Its long survival into Christian times might lend weight to the theory that it was purely a traditional ritual, without any overt connection with a specific pagan god.

Other evidence for the cult of Faunus

It will be seen from the above that though the literary references to Faunus are not infrequent, the amount of information we can glean from them is not very great; we can acquire only a very general idea of the nature of the deity. Archaeological evidence is scanty in the extreme. A fragment of a calender from the Esquiline refers to the temple dedication festival on 13 February,[18] while a marble altar found in the Campus Martius has a long inscription mentioning Fauns (in the plural) and nymphs.[19] There is no visual image which would help us to recognise representations of Faunus.

Some small bronze statuettes have been identified as Faunus,[20] but without any definite evidence. They show a dignified, bearded god wearing boots and a goatskin, and carrying a cornucopia and drinking-horn. Certainly these attributes seem appropriate, but it is difficult to see how such an image can be distinguished from one of Silvanus. Dogs, wolves or goats would also be suitable additional attributes,

as presumably would woodpeckers. Some sources imply actual horns and goats' legs, like Pan himself; a representation of this kind could not be told apart from one of Pan. This lack of iconographic information may well be the key to the apparent obscurity of the cult of Faunus. The problem may turn more on the use of the ancient Latian name than on the concept of the god himself.

The fourth century

As we have already seen, there is at least one literary source in the fourth century which makes reference to Faunus; Arnobius of Sicca, in his clumsy and ill-informed diatribe against paganism, *Adversus nationes*, mentions the god several times. Apart from this, our evidence for a Faunus cult in this increasingly Christian period was absent until the discovery of the inscribed spoons from Thetford.

The key, as hinted above may lie simply in the fact that we do not know what Faunus looked like in the imaginations of his worshippers. There is no lack of archaeological evidence for the worship of Silvanus throughout the Roman period, including much evidence from the Celtic areas, where this god was often worshipped in Celtic guise, and given Celtic by-names. Nor is there any absence of visual evidence for the worship of Pan, together with the whole Bacchic cult, in the later Empire. If, in both the Celtic and the Roman traditions, the concept of Faunus had become profoundly interwined with those of these better-known and more widespread deities, all the difficulties disappear. If the satyrs which we so often find in late-Roman Bacchic decoration, for example on sarcophagi, and on objects such as the Mildenhall great dish, were really thought of equally as fauni, or if the representations of Pan could be referred to alternatively as Faunus, then the place of the cult becomes perfectly clear. It fits into the context of Bacchic worship at this period, probably the most important aspect of paganism in opposition to the growing influence and status of Christianity in the fourth century.

The worship of rustic fertility deities did not wane even with the growth of Christianity, and indeed continued throughout medieval and into post-medieval times in various guises. The cult which is represented by the inscribed spoons from Thetford was probably Celtic at root, but was Romanised into the Bacchic religion, and then overlaid with some conscious harking-back to earlier Italian models. In this sense, there is an element of revival, but the basic religious feeling had probably been constant and uninterrupted for many centuries. Virgil and other authors of the early Empire were read even in fourth-century Britain, as we are reminded by objects like the mosaic from the Low Ham villa, with its quotation from the *Aeneid*. One may even wonder whether one or two of the Thetford inscriptions are directly inspired by literary quotations concerning Faunus. An epithet frequently applied to Faunus or Fauni was *agrestis*,[21] and another, referring to his connections with woodland, was *silvicola*.[22] AGRESTE VIVAS and SILVIOLA VIVAS, on spoons 72, 68 and 69, may at the very least contain some echo of such epithets, used because of their appropriateness to the god.[23] The Celtic names or descriptions stress the background of the cult, in which ancient Celtic nature spirits clearly displayed the same characteristics as the Romanised Bacchic deities which were worshipped. The combination of Roman and Celtic names for gods in the Celtic provinces of the Roman Empire is so common as not to require any detailed discussion.

There can be no doubt that the Thetford material as a whole fits into a Bacchic context; in Chapter 2, while discussing the possible links between the jewellery and the silverware, we have pointed out the Bacchic visual references, some ambiguous, but others quite definite. In the jewellery, they include the satyr (or faun?) on the buckle, and the Pan head — or Faunus head — on ring **23**; in the silver, the panther on spoon **66** is unequivocally Bacchic, the Triton on **50** more vaguely so. As we have seen from the discussion above, the woodpeckers on ring **7** fall into a different category again. They are quite specifically linked with Faunus himself, rather than generally with the worship of Bacchus, and as such, constitute the strongest evidence that the jewellery, as well as the silverware, was in some way connected with the worship of this god.

Obviously we cannot say with any confidence what kind of ritual may have been involved in the worship of Faunus in a Celtic province in the fourth century AD. It would have contained elements of the Celtic traditions which had been combined with the Roman, but the overall picture would presumably have been that of a Bacchic cult, and would therefore have involved feasting, drinking and dancing — as did the rustic Faunalia described in an earlier century by Horace. This would have taken place at a sacred site, but we cannot assume that there would have been a temple in the form of an actual building. There might well have been a small shrine or altar, but it is also possible that the focus of the site may have been a natural object such as a tree or cave.

The spoons and strainers must have been used in the eating and drinking part of the ritual. It may well be that the names on them were linked with individuals who formed part of the group of worshippers; the idea of a *collegium* (or perhaps a coven?) may well be correct.[24] The link with the witch cult in later times undoubtedly exists, but it would be inappropriate to pursue it here.

In summary, we can say that the appearance of the name of Faunus on our late-Roman spoons is perhaps not as astonishing as it appeared at first sight. Faunus was indeed an ancient and local earth deity of Latium, but his nature was a universal one, finding echoes not only amongst other Graeco-Roman deities (sometimes so close as to amount almost to identity), but also undoubtedly with the now unknown spirits of the Celtic woods and fields. The fact that our fourth-century Gauls or Britons saw themselves as worshippers of Faunus, within the Bacchic thiasos, rather than worshippers of Pan or of a purely Celtic deity, is probably mainly a comment on their view of themselves as part of a Roman Imperial tradition, as readers of the great Latin writers of earlier centuries, and as opponents of the growing cult of Christianity which was inexorably changing their culture and their world.

NOTES

1. See Roscher *et al.* 1886–90; Ziegler and Sontheimer 1967, 521; Reifferscheid 1866; Smits 1946. The last mentioned is a very detailed discussion, with extensive quotations from the ancient sources, but her general conclusions should, in the opinion of the present writer, be treated with some caution, if not scepticism.
2. Warde Fowler 1899, 258–9 has a discussion of the main possible derivation of *Faunus*; Smits 1946, 8–9 suggests a link with the name of another deity/king, Daunus.
3. Livy 1, 5.
4. Virgil, *Aeneid* 7, 45.
5. Dionysius of Halicarnassus, 1, 31.
6. Roscher *et al.* 1886–90, 1454, 51.
7. Smits 1946, 16–17.
8. Smits 1946, 16–17.
9. Smits 1946, 14–15.
10. Virgil, *Aeneid* 7, 81–91; Ovid, *Fasti* 4, 649 relates a similar story, but the suppliant is Numa, not Latinus.
11. Tilly 1947, Chapter 6.
12. Arnobius, *Adversus nationes* 5, 1; an earlier version is in Ovid, *Fasti* 3; Smits devotes a section to this myth, Smits 1946, 11–13.

13. Livy 33, 42.
14. Horace, *Odes* 3, 18.
15. Warde Fowler 1899, 310–21 refers to the ancient sources; see also the relevant entry in Ziegler and Sontheimer 1969, 780–3, where recent publications are cited.
16. Ovid, *Fasti* 2, 282.
17. Smits 1946, 25. She remarks that the name of the god may originally have been secret, not to be spoken, and then goes on to the further possibility; 'Het is mogelijk, dat er in de oudste tijd bij dit feest geen god voorkwam'. But she has no doubt that in due course, Faunus became firmly connected with the Lupercalia.
18. *Corpus Inscriptionum Latinarum* 6, 2302.
19. *Ibid,* 23083.
20. e.g. Roscher *et al.* 1886–90, 1459–60.
21. e.g. Ovid, *Fasti* 2, 193; 3, 315; Virgil, *Georgics* 1, 10.
22. e.g. Virgil, *Aeneid* 10, 551.
23. This point has been made, though somewhat cautiously, by Hassall 1981, 392, footnotes 102 and 106.
24. See Hassall 1981, 390, footnote 95.

8

The Silver Strainers

Silver strainers, amongst them a curious form of instrument with a curved prong at one end, are a conspicuous feature both of several late-Roman hoards and of a number of graves of late-antique date.[1] While the time is perhaps not yet ripe for a full study of this class of object, nevertheless it should be noted that the three examples from Thetford (47, 48, 49) form an important addition to the series, not least because of their firm association with a large group of other, presumably contemporary, objects.

Various types of metal strainer are well attested throughout classical antiquity.[2] They could serve a variety of functions in the filtering of sediment — not least wine dregs — and were also used for cooling wine. However, as Strong has pointed out,[3] very few silver strainers have been found at Pompeii or Herculaneum and it may be, as he suggests, that in Imperial times the wine was strained with bronze vessels in the kitchen rather than at table. On the other hand, some very elaborately made Roman strainers are known and it is to be doubted whether these display pieces were confined to domestic quarters. Moreover, from late-Roman times, both strainers and spoons may have played a role in Christian liturgy.[4] This religious aspect is manifested by several strainers from late-antique or early medieval contexts, which have unequivocal Christian associations. Amongst them is a fine example in the Water Newton Treasure, a remarkable set of objects which is most convincingly explained as Church plate.[5] This strainer, which has a fairly small bowl and a long, rather wide, handle, has a circular disc as its terminal. On it is engraved a Chi-Rho, flanked by an alpha and an omega, a clear indication of its Christian affinities. Similarly, in the Traprain hoard, concealed c. AD 400, there is the bowl of a strainer together with the base of its handle, formed by two engraved dolphins.[6] Here the Christian associations of this piece are suggested both by a Chi-Rho, formed by the perforations, and by the words IESVS CHRISTVS, also in perforations, placed immediately below the rim. In these cases, then, it is reasonable to assume that they played a specific part in Christian religious ceremonial. A much later example in gilt bronze was found in 1980, together with a chalice, paten and stand, at Derrynavlan, County Tipperary, Ireland.[7] No firm date for the hoard has yet been demonstrated; but the stainer, although provided with a pierced partition within the bowl, is evidently in much the same genre as those from Water Newton and Traprain Law, and, equally clearly, must have been used in Church liturgy. Indeed, a not dissimilar strainer appears to be illustrated on the first page of text of St Luke's Gospel in the Book of Kells.[8] Here can be seen two men, one holding a cup and the other a ladle or strainer of much the same shape as the Derrynavlan example, from which wine is being poured.

By way of contrast, another strainer would seem to have equally explicit associations with pagan religious sites: it is the silver-gilt example found within a circular casket, concealed in the Walbrook Mithraeum at London.[9] Its form is unusual, being cylindrical with three bars across the top so that it could be lifted out and with an elaborate design made up by the perforations in the bottom. Assuming that it was intended to go with the elaborately decorated casket (and this is not certain) it is likely to have been used in the celebration of the Mithraic ritual. Indeed, Professor Toynbee has suggested that it could have been employed as a container for strained honey, since the initiation rites for the Mithraic grade of *Leones* involved the taking of honey.

With most strainers, however, there is nothing to indicate whether they were intended for secular or religious use. Instead, the surviving examples demonstrate a quite wide variety of forms and a considerable diversity in the degree of elaboration. One very unusual example, where the strainer is hinged with a funnel, was found in the Chaourse Treasure, buried about AD 270.[11] Others, like those from Kyngadle (Dyfed) and Moylarg (Co. Antrim),[12] appear to owe much in their shape to the standard form of skillet.[13] Some strainers, on the other hand, take a somewhat different form. Exemplified by those forms at Abergele (near Bangor),[14] Kaiseraugst,[15] Richborough,[16] Water Newton[17] and, indeed, Thetford, this type of strainer has a comparatively small bowl and an elongated, often decorated, handle. Normally there is also a quite elaborate effect between the bowl and the handle, as well as many variants of terminal. Moreover, it was not uncommon to provide a ring or suspension loop as on our strainer 48 and on examples from Richborough, Cologne or from a number of Saxon graves.[18] Within these broad parameters, however, there is a quite considerable diversity of design, suggesting (although on the basis of much too small a sample) that a good many workshop traditions are represented by the surviving examples of strainers.

The three Thetford strainers cannot be paralleled exactly but they do share many points of similarity with other examples. In the first place, the twisted rod handle — a feature, as we have seen, of some of the spoons in the assemblage — can be matched by two strainers from the Kaiseraugst Treasure and by an example recovered from the inner ditch of the stone fort at Richborough: this is a firm late- to post-Roman context.[19] The baluster mouldings of 47, and 49, can also be compared with those on the Richborough 'implements' and on the Kaiseraugst strainers. Secondly, the beaded bowl-rim (which was made separately and had in fact become detached when found) is not unlike the milled ring — also made separately — around the bowl of the Water Newton strainer and is close to an example found in Tomb 217 at the Severinskirche at Cologne.[20] The neatly laid-out perforated design of **48** also recalls the carefully drawn motif in the Water Newton strainer and the Chi-Rho of the Traprain example.[21] However, we have tried in vain to detect an overall pattern in the holes that pierce the bowl of **43**. Thirdly, the comma-shaped terminal of **49**, is a design that is well represented on objects of this period and has provoked a certain degree of controversy about its function and purpose.

These pronged implements, which occur frequently in association with late-Roman spoons, take a number of forms. The combination of a curved terminal with a strainer, exemplified by **49**, is found both in the Kaiseraugst Treasure and at Richborough. On the other hand, Kaiseraugst and Richborough also provide instances where the prong is found together with a small spatulate end, and there is a not dissimilar ligula-spoon arrangement on pronged instruments from Canterbury and Kertch in the Crimea and on one now in the National Museum, Dublin.[22] An unprovenanced ligula-spoon, probably from south-east England, further emphasises the frequency of these artifacts, while there are related forms from both Lydney and Dorchester (Dorset).[23]

Some sort of Christian association is presumably implied by Chi-Rho monograms on the disc of the prong on implements in both the Canterbury and Kaiseraugst Treasures. However, as Painter has pointed out, these were natural vehicles for decoration, and it is unclear exactly what significance should be attached to these Christian motifs.[24] What does seem certain — and the Thetford find underlines the point — is that these objects were neither exclusively Christian nor, one suspects, exclusively religious in purpose. It seems more likely that they were developed as an albeit elaborate addition to sets of tableware which, under certain circumstances, were absorbed into both pagan and Christian liturgy. In fact, the diversity in the form of the prongs emphasises the variety of ways in which they could have been used. The Thetford example, which has a fairly sharp edge along one side, would have been effective both as a small knife and as a hook for shellfish and the like.[25] By contrast, the curve of the prong on the Kaiseraugst implements would appear to have rendered a cutting action extremely difficult. We cannot argue, therefore, for any restricted interpretation of the function of these curious objects.

This question has come into particular focus with recent discussions of a pronged implement and a spoon found in the St Ninian's Isle Treasure.[26] Concealed in c. AD 800 beneath the floor of a Pictish church, they form part of a group containing secular and, in all probability, ecclesiastical objects. It has been suggested that the spoon was used in giving communion, as is still common practice in the Eastern Orthodox Church today, while the pronged instrument was employed to cut up the host — the 'complicated *Fractio panis* envisaged in the Stowe Missal'.[27] This seems to be supported by the fact that the St Ninian's implement has a small projecting cutting edge at the base of the prong. However, it should be emphasised that not all scholars would accept this conclusion, especially as the hoard contains no chalice or paten but does include some secular objects.[28]

This discussion of these strainers and pronged implements underlines the many difficulties involved in their interpretation. However, the Thetford find is useful in that, assuming that the strainers *are* associated with spoons and thus with rites connected with the worship of Faunus — and there seems to be no good reason to doubt this — then here at least we can envisage a role in some sort of pagan ritual. Just what form of ritual this may have been it is impossible to say; but it is another reminder of the intricate blend between paganism and Christianity that is so characteristic of this period.[29]

To these remarks should be added a brief postscript. Spoons are well-known as grave goods in both Roman and post-Roman tombs;[30] but it is also worth remembering that strainers were also not uncommonly used as burial accessories. Milojčić cites over twenty instances, a number from Saxon graves in England.[31] Although in a typological sense, many of these strainers represent a distinct development from the fourth-century forms that we have been discussing, they are nevertheless very much in the same genre and often include suspension rings. They furnish another remainder that strainers are as home in a pagan context as they are in one that is overtly Christian.

NOTES

1. Many of them have been usefully catalogued by Milojčić 1968.
2. Strong 1966, 91f. (Hellenistic strainers), 144–5 (early Imperial strainers).
3. Strong 1966, 145.
4. Cf. Curle 1923, 65, but note his *caveats;* also Richardson 1980, 95. As Curle observes (76), strainers — *colum* or *colatorium* — appear frequently in early church inventories.
5. Painter 1977b; the strainer is no. 7. See also Thomas 1981, 113f.
6. Curle 1923, no 111 and pl. XXVIII.
7. Richardson 1980.
8. Richardson 1980, fig. 31.
9. Toynbee 1963; 1964, 315f. For a parallel from Stráže (Czechoslovakia), cf. Strong 1966, 170.
10. Toynbee 1964, 317.
11. Illustrated in Strong 1966, pl. 46B.
12. Cf. Richardson 1980, figs. 28, 29.
13. Cf. Strong 1966, 145f. for the type.
14. Richardson 1980, Fig. 29c and 113.
15. Laur-Belart 1963, Abb. 20.
16. Bushe-Fox 1949, Pl. XXXVII, no. 126.
17. Painter 1977b, no. 7, pl. 7.
18. Richborough: Bushe-Fox 1949, pl. XXXVII, no. 126; Cologne: Doppelfeld 1960, Taf. 27. The Saxon examples include several examples from Bifrons, e.g. *Arch. Cant.* 10. 1876, pp. 303, 314; *Arch. Cant* 13. 1880, p. 552, and an instance from Lyminge (*Arch. Cant.* 69. 1955, pl. XIII). Presumably our strainer **47** was also intended to have a ring.
19. Kaiseraugst: Laur-Belart 1963, Abb. 20; Richborough: Bushe-Fox 1949, pl. XXXVII, no. 126. For the dating evidence cf. p. 70f.; the coins include issues of Theodosius.
20. Water Newton: Painter 1977b, no. 7; Cologne: Doppelfeld 1960, Taf, 27.
21. Curle 1923, no. 111.
22. Canterbury: Painter 1965, 8; Kertch: Cabrol and Leclerq 1914, 3180 and fig. 3459; Dublin: Painter 1965, Martin 1976, Abb, 3, no. 5.
23. Unprovenanced example: Potter, *forthcoming;* it has a sharply curved prong, a partly twisted and partly plain stem and a baluster moulding (photographs held by the British Museum); Lydney: Bathurst 1879, pl. XXV, no. 1; Dorchester: Dalton 1922, 90.
24. Painter 1965, 8–9.
25. For the possibility that some may have been used as toothpicks, cf. Martin 1976.

26. Cf. Richardson 1980, 95f.; McRoberts 1965; Painter 1965, 9; Painter 1977a, 20–21.
27. Richards on 1980, 96.
28. Cf. particularly Wilson 1973.
29. Well epitomised by the Hinton St Mary pavement (cf. most recently, Thomas 1981, 105f.) or the Water Newton plaques ('indubitably Christian in nature, but pagan in form': Thomas 1981, 31).
30. Böhme 1970.
31. Milojčić 1968.

9

The Scientific Examination of the Thetford Treasure

Part 1: Analyses of materials

by M. R. Cowell, S. La Niece and
N. D. Meeks (British Museum Research
Laboratory)

This part of the scientific examination of the Thetford Treasure was undertaken in order (1) to determine the compositions of the metal; (2) to obtain information on the methods of decoration (gilding and niello); (3) to identify the stones and backing pastes in the jewellery; and (4) to establish whether the gold jewellery is in a pristine condition or if it had been worn.

Analytical techniques

Energy dispersive x-ray fluorescence (XRF) was used to determine the elemental composition of all items in the Thetford Treasure (Table 5). XRF is a surface technique; therefore, to ensure that the surface composition is representative of the interior, it is usually necessary to prepare a small area on the item being analysed. This would normally involve abrading and polishing a circular zone about 2–3 mm in diameter to remove any surface enrichment and produce the smooth surface which is a requirement of the technique. This was not possible, or desirable, on all the items in the treasure and consequently only a representative selection were given this full pre-treatment. These analyses will subsequently be referred to as 'quantitative' (QU in Table 5). All the remaining items were analysed without prior treatment other than de-greasing and their analyses will be referred to as 'semi-quantitative' (SQ in Table 5). For purposes of comparison all those items which were to undergo a 'quantitative' analysis were analysed 'semi-quantitatively' first.

The precision (reproducibility of a series of measurements) of the quantitative analyses depends on the element being determined and on its concentration in the alloy. However, it is generally in the range +/− 0.5–1% absolute for concentrations in excess of 2% and about +/− 25–50% relative for concentrations below this. A feature of the XRF analyses is that they are scaled to total 100% so that the precision ranges are not exactly symmetrical about each element concentration. Generally, the accuracy would be similar to the precision. As far as the semi-quantitative analyses are concerned, their precision should be only slightly poorer than that of the full quantitative technique. Their accuracy, however, is very difficult to assess since this depends primarily on the homogeneity of the individual item, particularly whether or not there is some surface enrichment, and also on the geometry of the area examined. Furthermore, each element will be affected to a

different extent by these factors. For the sort of alloys involved here, experience seems to justify expecting accuracies typically up to five items worse than that of full quantitative analyses. The format in which the semi-quantitative results are reported in Table 5 attempts to reflect this by rounding the major element concentrations to the nearest whole number. Certainly, the semi-quantitative results must be interpreted with caution; they are primarily intended to give an overall picture of the composition of the treasure and to identify any distinctive items.[1]

SILVER OBJECTS

Metal Composition
The majority of the silver items in the treasure are spoons, the three exceptions being the strainers (47–49). Six of the spoons (50, 51, 56, 66, 75 and 80) were analysed quantitatively (after the semi-quantitative survey) on representative areas of the bowl and handle in each case. For this group there is only one instance (66) where there is a significant difference between the composition of the two components. The handle here has a lower silver content (by 1.7%) than the bowl and the copper contents are correspondingly different. This would suggest that different batches of silver alloy had been used in the manufacture of this particular spoon. From the semi-quantitative survey it seems that spoon 59 may also exhibit significant differences in composition between bowl and handle.

The remaining silver items were only analysed semi-quantitatively but reference to the results obtained for those spoons analysed by both procedures enables an assessment to be made of the accuracy of the semi-quantitative analyses. When comparisons are made of the results obtained by the two procedures on the same part of each item then systematic differences are apparent. With only one or two exceptions the semi-quantitative results have higher silver and gold and lower copper contents than their quantitative counterparts. This pattern is to be expected if there is a change in the composition at the metal surface caused by exposure to a mildly corrosive environment. Under conditions of burial, because of their differing reactivities, copper is most readily leached out, silver much less so and gold almost not at all. This leads to a progressive enrichment of the less reactive metals, gold and silver, at the expense of the most reactive, copper. It seems that lead is similarly leached, although only two examples are available for comparison. The overall effect on the semi-quantitative analyses is for the silver to be overestimated by up to about 1%, the copper content to be underestimated by a similar amount and the gold to be overestimated by up to about 0.4%. However, it should be stressed that these are

Table 5 XRF analyses of the objects

No	Description	Part	Method	AU	AG	CU	PB	ZN
1	buckle	clasp	QU	87.1	10.3	2.6		
1	buckle	clasp	SQ	98.0	2.5	<0.1		
*2	ring		QU	95.5	3.4	1.1		
2	ring		SQ	95.0	4.2	1.0		
3	ring		SQ	96.0	3.0	1.1		
*4	ring		SQ	94.0	5.0	0.7		
*5	ring		SQ	93.0	6.1	0.9		
6	ring		SQ	94.0	5.0	1.0		
7	ring		SQ	97.0	3.3	0.1		
8	ring		SQ	96.0	3.4	0.8		
*9	ring		SQ	97.0	2.7	<0.1		
*10	ring		SQ	95.0	4.0	1.4		
11	ring		SQ	94.0	5.2	1.3		
*12	ring		QU	96.0	3.7	0.3		
12	ring		SQ	91.0	6.2	3.1		
*13	ring		SQ	94.0	5.0	1.3		
*14	ring		SQ	94.0	4.2	1.9		
15	ring		QU	92.5	5.2	2.3		
15	ring		SQ	95.0	2.9	2.3		
*16	ring		SQ	98.0	1.8	<0.1		
17	ring		SQ	95.0	3.4	1.8		
18	ring		SQ	94.0	4.2	2.1		
19	ring		SQ	96.0	2.5	1.8		
*20	ring		SQ	95.0	4.5	0.2		
21	ring		SQ	96.0	3.8	0.5		
22	ring		SQ	95.0	4.4	0.5		
23	ring		SQ	90.0	9.7	0.7		
24	bracelet		QU	96.1	3.1	0.8		
24	bracelet		SQ	97.0	2.9	<0.1		
25	bracelet		SQ	94.0	5.5	0.4		
*26	bracelet		SQ	95.0	4.3	0.5		
*27	bracelet		SQ	92.0	7.5	0.3		
*28	pendant		SQ	94.0	4.5	1.8		
29	pendant		SQ	95.0	3.5	1.0		
*30	amulet case		QU	92.5	4.5	3.1		
30	amulet case		SQ	95.0	3.0	2.4		
31	chain		SQ	95.0	4.7	0.3		
*32	chain		SQ	89.0	10.2	0.6		
33	chain		SQ	89.0	10.5	0.5		
*34	chain		SQ	92.0	6.6	1.0		
*35	chain		SQ	94.0	4.8	0.9		
37	terminal		SQ	93.0	6.2	0.9		
*39	pendant		SQ	94.0	5.3	1.2		
*40	pendant		SQ	94.0	5.0	1.4		
47	strainer	handle	SQ	0.8	96.0	2.7	0.5	<0.1
48	strainer		SQ	0.9	96.0	3.0		
49	strainer		SQ	1.0	96.0	2.8		
50	spoon	bowl	QU	0.5	95.8	3.1	0.7	<0.1
50	spoon	handle	QU	0.6	94.7	3.9	0.8	<0.1
50	spoon	handle	SQ	1.0	97.0	2.0		
51	spoon	bowl	QU	0.6	97.2	1.8	0.5	<0.1
51	spoon	handle	QU	0.5	97.2	1.9	0.5	<0.1
51	spoon	bowl	SQ	0.9	98.0	0.9	<0.1	<0.1
51	spoon	handle	SQ	0.6	98.0	1.2	0.2	<0.1
52	spoon	handle	SQ	0.8	98.0	1.5		
53	spoon	handle	SQ	0.8	97.0	1.7		
54	spoon	handle	SQ	1.2	97.0	1.5		
55	spoon	handle	SQ	0.9	98.0	1.3		
56	spoon	bowl	QU	0.6	96.3	2.8	0.3	<0.1
56	spoon	handle	QU	0.7	95.9	3.2	0.3	<0.1
56	spoon	bowl	SQ	0.6	96.0	3.1	0.2	<0.1
56	spoon	handle	SQ	0.6	97.0	2.4	0.1	<0.1

Table 5 *Continued*

No	Description	Part	Method	AU	AG	CU	PB	ZN
57	spoon	handle	SQ	0.8	98.0	1.7		
58	spoon	handle	SQ	0.9	98.0	1.2		
59	spoon	bowl	SQ	0.5	95.0	3.5	0.3	0.8
59	spoon	handle	SQ	0.5	97.0	1.9	0.2	0.4
60	spoon	handle	SQ	0.5	97.0	2.0		
61	spoon	handle	SQ	0.9	96.0	3.0		
62	spoon	handle	SQ	0.8	99.0	.6		
63	spoon	bowl	SQ	0.6	95.0	4.0	0.4	0.1
63	spoon	handle	SQ	0.6	96.0	3.3	0.3	<0.1
64	spoon	bowl	SQ	0.6	98.0	1.6	0.2	0.2
64	spoon	handle	SQ	0.8	97.0	1.4	0.1	0.1
65	spoon	handle	SQ	0.8	98.0	1.5		
66	spoon	bowl	QU	0.9	96.9	1.8	0.4	<0.1
66	spoon	handle	QU	0.6	95.2	3.9	0.4	<0.1
66	spoon	handle	SQ	1.0	97.0	2.1		
67	spoon	bowl	SQ	0.3	98.0	1.0	0.3	0.1
67	spoon	handle	SQ	0.4	98.0	.8	0.2	0.1
68	spoon	handle	SQ	0.7	98.0	1.6		
69	spoon	handle	SQ	1.3	98.0	.6		
70	spoon	handle	SQ	1.8	96.0	2.3		
71	spoon	bowl	SQ	0.5	98.0	1.4	0.2	<0.1
71	spoon	handle	SQ	0.8	98.0	1.2	0.3	0.1
72	spoon	handle	SQ	0.8	97.0	2.2		
73	spoon	handle	SQ	0.7	97.0	1.7	0.2	<0.1
74	spoon	handle	SQ	0.9	97.0	1.7		
75	spoon	bowl	QU	0.5	97.2	2.0	0.3	<0.1
75	spoon	handle	QU	0.7	97.3	1.7	0.3	<0.1
75	spoon	handle	SQ	0.8	97.0	1.8		
76	spoon	handle	SQ	1.3	97.0	1.3		
77	spoon	handle	SQ	0.6	98.0	1.2	0.3	<0.1
78	spoon	handle	SQ	0.8	97.0	1.7	0.5	<0.1
79	spoon	handle	SQ	0.8	97.5	1.8		
80	spoon	bowl	QU	0.5	96.6	2.6	0.3	<0.1
80	spoon	handle	QU	0.5	96.8	2.3	0.3	<0.1
80	spoon	handle	SQ	0.8	97.0	2.0		
81	spoon	handle	SQ	1.1	97.0	1.4		
82	spoon	handle	SQ	1.1	97.0	2.3		

* = Platinum group metal inclusions observed using optical microscopy

ranges; the exact effect on any individual determination is impossible to estimate.

The majority of items have silver contents in the range 96–98%; there are no significant outliers, and copper is the principal alloying element. This composition range is similar to that found for the Mildenhall and Water Newton Treasures and for other fourth-century silver.[2] The amount of gold and the presence of small amounts of zinc are also typical. Zinc is often present in argentiferous lead ores from which the silver would have been extracted and this may account for its occurrence in the finished product. However, zinc is normally removed very effectively by cupellation and an alternative explanation is that it was introduced with copper in the form of brass.

The amount of lead in the Thetford Treasure is occasionally somewhat lower than that generally found in other fourth-century Roman silver. The presence of lead is due to the use of silver-rich lead ores as the source of silver and the practice of cupellation to recover the silver from the ore. McKerrell and Stevenson[3] have found by experiment that the lead content of silver can be reduced quite easily to 0.5% but that extensive cupellation would be required to achieve lead contents much less than this. In fact, many items have less than 0.3% lead although, since these were only analysed semi-quantitatively, this may not be of any significance. The average in those items analysed quantitatively is about 0.4% which is within the range but below the average value found by Hughes and Hall.[4]

Gilding

Two of the spoons are gilded: the duck-handled spoon, **50**, with a gilded Triton, and long-handled spoon, **66**, with a gilded panther. In both cases mercury was detected in the gold using x-ray fluorescence analysis which indicates that the method of gilding used was the mercury amalgam method.

Mercury-, or fire-gilding, is a technique by which the gold is applied as an amalgam, or alternatively, gold leaf is placed on a surface already coated with mercury to form an amalgam *in situ*. In either case the mercury is then evaporated by heating the object, leaving a firmly bonded layer of gold on the surface. The mercury-gilding technique was widely used in the Roman world from about the third century AD onwards.[5]

Niello

Twenty-six of the spoons have some niello surviving in their inscriptions. Four spoons (51, 58 and 73 with inscriptions in the bowl and 66 with inscription on the handle) were chosen as representative of the group and samples of the niello (approximately 0.5 mg) were taken for analysis by x-ray diffraction and x-ray fluorescence. The results showed that, in all four samples, the niello was the silver sulphide, acanthite (Ag_2S).

Silver sulphide is the commonest form of niello to be found at this date. All Roman niello is of the single sulphide variety, either silver or copper sulphide. Generally the composition of the niello is related to the composition of the metal in which it is employed; thus, silver sulphide is found in silver objects and copper sulphide in bronze objects. It was not until the sixth century AD that mixed copper-silver sulphides were introduced. This combination effectively lowers the melting point of the niello. However, silver sulphide niello continued in use until about the eleventh century when both the single sulphides and the binary sulphides were superseded by a mixture of lead, copper and silver sulphides. After the fifteenth century, the use of niello declined in Western Europe but it continued to be used in the Middle East and in Russia into this century.

GOLD OBJECTS

Metal Composition

In all, thirty-eight items were analysed, six of them quantitatively. Similar considerations apply to the gold as to the silver regarding the comparisons between the quantitative and semi-quantitative analyses. Where there is a significant difference between the two procedures then, as expected, the gold content is generally higher and the silver and copper lower at the metal surface compared with the interior. The greatest difference between the semi-quantitative and quantitative analyses occurs for the buckle (1) where the gold content is 11% higher at the surface. The extreme difference here, coupled with the fact that it does not seem typical, suggests that this was brought about by exposure to a particularly corrosive environment not experienced by the majority of the items in the hoard. This might suggest a non-uniform burial environment or perhaps chemical cleaning subsequent to discovery.[6]

Considering those items analysed quantitatively, two features are apparent: the gold content is usually high (mean 94.5%, excluding 1 with 87% gold) and silver is always the dominant alloying element over copper. Typically the silver content is 2 to 4 times that of copper. It is of some interest to note the similarity in the composition of ring 12 with bracelet 24 which have clear typological parallels. The buckle (1) is the least typical of these items because of its conspicuously low gold content which is 6% less than the norm. However, the semi-quantitative survey shows that there are probably at least two other items (chains 32 and 33) with less than 90% gold and one close to 90% (ring 23). Nevertheless, the atypical compositions highlighted by the semi-quantitative survey must be treated with caution because of the difficulty in some cases of finding representative areas for analysis. This is particularly true of the rings (10–15) with extensive granular and/or spiral applied decoration where it is possible that the surface of the item is contaminated by solder of low gold content. An illustration of this is the pair of analyses for ring 12 where, contrary to what would be expected for surface enrichment, the quantitative gold content is higher than that by the semi-quantitative procedure.

Unfortunately there are few published analyses of Roman gold jewellery from Britain contemporary with the Thetford Treasure with which comparisons can be made. Two fragments of necklace from Canterbury, probably of third to early fourth-century date, have been analysed by XRF.[7] Their gold contents (95 and 97%) are compatible with the Thetford material and there are similar relationships between the silver and copper contents. Isolated finds examined at the Research Laboratory for purposes of Treasure Trove investigation, but unpublished, generally have similarly high gold contents with silver the dominant alloying element. The contemporary gold coin of the period was the *solidus* introduced by Constantine I early in the fourth century. *Solidi* of the fourth and early fifth centuries have been analysed by Caley,[8] using SG measurements. The average gold contents for the first and second halves of the fourth century were 96% and 96.4% and during the first half of the fifth century it was slightly higher at 97.4%. The average gold content of the Thetford Treasure is slightly lower (93.3% for all quantitative items) but this is not surprising since jewellery would benefit from the improved mechanical strength which results from alloying.

Platinum group metal inclusions

Silvery coloured platinum element inclusions were located by optical microscopy in nineteen gold items (Table 5). Analysis of the inclusions in three items (12, 16, and 26) using the x-ray spectrometer attached to the scanning electron microscope showed that they were all of the iridium-osmium-ruthenium alloy type and were comparable in composition to inclusions previously analysed in gold antiquities.[9] The presence of platinum group element inclusions confirms that the gold was obtained from placer deposits. However, because of the wide range of inclusion compositions frequently observed within a single object,[10] the analytical data for the inclusions do not provide a basis for identifying or characterising the actual placer deposits used.

Stones and backing pastes

The stones were all examined by optical microscopy and where necessary their identification and that of any remaining backing material was carried out by x-ray diffraction. The results are summarised in Table 6.

The stones are amethysts (purple), garnets (red), emeralds (green) and various chalcedonies. Many of the green 'stones' are coloured glass. The weathered millefiori glass beads in necklace **31** now appear to be composed of green with yellow or white marbling; however x-ray diffraction and x-ray fluorescence analysis both indicate that the opacifier present is lead antimonate and therefore the white areas were probably originally yellow.

Table 6 Stones and backing pastes

No.	Stone	Backing material
2	Purple: quartz, var. crystal (amethyst)	Sulphur filling hoop of ring
3	Purple: quartz, var. crystal (amethyst)	
4	Dark brown/black: quartz, var. chalcedony	
5	Green: beryl (emerald) Red: garnet Purple: quartz, var. crystal (amethyst)	Sulphur (also in hollow dolphins on hoop)
7	Blue-green: glass	Sulphur
8	Red: garnet	
9	Green: beryl (emerald)	
13	Red/green: quartz, var. chalcedony (jaspar)	
14	Green: glass	
15	Green: glass	
16	Banded blue/black: quartz, var. chalcedony (onyx)	
17	Green: glass	Cotton fibre (modern)
18	Red: garnet	
19	Green: glass	Sulphur
20	Green: beryl (emerald)	
21	Green: glass	
22	Red: garnet	Sulphur
23	Red: garnet	
27	Green: glass	Sulphur
28	Blue: glass	
29	Red: garnet Green: glass	Sulphur
31	Green: small broken green stone at hook end of chain is beryl (emerald). Other 3 beads are millefiori glass (probably originally green and yellow; opacifier of 'yellow' is lead antimonate)	
36	Blue: glass	
39	Black and white cameo: quartz, var. chalcedony (onyx)	
40	Milky, translucent: quartz, var. chalcedony	
41	Red: quartz, var. chalcedony (cornelian)	
42–46	Green: bright green bead is beryl (emerald) The other four are millefiori glass, see **31**	

The ring **21** and pendant **28** have designs in gold set into the surface of the glass. The design in ring **21** is made up of four pieces of wire. These designs were probably pre-formed, laid on the base of a mould and the glass introduced from above, either in the form of molten glass or powered glass which was subsequently melted. After removal from the mould, the surface was ground flat through half the thickness of the wire, leaving the wire in cross section on the surface of the glass. The design in the blue glass pendant, **28**, consists of five strips of gold which were probably incorporated into the glass by the same method as that proposed for the ring **21**. It is impossible to ascertain the thickness of the gold without damaging the pendant, but it is likely to be of the order of 0.1 mm as there is a very shallow depression forming a ring around the design which probably held another strip of gold, now missing. The glass in the depression is considerably less weathered than the rest of the surface; but this does not necessarily suggest that the gold was lost recently, as the rest of the surface would have been ground and a ground glass surface frequently shows an enhanced rate of weathering when compared with the original surface.

A number of the settings were partially filled with sulphur. In most cases, the sulphur seems to have been used to fill up unwanted space and prevent the poorly fitting stone from slipping too far back into the settings. It was thus possible to mount stones and glass which were often unsuitably shaped and which may therefore have been reused. Sulphur was also used to fill at least one of the hollow ring hoops (**2**) and thus provide support for the shell of gold. There may also be sulphur in other ring hoops but it is not readily accessible for sampling. Parallels for the use of sulphur as backing and filling material are rare. Parts of the great gold buckle from the seventh-century Anglo-Saxon ship-burial were found to be filled with sulphur and sulphur has also been reported as occurring, though very rarely, in the settings of garnets in migration-period jewellery.[11] Though there are no reports of sulphur in jewellery of comparable date to the Thetford Treasure, this may be because it is more usual for Roman gems to be found in tightly fitting settings which conceal any backing materials. Volcanic areas of Italy were the major source of sulphur but there are minor deposits in Great Britain associated with gypsum at Newark, Nottingham and in Cornwall, Derbyshire and Cumbria.[12]

Wear
The gold jewellery was examined under an optical microscope for evidence of characteristic areas of wear associated with use. On the basis of the relative degree of wear observed on the jewellery, the four following categories were defined: 1: no significant wear; 2: slight wear; 3: moderate wear; and 4: extensive wear. The results are presented in Table 7.

Sixteen of the twenty-two rings show no significant wear but where present, it is fairly obvious and on one ring (**15**) it is extensive. Only one of the four bracelets (**26**) shows any significant wear. In contrast, four of the five necklaces and all the necklace clasps and pendants show definite signs of wear.

The absence of wear on the majority of the rings and bracelets is consistent with at least this component of the hoard being the 'stock-in-trade' of a merchant or goldsmith rather than an assemblage of an individual's personal jewellery. If the hypothesis of a merchant's or goldsmith's 'stock-in-trade' is to be extended to cover the entire hoard, then those items which exhibit wear associated with personal use must be interpreted as items acquired by the merchant/goldsmith either for reuse of the metal or for modification, including reassembly from among the diverse component parts.

Table 7 An assessment of the amount of wear on the jewellery

No.	Object	Extent of wear		Location
1	Buckle	Slight		See note a.
2	Ring	No		
3	Ring	No		
4	Ring	No		
5	Ring	No		
6	Ring	No		
7	Ring	No		
8	Ring	No		
9	Ring	No		
10	Ring	No		
11	Ring	Moderate	1.	Bottom outside of ring loop;
			2.	Rim of stone setting.
12	Ring	Slight		Bottom outside of ring loop.
13	Ring	Moderate		Outer edges of ring loop.
14	Ring	No		
15	Ring	Extensive	1.	Over all of the outside of ring loop but particularly on bottom;
			2.	Inside of finger-ring loop — rounded edges.
16	Ring	No		
17	Ring	No		
18	Ring	Slight	1.	Outside edge of ring loop;
			2.	Rim of stone setting.
19	Ring	No		
20	Ring	No		
21	Ring	Slight		Outside of ring loop
22	Ring	No		
23	Ring	No		
24	Bracelet	No		
25	Bracelet	No		
26	Bracelet	Moderate	1.	Both inside and outside of the bracelet loop;
			2.	Two areas on fixture loop. See note b.
27	Bracelet	No		
28	Pendant	Moderate	1.	Top inside edges of loop. See note c;
			2.	Outside of wire rings;
			3.	Bottom of pendant body.
29	Pendant	Moderate	1.	Top inside edges of loop. See note c;
			2.	Outside of wire rings;
			3.	Bottom of pendant body.
30	Pendant	Moderate	1.	Top inside and outer edges of 2 loops. See note c;
			2.	Outer edges of wire at cylinder ends.
31	Wire chain necklace	Moderate	1.	Links rubbing together;
			2.	Slight wear on inside edges of clasp.
32	Wire chain necklace	Moderate		Links rubbing together (no clasp).
33	Wire chain necklace	Moderate		Links rubbing together.
34	Conical chain necklace	Moderate		Clasp ends but not on links (NB Clasp ends and chain may not belong together).
35	Wire chain necklace	Moderate		Links rubbing together (no clasp).
36	Clasp for chain	Moderate	1.	Loops and hooks;
			2.	Tube ends of clasp.
37	Clasp for chain	Slight	1.	Loop and hook;
			2.	On decoration.
38	Clasp for chain	Slight	1.	Loop and hook;
			2.	On decoration
39	Cameo pendant	Moderate	1.	Inside of Loop. See note c;
			2.	On cameo surround.
40	Cameo pendant	Moderate	1.	Inside of loop. See note c;
			2.	On cameo surround.

a. The buckle plate and hinge cylinders show no significant wear and sharp detail is seen inside the ends of the latter. The buckle loop also shows no significant wear except for one area of slight wear in the centre of one side where the buckle tongue would have once rested. The tongue and the hinge wire are both now missing. On the basis of these observations, the buckle appears to be essentially unused but shows signs of handling.

b. The extent of wear on the hook and eye is less than might be expected if the clasp was always used. This suggests that when in use the bracelet ends were not hooked together which, in view of the thickness of the gold and the difficulty of engaging the hook and eye, is perhaps not surprising.

c. The nature and extent of the wear on the pendant loops suggests that the pendants were suspended from a leather thong or cord rather than from a metal chain or wire.

Part 2: Gold wire on the Thetford jewellery and the technology of wire production in Roman times

by W. A. Oddy
(Conservation Division, British Museum)

Introduction

By the Roman Imperial period gold wire had been used in the manufacture of jewellery for at least 2500 years,[13] and six different techniques of making wire during this period have been recognised by using modern laboratory methods of examination. These techniques have been designated as hammering, block-twisting, strip-twisting, strip-drawing,[14] folding[15] and casting.[16] Furthermore, once a wire had been made it was sometimes modified before being used to give it a beaded appearance.[17] None of these six techniques is, however, used to manufacture wire today as all modern wire is made by drawing, a technique which was certainly in use by the early Middle Ages, although the date and place of its invention are unknown.

Several authors have claimed, on the basis of scientific evidence that true wire-drawing was known before the Middle Ages. In particular Anastasiadis[18] and Epprecht and Mutz[19] presented metallurgical evidence which they interpreted as proof of drawing by the Greeks and Romans respectively, although the evidence is open to other interpretations. More convincing is the surface on the pin of a first-century BC Celtic brooch, which is covered with fine parallel scratches[20] very like those produced by a wire-drawing die. However, it is more likely to have been hammered and the surface scratches to result from the finishing process.

A second approach to finding the origin of wire-drawing is to look for surviving wire-drawing dies. Jacobi[21] has published what he believed were wire-drawing dies from a Celtic site, and Rump, after questioning whether similar implements might not be nail-making irons,[22] decided that they were actually used for making wire.[23].

Nevertheless, the final proof of whether wire-drawing was known at any particular time is the identification of actual drawn wire, on the surface of which fine parallel scratches are always created by the drawing die. As this evidence is lost if the metal corrodes, gold wire, which does not corrode, offers the best chance of determining whether the wire was drawn.

Of the six techniques of making wire before the invention of drawing, casting was used by the pre-Columbian civilisation of South America to make false-filigree,[24] and has not been identified on jewellery in the Old World. As far as the other five techniques of hand-making wire are concerned, which were used in Europe before the Middle Ages, each leaves characteristic marks on the surface of the wire which can be studied under low-power microscopy ($<75\times$) as a means of identifying the method of manufacture.[25] Five factors, however might inhibit the identification process:

1. The extent of polishing applied to the wire during the finishing process, as polishing tends to obliterate the characteristic marks of manufacture.
2. The extent of corrosion, as the formation of layers of corrosion products also obliterates the characteristic surface markings. This is not a problem with gold wire.
3. The amount of soldering to which wire has been subjected, as a layer of solder will also obliterate the characteristic marks. This is a particular problem when studying wire used as filigree.
4. The extent of wear to which the wire has been subject, as this has the same effect as polishing.
5. Any further manufacturing process which has been applied to the wire before use. Examples are wires which have been swaged to make a D-shaped cross-section[26] or beaded wire.[27]

Although these factors complicate the technological study of wire in antiquity, the first attempts at commenting on the technology of wire were made as long ago as the 1920s by Caroline Ransome Williams.[28] However, it is only in recent years that the various manufacturing techniques have been fully described and almost no systematic studies have yet been published of the occurrence of the techniques in different cultures or of their presence in the various geographical areas of the Old World.[29]

Gold wire on the Thetford jewellery

Gold wire occurs on twenty-one of the items of jewellery from the Thetford Treasure and in all cases where the technique of manufacture can be determined with certainty, either hammering or block-twisting have been used.

Hammered wire is made by beating out a cast rod, or other suitably shaped ingot, on an anvil and thus gradually extending its length and reducing its diameter. The characteristic marks left on the surface are facets and short striations or creases. Sometimes partly detached flakes of metal are also present. Some hammered wire is very smooth and round in cross-section, for example the Snettisham torc[30] which dates from the end of the first century BC, and in such cases it seems likely that a swage-block was used in the manufacture of the wire, as this would eliminate the faceting which is inevitable with simple hammering.

Block-twisted wire is made by first hammering out an ingot to make a wire with a square cross-section, which is easier to manufacture than a round wire, and then tightly twisting it to produce a 'barley-sugar' effect. The wire is then rolled between two hard flat surfaces, producing a smooth wire with two independent helical creases running along its length.[31] When this technique is used to make wire from pure gold, which is soft, extensive rolling will completely eliminate the helical creases, producing a perfectly smooth round wire. In such cases, the wire should not be confused with drawn wire which invariably has a surface covered in very fine longitudinal scratches running the length of the wire, produced by the drawing die.

Numerous pieces of Thetford jewellery are made or decorated with beaded wire, but in no case did the surface preserve any evidence of how the wire was made before the beading operation was carried out. In recent years several studies of the techniques for making beaded wire have been carried out[32] but, although at least three methods of beading have been described, it is difficult to determine which was used in many cases. Unfortunately this is particularly true of the beaded wire on the Thetford jewellery, and the meagre comments on beading offered in the following list of all the Thetford wire are given for the use of technologists in the future, rather than as a means of drawing any useful conclusions about the hoard now.

RING (10)
The filigree consists of wire which was made by block-twisting. Round the finger-loop are two strands of beaded wire on which the beads are very uneven and may result from some sort of rolling technique, rather than swaging.

RING (11)
The filigree consists of loosely twisted block-twisted wire. In this case the first stage of manufacture produced a wire with an oblong, rather than a square, cross-section, so that twisting and rolling have not produced a typical block-twisted wire. The finger-loop consists of unevenly beaded wire.

RING (12)
The filigree consists of block-twisted wire. The finger-loop consists of unevenly beaded wire.

RING (13)
The finger-loop is made up of five components, three of which are unevenly beaded wires, while the other two consist of a pair of wires twisted together. Unfortunately, details of the original surface have been abraded by wear or obscured by solder and it is not possible to say how the wire was made (Plate 16a).

RING (14)
The finger-loop is made up of three pairs of twisted wires. Spiral creases are visible on the central pair of wires which were probably made by block-twisting. The other two pairs show no evidence for how the individual strands of wire were made. The ring is decorated with spiral filigree which was made by block-twisting.

RING (15)
The finger-loop is made of two beaded wires with uneven beading and two pairs of twisted wires which were made by block-twisting.

RING (17)
The filigree consists of block-twisted wire (Plate 16b).

RING (21)
The finger-loop consists of a beaded wire. The beads are evenly spaced with a groove round the middle. The tops of the beads are flat and would appear not to have been made by swaging.

RING (22)
The finger-loop consists of four pairs of twisted wires which were made by block-twisting.

RING (23)
The finger-loop consists of beaded wire which is very similar in appearance to that on ring 21 (Plate 16c).

BRACELET (26)
The clasp is decorated with twisted wire filigree, but there is no evidence for how the wire was made.

BRACELET (27)
Fragments of crudely made beaded wire have been soldered into the numerous crevices on the bracelet.

PENDANT (28)
The pendant is decorated with two circles of beaded wire. The beads are fairly evenly spaced with grooves around them.

PENDANT (29)
The pendant is decorated with two circles of well-made beaded wire with grooves round the beads.

PENDANT (30)
The pendant is decorated with two circles of fairly even beaded wire.

NECKLACE (31)
This is a loop-in-loop chain made of block-twisted wire.

NECKLACE (32)
This is a loop-in-loop chain made of block-twisted wire (Plate 16d).

NECKLACE (33)
This is a loop-in-loop chain made of block-twisted wire (Plate 16e).

FRAGMENT OF NECKLACE (35)
This is a length of loop-in-loop chain made of block-twisted wire.

NECKLACE TERMINALS (36)
The animal heads are decorated with loops of evenly spaced beaded wire, but the surfaces are obscured by solder and wear. The s-shaped wire loop has the appearance of hammered wire, with facets and short longitudinal striations on the surface.

NECKLACE TERMINALS (38)
The hooks is a short length of hammered wire.

Gold wire on other Roman jewellery from the British Isles

Block-twisted wire has been identified on several other pieces of Roman gold jewellery found in the British Isles:

i.   Chain necklace from Wincle hoard.[33]
ii.   Fragment of chain necklace from Wincle hoard.[34]
iii. Fragment of chain necklace from Wincle hoard.[35]
iv. Wire suspension loop on ear-ring (BM PRB 1856.7-1.810).
v.   Wire suspension loop on an ear-ring from the Walbrook, London.[36] The filigree on this ear-ring is more difficult to classify; it may be strip-twist, or a combination of strip- and block-twist in which the filament before twisting is neither square in cross-section nor a ribbon, but consists of a thick strip of an oblong cross-section.
vi. Triple gold chain necklace from Newton, near Carlisle (BM PRB 1904.11-2.2).

vii. Chain necklace found at New Grange, Co. Meath, Ireland (BM PRB 1884.9-20.4) (Plate 16f).
viii. Wheel pendant on gold chain found at Dolaucothi (Payne Knight Collection 1824).
ix. Gold bracelet with spherical hollow gold beads on a chain from Backworth, Northumberland.[37]
x. Gold bracelet from Rhayader, Radnorshire.[38]

Hammered wire is less common, but has been identified on:
xi. Interconnecting loops between the separate sections of a necklet from Rhayader.[39]
xii. Two pieces of wire attached to a pierced square plaque from the Wincle hoard.[40]
xiii. Finger-ring made of a loop of plain wire (BM PRB 1883.12–13.491).
xiv. Bracelet, found at New Grange, Ireland, and made of a pair of thick wires twisted together (BM PRB 1884.9-6.2).

Beaded gold wire is very common on Roman jewellery but, as yet, no criteria have been developed which will distinguish between the different methods of manufacture. It is present on ix, x and xi above, and on several rings with provenances in the British Isles. On some of these the beading is uneven, e.g. rings from New Grange (BM PRB 1884.9-6.2), Havering (BM PRB 1869.3-24.1), Richborough (BM PRB 1936.2-4.1) and Brough (BM PRB 1936.12-11.2), while the Roman ring found in a Jutish grave at Howletts, Kent (BM PRB 1936.5–11.22) is decorated with very even beaded wire.

The filigree on ear-ring (iv) above is made of rather unusual 'beaded' wire which consists of a continuous 'screw thread', rather than individual beads. The technique of manufacture is not clear.

Discussion

Taken as a whole, these examples of gold wire used to make Roman jewellery which has provenance in the British Isles were made either by hammering or block-twisting. Hammering is the oldest technique of making wire and hammered gold wire was used extensively to make necklaces and hair ornaments by the Sumerians[41] in the middle of the third millennium BC. It was probably in continuous use from then onwards, and its occurrence alongside block-twisting in Roman Britain can be exactly paralleled in Bronze Age Cyprus, where an ear-ring from tomb 61 at Enkomi,[42] which has a hammered wire suspension loop, is almost identical with the ear-rings from tomb 2 at Hala Sultan Tekke,[43] on which the loops are made of block-twisted wire.

Block-twisting was certainly an established technique of making wire in Crete by the seventeenth to sixteenth centuries BC, where it occurs on the gold wire chains of the Aegina Treasure.[44] Soon afterwards it is found in Mycenean contexts in Cyprus, and it then continued in use in the Mediterranean area, where it has been noted on Etruscan necklaces,[45] a Greek ear-ring[46] and a Roman jewellery setting from Cyprus (BM G&R 1871.6-16.60). In Europe, block-twisted wire from Roman contexts has been examined metallurgically by Raub.[47] In Egypt it has been recorded on typically Hellenistic ear-rings (BM EA 266329 and 65408) and on a necklace of the Hellenistic or Roman period (BM EA 26332). Further East it occurs on wire in the Oxus Treasure of the mid-first millennium BC[48] and has also been observed on a Parthian necklace dating to the first to second centuries AD.[49]

The identification of these occurrences, however, are the result of random 'sampling' of the jewellery collection in the British Museum, and do not result from a systematic survey. Thus, although it seems likely that block-twisting was a widespread wire-making technique in the Mediterranean area by the end of the first quarter of the second millennium BC, much more systematic work is necessary before the theory can be regarded as fact. As to whether the technique is originated in that area, or was introduced from elsewhere, no information is yet available.

What seems to be the most significant fact about the wire on the Thetford Treasure is that none of it was made by drawing. As drawing, once mastered, is such an easy way of making very good wire, and of making long lengths of wire, it seems unlikely that 'old-fashioned' methods would persist once details of a much improved new technique became known. Thus the wire on the Thetford Treasure may well be yet another piece of evidence to indicate that wire-drawing is a post-Roman invention.

Part 3: Some Observations on the Techniques of Manufacture

By R. Holmes
(Conservation Division, British Museum)

The spoons

There are three basic groups in this collection, seventeen conventional long-handled spoons, sixteen 'duck-handled' spoons and three strainers. Smaller groups may be found within these, and in some cases there are definite pairs and cross-links between the groups.[50] The seventeen conventional spoons can be sub-divided thus: eight plain-handled, four twisted-handled, and five square-handled with filed decoration ('chip-carved'). In the first group of plain spoons no definite pairs can be found; amongst the twisted-handled spoons, 73 and 74 appear to be a pair, and in the square/filed-handled group, 72 and 78 would seem to be a pair. It was noted that 80 and 75 bear the same inscription, although the styles of the spoons are different. Amongst the duck-handled spoons no definite pairs were found, but two basic styles exist; five have a bead in the bird's beak whereas the rest are plain. The most interesting cross-link between the groups is with duck-handled spoon 50 and plain-handled spoon 66; these are both finely chased and gilded, and although the subject and spoon types are different, the style is identical. These spoons are almost certainly by the same hand.

The strainers are all of different sizes and styles. The handles of 48 and 49 are made by simply twisting a square wire. The handle of 47 is more involved in manufacture. A square wire is given a v-shaped groove down each face, probably with a fine chisel, and is then twisted as in the other cases. In this instance the twisted section is one with the bowl and not made separately and joined on. All the spoons with twisted handles are made in a similar fashion.

The majority of the spoons carry inscriptions, of which a number are filled with niello. There is no evidence that *engraving* was used at all on any of the objects: all the lettering seems to have been applied with punches. Very few tools were used, much of the work being carried out with a small chisel-ended punch. By using this at different angles, different parts of letters could be formed. The most noticeable features are the triangular serifs on the majority of the letters. These are easily formed by using such a punch at an angle. An experimental punch was made to test the technique and gave comparable results. The designs in the bowls of spoons 50, 66 and 67 are all chased, but in 67 the work is of a poor standard.

All the spoon bowls have been finished by scraping. In many cases this has been carried out fairly crudely. It is hard to tell how much finishing was carried out before the niello was applied or even before the lettering, but there is evidence that fairly heavy scraping was done after the niello was applied. Heavy scratches on the silver can be seen to extend over the niello on several of the spoons. The evidence therefore confirms that the addition of the inscriptions was part of the process of manufacture, and was not a secondary feature.

The technique of lettering on the spoons does not vary widely, but on some the work has been carried out with more care and a tidier result obtained.[51] It is certainly possible that many of the spoons are from the same workshop, but except in one or two cases, it would be hard to prove that they were by the same hand.

The jewellery

Even at first glance the Thetford jewellery appears to be made up of groups of similar objects and in some cases of definite pairs. The bracelets 24 and 25 are identical, the pendants 28 and 29 are very similar to each other in construction, varying only in detail, whilst many of the rings fall into distinct groups. It is possible to find numerous links between the objects.[52]

Most of the jewellery is made up from fine sheet metal, but certain pieces are worked from the solid. There is no evidence that any casting was used. The objects most likely to have been cast would be the rings 5, 6 and 7: the dolphins and birds forming the shoulders of these, and the vase-shaped setting of ring 7 all appear at first sight to be cast, but close examination shows them in fact to have been fabricated. Some of the objects have been built up from a very large number of separate parts. The buckle (1) is made up from twenty-one separate parts, and this does not include the large number of heavy granules around its edge. Use has been made of thin folded gold sheet to obtain a special effect on four objects, 2 and 25 (bracelets) and 10 and 1 (rings). The sheet is creased one way and then again at right angles, producing a pleasing reflective effect. Other surfaces have been enriched with chased and punched decoration and several of the pieces bear very similar round punch-marks (2, 4, 9, 28, 29).[53] In fact, much use was made of punches in the decoration of the jewellery. In general, the Thetford material demonstrates a mastery of the art of fabrication: everything is built up from sheet and solid metal, wires and granules. There appears to be little pierced work, and, as already stated, no cast work.

The soldering may have been carried out by the 'reaction' method. Using this technique, a fine paste made up from a copper compound, such as verdigris or malachite, gum and water. This mixture is applied to the metal surfaces at the proposed joint and then the object is heated. As the temperature is raised the gum burns to carbon, which reduces the copper compound to copper metal. This copper then alloys with the surface of the gold and thus causes it to melt at a lower temperature than the surrounding metal. The surface 'swims' or melts and the joint is made without the addition of extra solder. This method of soldering was discovered earlier this century by H. A. P. Littledale and was proposed by him as the method by which fine filigree and granulation work was carried out in antiquity.[54] Jochen Wolters has drawn attention to a mention by Pliny (AD 23–79) that the Romans were using malachite (which they called crysocolla) for this type of soldering.[55]

Examination of soldered joints within the hoard show no visible traces of extra solder having been used — there are no fillets or flashes and no semi-melted pieces of solder. Replication tests were carried out using a malachite/gum mixture on gold and almost identical effects were noted. The amulet

(30) shows the 'swim' effect in several places. It would of course be hard to prove that any particular method was used to solder the work, but the lack of evidence for extra solder being fed into the joints and comparison of the ancient work with modern samples of the reaction method would seem to suggest that this method might have been used.

One object demands attention for the unusual method of construction. The necklace, 34, consists of two end terminals, a central bead and over a hundred segments. These are funnel-shaped and fit into each other; they are beautifully made and virtually flawless, and when strung together form a snake-like necklace. These beads can only have been made with some form of punch and die, since joining them by hand would be almost impossible. The design of a punch and die (and it would probably require two sets) would not be easy, and this object demonstrates great skill.

Many of the hollow objects have a sulphur core which has been used to fill hollow spaces and support thin metal. It has also been used for supporting gems in their settings. In addition to those occurrences listed in the Research Laboratory report (2, 5, 7, 19, 23, 27, 29) the amulet, 30, was found to contain a filling of sulphur. As the metal from which this object is made is fairly thick, the sulphur is obviously not needed for support; its purpose remains obscure.[56]

The use of sulphur for setting gems has no parallel in modern jewellery, but it is ideal for the purpose because of the ease which it can be melted. The technique is to introduce powdered sulphur into the setting, place the stone on top and close the bezel. The whole object is then gently heated until the sulphur melts, thus locking the stone in place. The large hollow rings (i.e. 2) also appear to be filled to give support to the thin gold.

All the chain work is of an impressive standard.[57] The chains or cords are not, in fact, plaited but are made from separate links. The method is one of cross linking a double loop-in-loop chain so that it has four, six or even eight principal faces. The links are closed by soldering before assembly, and formed with the fingers to a dum-bell shape. The links are built up in a spiral with each new link passing through both ends of the two underneath it. A small jig in the form of a short length of thick tube was used as a support, and to close the links together as work progressed. The chain was finished by rolling on a flat piece of wood. This has the effect of 'condensing' the chain. The method described above was used to produce an experimental length of chain.

Is it possible that some of the items in the hoard are from the same workshop? There are several groups of objects that may well be by the same hand, for instance the two bracelets made of folded sheet, the pendants and several of the rings. Except where two objects are identical it would be hard to prove by style alone that any of the objects were by the same hand. Many of the objects bear small round punch marks and it was hoped that perhaps one of the punches used would bear a defect that would repeat on any object on which it was used. However, no such mark was found.

In conclusion, therefore, some of the objects, in particular pairs, may well have been produced by the same hand. However, it would be very difficult to prove beyond doubt, on technological grounds alone, that the whole treasure, excluding worn pieces, came from the same workshop. In saying this, it must be remembered that a workshop might well consist of more than one man and that styles of work might differ, as might metal compositions. Also, while tool types might remain similar, the *actual* tools of different workers would differ. It is for these reasons that proving the objects came from one workshop remains almost impossible.

An examination of punch-marks on five objects: the possible use of the same tool

All five objects, 2, 4, 9, 28 and 29, bear a number of circular punch impressions. These impressions are all of similar size and shape, and applied singly, with the exception of those on ring 9, where they have been applied in series to form a decorative band.

Ring 2: a gold ring constructed of thin sheet and almost certainly filled, probably with sulphur. The punch decoration appears to have been applied after assembly and filling, but presumably before the gemstone was set. The round punch impressions (eight in number) appear to have been applied with a small hollow-ended round punch. As the metal is thin and has a fairly soft backing, the punch impression is shallow, and there is a tendency for the metal around the impression to be pulled down. It would be safe to assume that all the round punch impressions on this ring were produced with the same tool. One of the impressions on the underside appears to have been struck at least twice, as the area of the impression is larger than the others and has all the signs of a double strike.

Ring 4: this ring bears twenty punch impressions of exactly the same type and scale as those on ring 2. The upper half of this ring on which the decoration is applied is constructed in a similar fashion to 2, and the punch impressions present the same characteristics. However, where the metal is thicker, towards the lower half of the ring, the impressions have a little more definition. One of the impressions is a mis-strike, its position having been altered before being struck again. Taking into account the general style of the ring as well as the punch impressions, it is certainly possible that these two rings are by the same craftsman.

Ring 9: the style of decoration on this ring is very different from the previous two. The shoulders of the ring are plain except for a small human face. The shank is solid and bears a band of overlapping round punch impressions; because of this overlap, a 'bite' is taken from each one. As the punch is here used on solid metal of some thickness, the effect is different: the impressions are much sharper in detail and there is no tendency to drag down the surrounding metal.

An experiment was carried out to determine the range of impressions that could be produced from a single punch by varying the metal thickness. A small steel punch was made that would produce impressions more or less identical to those on the Thetford objects. The results suggest that the impressions on items 2, 4 and 9 could have been made by the same tool.

Pendants 28 and 29: these gold pendants are again made from thin sheet and apparently filled. They bear six and four punch impressions respectively. The impressions are of the same size and have the same characteristics as those on rings

2 and 4. The two pendants are of very similar style and it would be reasonable to suggest that they are by the same hand, with a further possibility that they come from the same workshop as items 2, 4 and 9.

Conclusions

The punch impressions examined on the five objects are all certainly made by the same type of tool; the variations are caused by different thicknesses of metal, the strength with which the punch was struck, and the number of times it was struck. There is evidence of double striking in at least two places. It is not possible to state conclusively that the decoration on ring 9 was produced with the same punch, but was certainly made with one of the same size and type as the others, the final effect being different because of the thickness of the metal. It should be pointed out that any craftsman working with punches and chasing tools would probably have a very large selection, and this could well include several of the same type. Also, in a workshop each man would have his own collection of tools; new punches would be produced as jobs required them and the collection would be built up over the years.

The sample punch was tested on a variety of materials of different thicknesses including lead, gold and copper; the punch impressions produced were almost identical to those on the Thetford items. Opical examination was carried out with a $\times 10$ to $\times 40$ binocular microscope.

NOTES

1. Further details of the XRF procedure and equipment used here can be found in Cowell 1977.
2. Cf. Hughes and Hall 1979.
3. McKerrel and Stevenson 1972.
4. Hughes and Hall 1979.
5. Lins and Oddy 1975; Oddy 1981.
6. For further discussion of this point, cf. the catalogue entry.
7. Johns 1979(b).
8. Caley 1950.
9. Meeks and Tite 1980.
10. Meeks and Tite 1980.
11. Arrhenius 1971.
12. Mellor 1930.
13. E.g. Woolley 1934.
14. Oddy 1977.
15. Oddy, *forthcoming*.
16. Bray 1978, 36.
17. Foltz 1979, 218.
18. Anastasiadis 1950.
19. Epprecht and Mutz 1974/5.
20. Furger-Gunti 1978.
21. Jacobi 1979.
22. Rump 1967.
23. Rump 1968.
24. Bray 1978.
25. Oddy 1977.
26. Oddy 1980.
27. Maryon and Plenderleith 1954, 656.
28. Williams 1924, 39—44.
29. But see Carroll 1972.
30. Brailsford 1975, 55f.
31. Oddy 1979.
32. Maryon and Plenderleith 1954; Thouvenin 1971; Foltz 1979.

33. Johns *et al.* 1980, no 1.
34. Johns *et al.* 1980, no 2.
35. Johns *et al.* 1980, no 3.
36. Brailsford 1964, fig. 14. 4.
37. Brailsford 1964, fig. 7.5.
38. Brailsford 1964, pl. 3.
39. Brailsford 1964, pl. 3; Marshall 1911, 2797.
40. Johns *et al.* 1980, no 7.
41. E.g. Catalogue 1976, nos 12g and 13b.
42. Marshall 1911, 524.
43. Marshall 1911, 510 and 511.
44. E.g. Marshall 1911, 752; Higgins 1979, 56.
45. Marshall 1911, 1461 and 1463.
46. Marshall 1911, 1702.
47. Raub 1977, 1981.
48. Dalton 1964, nos 7, 124 and 152.
49. Ghirshman 1961, no. 740.
50. The complex stylistic links between the spoons are fully analysed in Chapter 5.
51. The possibility of different 'handwritings' being detectable is discussed in Chapter 5.
52. The stylistic links in the jewellery are further examined and analysed in Chapter 2.
53. See the full report on the punch marks in the final section of this discussion.
54. H. A. P. Littledale, 'A new process of hard-soldering and its possible connection with the methods used by the ancient Greeks and Etruscans', in *The Scientific and Technical Factors of Production of Gold and Silverwork*, Worshipful Company of Goldsmiths, London, 1936, pp. 44–63.
55. J. Wolters, *Zur Geschichte der Löttechnik Degussa*, Frankfurt, 1976.
56. See Chapter 2, and 30.
57. The techniques of wire manufacture have been dealt with in Part 2 of this chapter.

10

The Significance
of the Treasure

In this final chapter, it must be our aim to sum up the main threads of the argument traced through previous sections and to make some attempt to ascertain the factors that lie behind the concealment of the hoard. Naturally, we are all too aware of the difficulties that confront enquiries of this sort. It is to trespass upon dangerous ground where opinion holds sway over fact and where there can be no hope of a certain conclusion. Nevertheless, there are questions that must be posed and, if the result is not one but several hypotheses which could explain the hoard, that at least the reader has the chance either to select his preferred choice or to account for the treasure in some other way.

The composition of the treasure

That the Thetford hoard, as it stands, comprises an unusual and curious assemblage is unlikely to be in serious dispute. In the form in which it survives, it cannot be closely paralleled, especially with its apparently disparate components of, on the one hand, a collection of closely related items of jewellery and, on the other, of a set of silver objects, associated with an obscure religious cult.

Hoards of the fourth and early fifth centuries are, however, fairly well represented in the archaeological record[1] and it may be helpful to delineate the main categories. Of prime importance are the great plate treasures such as those from Mildenhall, Kaiseraugst, the Esquiline Hill in Rome, and, in all probability, Corbridge.[2] Most of these would appear to represent the possessions of some very wealthy and influential individuals; thus Painter's plausible suggestion that the thirty-four silver objects that comprise the Mildenhall find may have been brought to Britain by the Christian Lupercinus, who was *magister equitum per Gallias* when Julian, cousin of Constantius II, was Caesar of the Gallic provinces;[3] or the inscription on a dish in the Carthage Treasure, which links this find with the Cresconii, a North African family highly placed in the public service during the fourth and early fifth centuries.[4] Equally there are other sets of plate which are best explained as the property of a church. As many scholars have emphasised, it was not uncommon practice to make items of silver specifically for churches in the fourth century, and Constantine himself donated a patera weighing no less than 15 pounds, as well as nine other vessels, to the Basilica of SS Peter and Marcellinus.[5] One such set is, in all probability, represented by the Water Newton Treasure[6] while another is instanced by the twenty-four silver vessels discovered at Canoscio near Perugia, Italy.[7] However, it should be stressed that in many cases it is not always possible to decide what the associations of a set of plate may have been: just as the

Mildenhall Treasure or the Risley Park lanx[8] are neither unambiguously Christian nor pagan, so it is difficult to know what significance should be attached to a hoard of silver spoons, at least one with a Christian symbol, from Biddulph in Cheshire.[9] Such finds underline the fact that in the late-Roman period iconographical traditions were deeply intermingled, very often reflecting a deeply rooted eclecticism in taste.

Another very distinct category of hoard, particularly well represented in regions beyond the northern frontiers of the Empire, is conventionally known by the term *Hacksilber*. Typified by finds from sites such as Traprain Law (Scotland), Balline and Coleraine (= Balinrees) in Ireland, Whorlton (Yorkshire) in England, Høstentorp (Denmark), Gross Bodungen (Germany) and elsewhere,[10] the characteristic feature of such hoards is the inclusion of often large quantities of broken and squashed silver objects. The Traprain Treasure for example — one of the very few hoards to be identified and recovered under relatively controlled conditions of excavation[11] — consisted of fragments of well over one hundred silver items, most of them cut up or flattened. In addition, there were four coins which take the date of deposition into the reign of Honorius (AD 395–423) or later. Similarly, the Coleraine find also comprised pieces of a number of vessels, spoons and other objects, as well as six silver ingots, a silver bar and 1,506 coins, all but one being silver *siliquae*.[12] Silver ingots, although not coins, were a conspicuous feature of another Irish *Hacksilber* hoard, that from Balline[13] and are well-represented in many other finds. They are a particularly interesting series of objects, with over forty examples recorded from the European provinces alone.[14] Many can be shown to weigh the equivalent of one Roman pound and a number bear official stamps. Thus they can be firmly associated with the well-attested fourth-century practice of payment in the form of Imperial donatives, of which Julian's promise of five gold *solidi* and a pound of silver to each man on the occasion of his accession, in AD 361, provides a good instance.[15] The importance that was attached to quantification of the weight of gold and silver is further confirmed by inscriptions on items of precious metal and by the degree of control that is known to have been exercised over the official centres of production. As Kent notes, 'after 366, the central Treasury no longer accepted its gold issues in individual pieces; they were taken back only when converted into carefully refined and weighed bars.'[16] In this light, then, it is no longer acceptable always to regard the *Hacksilber* hoards — particularly those from beyond the confines of the Empire — as loot cut up for division amongst the plunderers. Rather, while some collections of late-Roman gold and silver, like that from Traprain, may represent the spoils of war, it is likely that many more were in fact payments of a certain weight of gold and silver: that, whatever its form, an item such as a crushed silver bowl could be a type of currency.[17]

Firm conclusions about the importance of mensuration in late-Roman hoards are, however, often frustrated by a lack of information. Accurate weights of the objects are not always available and, in many cases, there is no guarantee that a hoard was recovered in its entirety — or, for that matter, that it was interred complete. The *Hacksilber* treasure from Whorlton, Yorkshire, is a case in point. Found in 1810, it is said to have weighed as much as two stone. Little now survives but, to what must have been several thousand silver coins, held in a silver 'urn', there were also silver bars, a number of rings (mainly of silver), a silver spoon and part of a silver buckle.[18] On the other hand, there is much more precise information about the hoard found in 1974 at Water Newton (*Durobrivae*).[19] This comprised thirty gold *solidi* and two folded packets of silver, weighing 321 g and 642 g — namely, about one and two pounds of silver, respectively — underlining that it was a measured weight of precious metal that was buried, *c.* AD 350, for safe-keeping in the ground.

The plate and *Hacksilber* hoards can be generally distinguished from a third, somewhat miscellaneous group, characterised by the inclusion of various items of jewellery. Even a cursory search of the literature shows that such finds are by no means uncommon, especially in Britain. Apart from the New Grange find[20] of two gold rings, a gold necklace and two gold bracelets — a deposit almost certainly votive in intention — examples include Sully Moors near Cardiff; Amesbury, Wiltshire; Grovely Wood, Wiltshire; East Harptree near Bristol; Canterbury; and further afield, Beaurains near Arras (France) and Ténès, on the north coast of Algeria.[21] It is a list that could easily be extended, but it is the general points about these assemblages that are important. In the first place, the great majority contain coins in precious metals, often in very considerable number. Secondly, items of jewellery occur in every hoard, ranging from rings, necklaces, bracelets and brooches through to elaborate buckles. Thirdly, a few have silver ingots, while small objects of silver, particularly spoons, are also sometimes represented. However, it should be pointed out that hoards apparently consisting solely of coins and spoons are also not unknown, such as those from Dorchester (Dorset).[22]

By way of comparison, it may be helpful to take some of the larger 'jewellery hoards' of the later-Roman period and to set out the main components and their quantities, in so far as these are known[23] (see Table 8).

Whilst it would be incautious to draw any over-elaborate conclusions from the distribution of artefacts in these hoards, it is nevertheless of interest to see the many links that unify them as a group. If a distinction can be drawn between the Thetford Treasure and the other assemblages, it is certainly not one of composition: rather, it is the fact that the other groups could all be regarded as suites of jewellery and other possessions belonging to a single family or individual, whereas the Thetford set quite clearly is not. This is a matter that we shall pursue in more detail below.

Finally, we should mention a fourth category of hoard,

Table 8 Gold and silver objects from major 'jewellery hoards'

	Beaurains (early 4th cent.)	Thetford (late 4th cent.)	Canterbury (early 5th cent.)	Ténès (early 5th cent.)*
gold jewellery				
buckles	1	1		2
Other belt fittings				5
brooches				4
bracelets	5	4		4
amulet cases		1		2
necklaces	5	5	1	
pendants	6	2		
club of Hercules	1	2		
earrings	2			
cameo	1	1		
rings	2	22	1	
silver objects				
vessels	1			1
spoons	2	33	11	
strainers/ implements		3	1	
ingots	1		2	
pins			1	
candlestick	1			
other	2			
Coins	c. 700	?	?	

* = approximate date of deposition

namely those that comprise only coins. Two recent studies of late-Roman finds of gold and silver coin hoards make it clear that Britain is particularly conspicuous for the frequency of such finds, a feature which, as Carson notes, 'is in marked contrast to the pattern discernible in other western provinces of the empire.'[24] Presumably, this is in the main a reflection of the abrupt end to Roman administration of the island and the political upheavals that ensued. Indeed, numismatists take the view that the use of coinage *per se* effectively came to an end shortly after AD 420. Two principal conclusions emerge from these studies. One concerns the coinage in gold which turns out to be on the whole very rare. Apart from ill-documented finds like that from Cleeve Prior in Worcestershire, which allegedly contained between 450 and 600 *solidi*, and Eye, Suffolk (600 *solidi*), there are no properly authenticated discoveries of above fifty late-Roman gold coins. The figures are as follows with the number of *solidi* listed in brackets: Corbridge (48), Terling, Essex (30), Water

Newton (30), Chelmsford (26), Alcester (16), Carleton St Peter, Norfolk (4), Maiden Castle, Dorset (4), Springhead, Kent (4), Tower of London (3), Allington, Hants (1), Guisborough, Yorkshire (1), Reading (1), Sturmer, Essex (1), Wilton, Yorkshire (1).[25] The second principal feature of the finds seems to be the way in which they demonstrate a fairly well defined trend towards regional clusters so that there is (1) a group with gold or gold and silver focussing upon the Thames Valley; (2) a distinct Wiltshire-Gloucestershire-Somerset group; (3) a substantial cluster of finds from East Anglia; and (4) a small outlying group in the north-east. It is difficult to know precisely what significance should be attached to this distribution, beyond its general correspondence with some of the wealthier areas of Roman Britain. However, it is worth noting that recent discoveries from Thetford do fit comfortably into this overall pattern. Leaving aside the wholly unauthenticated possibility of gold and silver coins from the vicinity of the treasure, three hoards of late-fourth century silver *siliquae* are already known from the area, namely: (1) a find made *c.* 1962 on the north side of the town, comprising some twenty silver *siliquae* including issues of Julian and Magnus Maximus; (2) a discovery in 1978 of forty-seven *siliquae*, ranging in date from AD 355–61 to AD 385; and (3) a find in 1981, consisting perhaps of one hundred or more *siliquae*, of which latest issues are said to be of Eugenius (AD 392–4).[26] Whilst we cannot associate these hoards with the treasure itself, it is nevertheless striking that there should be such a concentration of more or less contemporary silver coinage buried so close to the main find. Given that, as we have seen, late-Roman gold and silver objects were very commonly interred together with *solidi* and/or *siliquae* (and, not infrequently, the rather larger denomination, the *miliarense*), it is tempting to wonder if there may not be some connection between these hoards — especially as both the Icklingham (Suffolk) and Shapwick (Dorset) appear to provide instances where contemporary collections of objects and coins were buried at more than one spot.[27] However, whatever way we interpret this remarkable series of discoveries, it is a clear illustration that there was a considerable amount of portable wealth in the Thetford area in the late fourth century; and, too, that there were factors that militated against the subsequent recovery of this gold and silver.[28]

To sum up, the Thetford Treasure is evidently best paralleled in terms of its composition by the 'jewellery hoards', like those from Canterbury, Beaurains and Ténès. These comprise a group of hoards which can be regarded as distinct from the plate, *Hacksilber* and coin assemblages, although, as one might expect, there is a fair degree of overlap. On the other hand, there are aspects of the Thetford group which cannot be readily paralleled, and it is to these matters that we must now turn.

THE JEWELLERY COMPONENT IN THE HOARD
In Chapter 2 we devoted a good deal of discussion to the question of stylistic links within the group of jewellery and to the condition of the objects. The arguments need not be reiterated in detail but the conclusions may be briefly summarised as follows:

1 A series of idiosyncratic decorative traits can be traced through many of the objects, suggesting that at least 75% of the jewellery was made in the same workshop. The form of other items such as the mounted gems, amulet case and necklaces is sufficiently plain and, to an extent, standardised so as to preclude conclusions about their stylistic affinities; however, one ring (no. 15) apart, there are no typological — or metallurgical — reasons for regarding any of the jewellery as the product of more than a single workshop. We therefore feel some justification in defining an *officina* of what we could aptly describe as the 'Thetford jeweller'.

2 The very pure and soft gold used by this workshop could normally be expected to succumb to traces of scratching and wear very rapidly. This is not the case with most of the objects and, of those that do, only a single item — ring 15 — exhibits any evidence of prolonged use. Unlike most hoards of ancient jewellery in gold the Thetford assemblage cannot therefore be regarded as a set of personal finery, brought together over a period of years or decades.

3 Equally striking is the fact that an unmounted gem, partly re-formed from its original shape, and a necklace comprise unambiguous instances of unfinished objects in the collection. There may be others but the evidence is not decisive.

4 The assemblage as a whole consists of items designed for women rather than men — ring 16 is an exception — and, surprisingly, does not include obvious late-fourth century objects associated with manly apparel such as cross-bow brooches.[29].

These observations seem inexorably to lead to one overall conclusion: namely that the Thetford jewellery is an expensive and flamboyant suite of objects, designed in the main for ladies, which remained either to be worn or, indeed, to be sold. Their owner, we must surmise, was either a high-class jeweller or, perhaps, some tolerably affluent merchant who purveyed these ostentatious examples of high-quality late-Roman metalwork to the high echelons of ancient society.[30]

One further point should be made. Despite the intensity of archaeological investigation and publication in Britain, close parallels for the Thetford jewellery remain comparatively elusive. It is the clearest pointer that we should look abroad for the workshop. As it happens, some of the best analogies come from Gaul, a Roman province which, apart from physical contiguity, has also brought to light a number of well-studied finds of this sort. However whilst we tend towards the view that Gaul — and perhaps the city of *Lugdunum* (Lyon) — may have been the centre of manufacture, the evidence falls far short of proof. It could be that an uneven level in the reporting of such finds (especially, perhaps, from the east Mediterranean) may mask the true origin of the 'Thetford jeweller': but only further research will tell.[31]

The cult of Faunus and the jewellery
The association of the jewellery with so many silver spoons bearing the name of the god Faunus naturally prompts us to wonder what relationship is shared by the two sets of objects. In a subsequent section, we shall consider some of the more esoteric possibilities, but here we must discuss the notion that the jewellery relates directly to the cult of Faunus. At the basis

of this view lies the assumption that either the jewellery was a votive collection, presented to the god in its unworn and unfinished state,[32] or that it was intended to be worn in the celebration of the ritual — a role that was never fulfilled. In this connection, it is interesting in view of the predominantly feminine associations of the jewellery that, of the personal names on the spoons, three are of men and three are of women. Were they, as Mark Hassall remarks, 'a guild of worshippers perhaps, whose activities included sharing a feast with their patron deities (*lectisternia*) perhaps once a month or at least, on the fifth of December, the date of the *Faunalia*'?[33]

We must, of course, look at the jewellery to see if the objects themselves embody by allusion to the deity, although we must bear in mind Martin Henig's point, that 'in the light of what we have said about colour replacing interest in gem-cutting, it is perhaps too much to expect any direct reference to the god Faunus in the group'.[34] The answer to this question is that there are some objects which *could* be interpreted in this way. These include:

1. The Bacchanalian satyr on the buckle.
2. The Faunus-like mask on ring 23.
3. The fact that Mars, shown on the gem of ring 16, is represented in some accounts as the father of Faunus.
4. That Diana, like Faunus, has associations with woodland.
5. That the birds on ring 7 may be interpreted as woodpeckers (= *picus*) and that Picus was the father of Faunus.

Whether one regards these links between the Thetford jewellery as tenuous or strong is entirely a matter of opinion. There are no inscriptions to help us (although the members of the cult were clearly not averse, as the spoons show, to disclosing their religious affiliation) and no wholly explicit iconographical reference. Probably the strongest piece of evidence associating the jewellery with the spoons is the fact that they were interred together; but we should recognise that a more obscure explanation for this curiously disparate collection of objects could exist, something that we shall consider further below.

THE SILVER COMPONENT IN THE HOARD AND ITS RELIGIOUS CONNOTATIONS

Study of the remarkable group of thirty-three spoons and three strainers in the Thetford Treasure yields a series of interesting, if tentative, conclusions. Leaving aside the question of weight, which we shall turn to below, the indications are that the spoons are, in all probability, the product of a single workshop. This we surmise from the stylistic traits that can be traced through each set of spoons, the duck-handled type and the long-handled form, the link between the two groups being provided by the Triton and Panther spoons. More subjectively, we are inclined to think that typologically they belong in a related but distinct tradition from most late-Roman silver spoons hitherto found in Britain[35] and were not therefore made in that province. Furthermore, we can demonstrate that some of the inscriptions were made before the spoons were given their finishing touches. Thus, since so many of the inscriptions embody Celtic names, we feel that this is one pointer towards a Gaulish source for this silverware — a conclusion sustained by the sheer *number* of

Celtic names.[36] The strainers, on the other hand, cannot be linked typologically with the spoons, although there is no reason to suppose that they do not have a common origin.

The inscriptions on the spoons fall into three main groups. Hassall[37] has characterised them as follows (1) twenty with religious inscriptions; (2) eight with personal names in either the vocative or genitive cases, six including the word VIVAS; and (3) three with mottos. No less than twelve of the spoons refer directly to the god Faunus, while others have names — particularly Agrestius, Ingenua, Primigenia and Silviola — which could be seen as containing allusions to the cult of Faunus. There seems little doubt, therefore, that the spoons form a homogenous set that was used in some way in the religious ritual of the cult. Notwithstanding the inscription on spoon 69, namely SILVIOLA VIVAS followed by a cross, and the fish on spoon 67 (both finds that, were they isolated discoveries, might be thought to have Christian connotations),[38] the whole set of spoons can safely be regarded as exclusively devoted to the celebration of pagan ritual.

The nature of these rites and the way in which the spoons may have been used must of course remain obscure. Spoons in the late-antique world undoubtedly served a variety of purposes, summed up by Kenneth Painter as follows: 'Some are grave-offerings, a custom having its origins in heathen antiquity. Others are memorials for, or good luck offerings for, individuals, or at least apotropaic in the devices. Some are parts of table-services, while others found a use in hoards of silver broken up for use as currency. A number had Christian uses, with inscriptions or graffiti, like those on brooches or gravestones or other materials, which prayed that God might grant the named person a happy life now or hereafter.'[39] In our case, we can probably assume that the spoons were intended partly as offerings, but also that they had a functional role. This much is clear from the traces of wear that are perceptible on many of the spoons, indicating that they may well have been used in some sort of ceremonial feast. The *Faunalia*, which took place on the 5 December (Horace, *Odes* 3, 18, 10), would have provided one obvious opportunity for such an occasion and meetings were no doubt much more frequent. Indeed, it is possible that the cult was organised into a guild or club of worshippers, a feature of religious life that is certainly attested in antiquity.[40]

THE DATE OF THE GOLD AND SILVER OBJECTS

Whilst the general late-antique character of the Thetford assemblage is abundantly clear, it is still not possible to arrive at any very close date for the treasure. This is partly the result of a dearth of published parallels of the later fourth and fifth centuries — the Ténès hoard is a notable exception — but it also reflects the fact that many of the objects appear to be unique. For example good parallels for the rings have proved on the whole to be surprisingly sparse, especially from well-dated contexts.

Nevertheless, it is clear from such analogies that we have been able to find that neither the gold jewellery nor the silver objects are, as collections, likely to be any earlier than the middle of the fourth century. Some types, it is true, are attested well before this; *inter alia* we may cite the amulet case and the chain necklaces. However, we can be certain that these objects were not old when buried and there is thus no reason to separate them chronologically from the rest of the assemblage; rather, they must represent archaic designs that still remained in the repertoire of the late-antique jeweller.

The central problem that confronts us, therefore, is to try to decide just how late in the fourth century we should assign the treasure. As far as the jewellery is concerned, the detailed discussion in the catalogue will make clear the numerous over-all similarities that individual objects share with late-antique styles. However, given that it *does* represent a jeweller's hoard, it is the pieces with the latest datable analogies that are of most significance. Amongst them we should include ring 15, with its parallels both with Canterbury and the Whorlton hoards (dated *c.* AD 400 and *c.* AD 410–25 respectively); ring 10, whose best analogies occur in the Terling hoard (*c.* AD 420); and ring 16, with a striking parallel in a hoard of the early fifth century from Tuddenham, Suffolk.[41] Similarly, rings 12 and 14 should belong in the later decades of the fourth century while the zoomorphic elements of rings 6 and 7 also imply a late date. When taken in conjuction with the gold belt-buckle 1, (which cannot be closely paralleled but is nevertheless quite certainly late-Roman in form), it seems reasonable to suggest a *terminus post quem* of at least AD 375 for the jewellery, and a *feeling* that it could well be a decade or two later. Indeed, it is striking that, as a hoard, it shares a remarkable overall similarity with the early fifth-century treasure found at Ténès on the north coast of Algeria.[52]

With the silver, closely dated analogies are equivalently sparse, although they are sufficiently numerous to be certain of a *terminus post quem* of *c.* AD 350. Due weight must be given, however, to the parallels with the Canterbury and Dorchester (Dorset) hoards,[43] both of which are near in date to AD 400; and to the distinctively late-Roman trait of zoomorphic offsets represented on six of the spoons. In other words, there is no good reason to regard the silver as being significantly different in date from the jewellery. A period of manufacture in the last couple of decades of the fourth century would, on present evidence, suit both sets of objects.

To these observations it seems germane to mention the general site evidence, in particular that of the coins. As we showed in Chapter 1, the vicinity of the Thetford Treasure has yielded a remarkable concentration of numismatic material, including a silver hoard buried *c.* AD 385 found in 1978; and second found in 1981 of the same general date; another which reportedly contained issues as late as Eugenius (AD 392–4); a fourth found in 1962 with coins of Julian and Magnus Maximus (AD 383–8); and an unproven possibility of gold and silver coins, including *solidi* of Magnus Maximus.[44] Whatever the uncertainties that lie behind the reports of some of these finds, it is quite certain that a remarkable volume of wealth was being buried in this area in the 380s–390s, in other words, at about the same time that (if our typological analysis is right) the Thetford Treasure was made — and concealed. This may of course be solely a matter of coincidence; but to infer a connection between these various discoveries does not seem to be stretching the bounds of possibility too far.[45]

THE QUESTION OF WEIGHTS
Both in Chapter 2 and Chapter 5, we drew attention to what appears to be a close correspondence between the weights of many of the objects and the subdivisions of the Roman pound. Naturally we were at pains to underline the difficulties in assigning an absolute value to the Roman pound since it is clear that, in practice, it could be a quite variable measurement. This much is quite evident from one-pound silver ingots which in fact range in weight from 301 to 340 g.[46] However, it is generally accepted that a weight of about 325 g represents a best approximation of the value of the Roman pound, so that one ounce would be in the order of 27 g.[47] This finds particular confirmation in the Thetford silver, as a study of the weights of the spoons quite clearly shows. Leaving aside one damaged spoon and six other anomolously large examples, the remaining twenty-six all weigh between 24.2 and 28.9 g, giving and average of 26.11 g. We can be certain, therefore, that the silversmith intended the great majority of the spoons to weigh one ounce and that the variation is due either to imperfections in his balance or, perhaps, because he estimated rather than weighed the silver for each object.

Similarly, there are some objects amongst the gold which also respond to this sort of analysis. The main difficulty is posed by the fact that most of the jewellery consists of composite materials, so that it is impossible to determine the weight of gold in each object with any precision. However, three items are both in perfect condition and made solely in gold, namely three of the bracelets. Of these, the matching pair 24 and 25 weigh 26.8 and 25.9 g, i.e. one ounce each, while bracelet 26 amounts to 108.1 g, the equivalent of four ounces (27.025 × 4). In these cases, therefore, we can be certain that the goldsmith intended to use a definite quantity of metal in the manufacture of each bracelet. With other items, as we saw in Chapter 2, there are some possible correlations but, without a more precise technique of measuring the weight of gold, it would be unwise to press the point too far. On the other hand, it is interesting to note that our estimate of the *total* amount of gold in the hoard, some 505 g, is close to 1½ Roman pounds (1.55 with a pound of 325 g), an equivalence that may not be accidental. Indeed, it is a figure that can be very closely matched by the weight of metal in the sixteen duck-handled spoons (497.5 g = 1.53 pounds). The long-handled spoons (which do not form an even-numbered set and may not, therefore, be complete) only come to 1.31 pounds (424.5 g). However, if the strainers are included with the rest of the silver, the total is 3.01 pounds, a figure which again could be meaningful. Alternatively, the addition of three spoons of 25 g weight each would also bring the overall figure for the long-handled spoons to 500 g, 1.53 pounds, and at the same time, would create an even-numbered set, with thirty-six spoons in all — the same total as in the Kaiseraugst Treasure.[48]

Further speculation is pointless since we do not know how complete the hoard may have been when it was buried; but there are sufficient hints of deliberate mensuration in the group as a whole to suggest that this is a valid line of enquiry. Moreover, it is a reminder of the quantity of wealth that is represented by the Thetford Treasure. Thus the silver would convert into over 430 *siliquae* and the gold into some 113 *solidi* — a considerable sum in a period when, as Kent observes, 'one gold *solidus* was enough to furnish bare subsistence for a year'.[49] When taken in conjunction with the other coin finds, discussed above and in Chapter 1, from the area of the treasure, it is a vivid indication of no small degree of affluence. As we saw earlier, of all the known late-Roman hoards with gold coins, only two — both ill-documented discoveries — appear to have contained more than forty-eight *solidi*, namely Cleeve Prior (Worcestershire) and Eye (Suffolk). This must surely prompt us to wonder how and why this wealth came to be interred in this remote rural area.

Some possible explanations

While further research will undoubtedly shed much more light upon the date, context, origin and, perhaps, the ownership of the Thetford Treasure, we may doubt whether there can ever be any final interpretation of this remarkable find. Nevertheless, certain possibilities need to be raised, if only to point the way for future enquiry.

There is no difficulty in finding a broad historical context to explain the burial of the treasure. As Crawford has shown,[50] the interment of wealth can often be shown to have a direct relationship with violent events, and there is no shortage of these in the history of the last few decades of the province. Apart from Magnus Maximus's coup of 383 (which brought about unsettled conditions until 389 or 390)[51] and the Pictish war of Stilicho, 396–8, there was, from 401, the rapid depletion of the Roman army in Britain to attend to crises in other parts of the Empire; all combined to create a situation of ever-increasing unease and confusion. Moreover, the immensely heavy overlay of Saxon sites in East Anglia is a further reminder of the vulnerability of this low-lying coastline to seaborne attack, which led ultimately to settlement.[52] However, it may be that there is a more specific reason for the concealment of so much wealth in the area to the north of Thetford. As we have seen, all of the coin hoards share as a common denominator issues of Magnus Maximus and at least three appear to terminate in his reign. Only in one is there a report of later coins, namely of Eugenius (392–4). Moreover, this is a date-range which would well suit the Thetford Treasure itself, so that we can conclude that the later 380s and perhaps the 390s witnessed the burial of a considerable sum of gold and silver in the Gallows Hill area.

Given the pagan associations of the Thetford spoons, this is of particular interest. Under Theodosius, who had become emperor in 379, 'the campaign against paganism was eventually intensified, despite the emperor's considerable tolerance of leading pagans.'[53] Many pagan sanctuaries were destroyed, and in an edict dated 24 February 391, all temples were closed to the public and sacrifice made illegal throughout the empire.[54] A year later, an even more harsh law was published: there was to be no domestic worship of the lares and penates; no incense could be burnt; nor could garlands be displayed. The fine for such activities in a public place was to be twenty pounds of gold, and the governor and his *officium* were to be fined even more heavily were these penalties not exacted.[55]

At the background of these punitive measures lay not only a strong opposition to paganism. Magnus Maximus was notorious for the severity of his fiscal policy,[56] while Theodosius was faced with a loss of revenue caused by the depredations of the Goths and by a heavy military expenditure. His taxation is thought to have been severe.[57] Consequently, the guardians of the wealth of a banned pagan temple may well have felt deeply threatened, even in a province as remote as Britain. It is by no means implausible, therefore, to see the concealment of the Thetford hoards, in the presumed vicinity of a sanctuary to Faunus, as a measure of the alarm that was caused by a new, harsh legislation and by repressive action against the old religion. A date of burial of the Thetford Treasure shortly before the more tolerant regime of Eugenius began in 392[58] might well suit both the typological arguments and the historical facts as we know them.

Who, then, was the owner of the jewellery? Given that it is a jeweller's hoard, containing in the main unused and, in some cases, unfinished pieces, it seems clear that, shortly before its burial, it must have been in the hands of a merchant. However, this does not necessarily mean that the merchant was the owner of the jewellery, since we know that craftsmen in valuable metals did work up material supplied by their customers.[59] Indeed, as Professor A. H. M. Jones remarks, 'dealers in luxury goods aspired, like the silversmiths and jewellers, to posts in the provincial *officium*. They cannot therefore have been very rich or important persons.'[60] Thus it is at least possible that the Thetford jewellery was a special commission, made up from some 1½ pounds of gold provided by the person or group who placed the order — perhaps, indeed, the devotees of the cult of Faunus. On the other hand, the composition of the jewellery (as it now stands) is such that it might seem much more like unsold stock-in-trade, including a ring (15) that was intended for reworking. Certainly there were *negotiatores* who, while of plebeian rank, were tolerably affluent. For example, there was a merchant of Alexandria who bequeathed to his two sons 5,000 *solidi* in cash, as well as clothes (high-costing items in antiquity) and slaves.[61] Moreover, many were capable of raising substantial loans, like the silversmith of Jerusalem who was robbed of 100 pounds of silver, not alas his own, the equivalent of 400 *solidi*.[62] These are trifling figures in comparison with the fortunes of the rich senatorial families whose yearly income could be as much as 1,500 to 4,000 pounds of gold;[63] but it is by means inconceivable that a well-to-do merchant might be in the possession of stock worth some 113 *solidi*.

To sum up these points, it is clear that the Thetford jeweller, while amounting to a conspicuously large sum of gold in comparison with most authenticated late-Roman gold finds from Britain, is nevertheless not a particularly substantial quantity in the context of the Roman world as a whole. Nor need we attribute to its jeweller or merchant any very special status. He was a plebeian, one of a group of craftsmen and traders who were accorded little rank in ancient society. What is important is the identity of the client or clients for whom he worked and it is to this matter that we must now turn. In essence, the problem is to explain how this unworn jewellery came to be associated with a set of spoons dedicated to the cult of Faunus. Here, there seem to us to be three main hypotheses. In the first place, we can follow Martin Henig's persuasive argument, advanced in Chapter 3, that the jewellery was commissioned for the temple of Faunus, as some sort of religious regalia. Rings made for Christian owners, appropriately inscribed, are well known, just as rings and intagli are common finds at pagan temple sites.[64] As an instance, we might cite the thirty-four gems found at the spring of Sul Minerva at Bath which appear to have been a votive gift to this healing deity: hence the themes of fertility and of life's pleasures that are most prevalent in the engravings upon the gems.[65] Given the several iconographical allusions to Faunus or related deities on some of the Thetford objects (particularly the woodpecker-like birds and the mask resembling Pan) this might seem a strong reason to associate the jewellery with this religious cult. If so, then we must remember that, save for ring 15, none of this jewellery has been worn (such wear-traces as there are cannot be said to be consistent with anything more than occasional handling and movement since manufacture) and that not every object is finished: it would have to be a temple regalia that had yet to serve any practical function.[66]

A second possibility might be that the merchant responsible for the jeweller was himself a devotee of Faunus and therefore chose to incorporate some hint of his religious beliefs into the products of his *officina*. From this it would follow that circumstances prompted him to place his wealth in the safe-keeping of the temple. One has only to remember the ruthless way in which Magnus Maximus suppressed the Priscillianists, and the trial and subsequent execution of their leader and principal followers to appreciate the potential danger to members of some pagan cults. As with the worshippers of Faunus at Thetford, there were women amongst this group, and Priscillian himself was convicted of 'magic and of studying obscene doctrines, frequenting nocturnal meetings of infamous women and praying naked'[67] — a parallel, perhaps, for the more Bacchanalian elements in the worship of Faunus, a cult that the moralistic Christian, Arnobius, was so anxious to denounce.[68] Our merchant, therefore, could well have found himself in danger of a punitive fine or worse, and hastened to safeguard his most valuable possessions by placing them in the care of the temple.

As a third possibility, we might discount these iconographical allusions of Faunus (satyrs, Pan-figures and the like were, after all, commonplace in late-Roman art) and consider the find more in its regional setting. Despite the concentration of wealth in East Anglia, it is a region that is noteworthy both for its apparent paucity of rich villas and for anything more than a few small market towns.[69] The *colonia* at Colchester and, perhaps, the affluent industrial centre of Water Newton (*Durobrivae*), may in urban terms be counted the only exceptions. One wonders, therefore, whether these towns with their wealthy landowners and high-placed officials, may not have been the most appropriate potential market for these no doubt costly products of the 'Thetford jeweller'. On the other hand, we should remember that a dearth of architectural pretension of the sort displayed, for instance, by the villas of the Cotswolds, does not necessarily mean a paucity of wealth. It is a point well made by the Cambridgeshire Fenlands today where a region of conspicuous individual affluence finds almost no expression either in the form of the houses or in the scale of the towns: unpretentious building tends to mask an exceptional degree of personal wealth. Given that centuries of intensive agriculture in East Anglia may have tended to

erode most traces of Roman country estates and their villas (built, as often as not, from easily destroyed materials such as flint and mortar), it could be that our archaeological understanding of the East Anglian region is at best misleading; that there were in fact many suitably well-off customers for the Thetford jewellery in the Norfolk area.

Nevertheless, it is tempting to see our jeweller/merchant more in an urban context that in a rural environment, especially as the finishing touches had still to be applied to his wares — no doubt because they awaited the specification of the client. We are thus bound to wonder whether the concealment of the material at Thetford might not ultimately be the result of a theft, the perpetrator taking advantage of the unsettled conditions that prevailed at the time. Indeed, we have as an example the case, cited above, of the silversmith of Jerusalem who was deprived of no less than a hundred Roman pounds of silver by an enterprising robber.

Plausible though this and other suggestions may appear to be, there can however be no certainty in our possible explanations of the composition of the hoard. They must be recognised for what they are: very tentative hypotheses, to be supported or discarded as more evidence becomes available and as perspectives sharpen with the passing of time. What is important is that the Thetford Treasure, with its wealth of new epigraphical and artistic material, all of it apparently of late fourth-century date, is now available for study and reflection. However one regards the conclusions that we have drawn, one thing is beyond dispute: that it must be counted amongst the most fascinating and noble treasures so far known from Roman Britain.

NOTES

1. Grünhagen 1954 summarises *Hacksilber* hoards; cf. also Kent and Painter 1977, 123f.
2. Painter 1977a; Laur-Belart 1963; Shelton 1981; Haverfield 1914.
3. Painter 1977a, 22–3.
4. Kent and Painter 1977, 50.
5. L. Duchesne, *Liber Pontificalis* i. 1886, p. 79; Strong 1966, 185f., Painter 1977a, 21.
6. Painter 1977b.
7. E. Giovagnoli, *Il tesoro eucaristico di Canoscio*. 1940.
8. Johns 1981b.
9. Painter 1975; Sherlock 1976.
10. Most usefully summarised by Grünhagen 1954; cf also Kent and Painter 1977, 123. For Whorlton, cf. Burnett and Johns 1979.
11. Curle 1923.
12. Mattingly, Pearce and Kendrick 1933; Kent and Painter 1977, 125f.; Bateson 1973, 63–4.
13. Bateson 1973, 73–4.
14. Cf. Painter 1972, to which add a new find from the beach near Reculver, to be published by Kenneth Painter.
15. Ammianus Marcellinus 10, 4, 18.
16. In Kent and Painter 1977, 160.
17. Kent and Painter 1977, 123.
18. Burnett and Johns, 1979.
19. Johns and Carson in Painter 1977b, 27f. The coins are listed in detail by Carson in *Recent Coin Hoards from Roman Britain*, British Museum Occ. Pap. no. 5. 1979, pp. 99f.
20. Bateson 1973, 70–1; Kent and Painter 1977, 128.
21. Kent and Painter 1977 and references; Beaurains: Bastien and Metzger 1977; Ténès: Heurgon 1958.
22. Dalton 1922.
23. References as note 21, plus Canterbury: Painter 1965.
24. Carson 1976. Cf. also Archer 1979.

25. The figures are from Carson 1976 and Archer 1979; there is also a find allegedly of 50 *solidi* from Great Stanmore, Middlesex (Gough's edition of Camden's *Britannia* 2. 1789, pp. 30–1).
26. For full discussion of these hoards, and a possible fifth hoard, cf. Chapter 1.
27. Usefully summarised in Archer 1979.
28. Cf. the final section of this chapter for further discussion upon this point.
29. As in the Ténès Treasure (Heurgon 1958).
30. For further discussion about the jeweller/merchant, cf. the final section of this chapter.
31. We should bear in mind the possibility that the jeweller could easily have been a travelling craftsman who produced these objects in Britain but in a foreign (Gallic) style. There was, after all, a mint in London under Magnus Maximus and gold-mining within the province.
32. For a probable votive deposit of jewellery at New Grange, Ireland, cf. Kent and Painter 1977, 128f.
33. Hassall 1981.
34. Cf. Chapter 3.
35. A good many of these spoons were themselves probably produced outside Britain: cf, for example, Painter's (1972) discussion of the Biddulph spoon.
36. Naturally, we recognise that Celtic names were by no means confined to north-west Europe; but, were the spoons, say, of eastern origin, one should probably expect a more heterogeneous range of names.
37. Hassall 1981.
38. Cf. Thomas 1981, particularly 91f., for a down-to-earth evaluation of the material evidence for Christianity in Roman Britain.
39. Painter 1975, 68; Thomas 1981, 109f.
40. Illustrated, for example, (as Hassall 1981 points out) by a ring inscribed COL/DEI/SIL = *col(legium) dei sil(vani)*, 'the guild of the gold Silvanus', *Britannia* 12, 1981, p. 384.
41. References in the catalogue.
42. Heurgon 1958, 76f.
43. Painter 1965; Dalton 1922.
44. Cf. Chapter 1.

45. Cf. the final section for some possible implications.
46. Painter 1972.
47. We are grateful to Dr Mansel Spratling both for a copy of his paper on the subject (1980) and to drawing our attention to Grierson 1964.
48. Laur-Belart 1963.
49. In Kent and Painter 1977, 160.
50. *Paper of the British School at Rome* 37. 1969, pp 76f.
51. Cf. M. Miller in *Britannia* 6. 1975, pp. 141f.
52. Cf. C. Hills and P. Wade-Martins in *East Anglian Archaeology* no. 2. 1976, fig. 1, p. 11.
53. Salway 1981, 408.
54. *Codex Theod.* 16, x, 10.
55. *Codex Theod.* 16, x, 12.
56. Jones 1964, 159.
57. Jones 1964, 162f.
58. Salway 1981, 409; Jones 1964, 168.
99. Jones 1964, 863.
60. Jones 1964, 865.
61. Palladius, *Hist. Laus.* 14.
62. *Cyr. Scyth.* 5, *Sabae*, 78, cited by Jones 1964, 863.
63. Jones 1964, 871.
64. Henig 1978,n37; Pliny, *Nat. Hist.* 37, 11.
65. M. Henig in B. Cunliffe, *Roman Bath* Soc. Ant. Research Report 140, 1969 pp. 71–88.
66. e.g. the Backworth Treasure: Henig 1978, 37. Whether we could interpret the site currently under excavation at Thetford as a religious complex is at present not clear.
67. Jones 1964, 164.
68. Cf. the numerous references to Faunus in the seven books of Arnobius's *Adversus nationes*.
69. R. R. Clarke's conclusions in *Norfolk Archaeology* 30. 1952, pp. 148f. are still not greatly altered by more recent work. For the apparent paucity of villas occupied in the post-367 period in the region cf. G. Webster in A. L. F. Rivet (ed.), *The Roman Villa in Britain*. 1969, p. 230, fig. 6.2.

11

The Catalogue

We have attempted to present the catalogue of the individual objects in the treasure in such a way that factual information is clearly differentiated from opinion and discussion. Each object is given a title and a brief descriptive heading; this is followed by a list of measurements, including the metal analysis, a paragraph of more detailed description, and finally a separate section of discussion, which includes our comments on parallels, both within and outside the Thetford Treasure, dating evidence, stylistic judgements, and any other material which seems interesting or relevant.

Measurements are given in centimetres and weights in grams. It will be noticed that the number and type of linear measurements listed vary, except in the case of the spoons, where they are standardised. This is because we have selected the measurements which seemed most useful and relevant in each case, and with varying types of object, these inevitably differ. Some rings are round, so a single diameter can be quoted, while others are not, so two measurements must be given. The size of rings depends on their *internal* dimensions, and it is therefore these which we quote. Many of the items of jewellery include gemstones or other settings, and sulphur used as adhesive or packing. It is not possible to separate these from the gold, and the weights include them. It should also be noted that the original total weight of objects which have lost settings cannot now be estimated.

The metal analyses were carried out by the x-ray fluorescence technique, which is fully described in Chapter 9. Where quantitative analyses have been performed, it is these figures which are listed in the catalogue entry, prefixed by (QU); the majority are semi-quantitative analyses (SQ). The full list of analyses, which includes both semi-quantitative and quantitative analyses of certain objects, will be found in Table 5.

The description of the appearance of each object is as full as seems necessary, bearing in mind that we have tried to show every important angle and detail in the enlarged drawings. The illustrations are of paramount importance, and the verbal descriptions cannot be more than a supplement to them.

It will be obvious that many types of information found elsewhere in the book are repeated in the catalogue entries. We have assumed that different users of the book will have different interests and priorities, and will therefore approach the text in different ways, so we have tried to make the various sections of the book, above all the catalogue, reasonably complete in themselves. Bibliographical references in the catalogue entries occur in the text, but in the general chapters, which are designed to be read as longer passages of prose, they are consigned to the footnotes. However, to avoid too much tedious repetition, some information in the discussion sections

of the catalogue entries is given by reference to other entries or chapters: in particular, the discussions of the spoons, which involve many very broad typological parallels, the same for each spoon, refer back to Chapter 5 and to the entries for the most important spoon of each type (**50** and **66**). Catalogue entries also refer back to the main chapters of the book in the cases of the gemstones and the inscriptions; the latter especially involve a highly specialised branch of study, and we felt it would make the catalogue entries unnecessarily complex if we repeated these discussions in them.

There are two final points to make. Firstly, the preparation of any catalogue of objects must entail a great deal of handling and physical examination of the items. Since the pristine condition of the Thetford gold and silver is such an important factor in the interpretation of the treasure, we have taken the utmost care to reduce the necessary handling to a minimum, and this approach will continue to be adopted towards the Thetford material.

Secondly, a word must be said about the numbering system. The catalogue numbers are the same as those which were assigned to the objects when they were listed on their first day in the Museum. For record purposes, this numbering had to be carried out before any detailed study could take place, and consequently there are one or two small anomalies. For example, the necklace and clasp, **35** and **36**, undoubtedly belong together, but as we were not perfectly certain of this at first, two numbers were given. One of the glass beads, **49/46**, was broken when acquired, and was also treated as two objects. Those bipartite objects which clearly belong together, the buckle and the shale box **1** and **83** were given single numbers from the beginning. On more mature consideration, there are certain groupings of objects which could have been better arranged, e.g. the rings **10** and **12** and some groups of spoons, but we have considered it wiser to retain the original numbers and avoid the potential confusion which tends to arise from changes and from numerical concordances. For the same reason, the full British Museum registration numbers of the objects match the catalogue: they consist of the catalogue number prefixed by P.1981.2–1. To quote an example, the gilded Triton spoon has the Museum number P.1981.2–1.50.

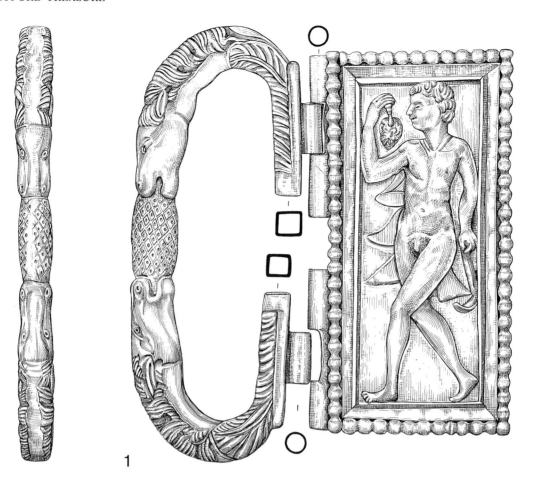

1

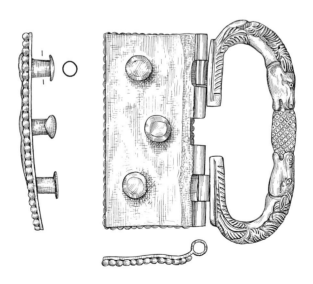

Fig. 6

1 Gold buckle

Buckle in two parts, a loop or bow with confronted horses' heads, and a rectangular plate decorated with a satyr in relief. *Measurements:* Loop: L 5.9 cm, w 2.4 cm; Plate: L 5.2 cm, w 2.8 cm; wT (together) 39.9 g. Metal (QU): gold 87.1%, silver 10.3%, copper 2.6%

Description: The loop or bow is cast in the form of two confronted horses' heads modelled in the round. Between them is an oval element, decorated with incised lattice and dot decoration. At the base of the loop are leaves from which the horses' heads emerge. Tubular sections of a hinge fit this loop to the rectangular plate, which is bordered by a bevelled frame and an edging of boldly beaded wire. In the centre is an applied relief depicting a young satyr dancing to the left, holding a small pedum in his left hand and a bunch of grapes in his right, which is raised. Folds of drapery, schematically rendered as triangles, billow behind him, but have no visible means of attachment to his body. On the reverse side of the plate are three studs with flat heads; they project about 5 mm, and would have served to attach the buckle to a belt. The separate hinge-pin and the tongue of the buckle are missing, but the presence of the latter is indicated by the very slight wear on the oval object between the horses' muzzles; the nature of this wear also establishes that the tongue was a single-pronged, not a double-pronged one. There are no traces of wear on the buckle which could result from actual use.

Discussion: There is no really close parallel for the Thetford buckle, but it belongs ultimately to a well-known category of late-Roman belt-fittings which has been much discussed and analysed. General studies of zoomorphic late-Roman belt-buckles and the other fittings associated with them, such as strap-ends, stiffeners and suspension-loops, include Heurgon 1958, 31–45, Hawkes and Dunning 1961, Bullinger 1969, and Clarke 1979, 264–91. The view put forward by Hawkes and Dunning was that belt-fittings of this type could be linked with the presence in the late-Roman army of German *foederati;* this opinion is no longer considered to be tenable, and indeed, the Thetford buckle and its closest parallels in gold, with their markedly classical style, must constitute part of the evidence against Germanic influence. In Britain and Gaul, bronze buckles with zoomorphic bows and decorated rectangular or oval plates occur fairly frequently in late-Roman contexts, but gold examples are extremely rare.

The best parallel in gold is an unprovenanced piece now in Berlin (Greifenhagen 1975, Abb. 34, 13). Its bow is formed of confronted ducks' heads arising from a leafy base, and the plate has, within a bevelled and beaded frame, relief floral ornament surrounding a beaded lozenge, which in turn encloses a medallion with an applied head of Alexander the Great. The overall form of the piece is very close to the Thetford buckle, with the one exception that the tongue is a double-pronged one.

Slightly less close, but important because of the many other parallels between the two hoards, is the larger of the two gold buckles from the treasure of Ténès (Algeria) (Heurgon 1958, pl. III, 1). This buckle is considerably larger and more massive than ours, but of the same basic form. The animal heads are again ducks, not horses, their eyes infilled with garnets, and holding cakes in their beaks, but they are turned away from each other, making the form of the loop more complex. The tongue is a double one, and the rectangular plate has a pierced floral scroll. Another gold buckle which should be mentioned is one with a plain bow, now in the cabinet des Médailles in Paris, and also illustrated in the Ténès volume (Heurgon 1958, pl. XVIII, 5 and 6). The buckle has relief ornament on the plate, and it has a name-stamp on the reverse, reading VICTORINVS.M, referring to the maker. It is discussed in Heurgon 1958, 39.

Most of the many zoomorphic late-Roman buckles in bronze are further removed stylistically and typologically from the Thetford piece than are the gold examples cited. The animals on the loop are generally very stylised, crested dolphins, which may be compared with the animals on rings **5** and **6** in the Thetford hoard, but one incomplete specimen from Richborough (Bushe-Fox 1949, pl. XXXII, 69) has horses which, although they are more crudely modelled, are very reminiscent of the Thetford beasts. This example from Richborough is omitted from the Hawkes and Dunning list, although several other buckles from the site which fit more closely into their typology are described.

The other bronze buckle which is particularly relevant is a gilded one (providing an even closer link with gold buckles) in the British Museum collections, Dalton 1901, no. 258. This is from a group of objects said to be from Palestine; in fact, the details given in the Museum register are so vague and ambiguous that it would be wiser to regard the object as unprovenanced. The bow of this buckle is broken, and it may therefore not even have been a zoomorphic one, but the general form of the loop and plate match Thetford, and the decoration of the plate, with a Bacchic motif (Bacchus himself, with a panther and thyrsos) in relief, and a crudely beaded border, is very reminiscent of the Thetford buckle.

The quality of craftsmanship and artistry of the Thetford buckle is high: the modelling of the horse-heads is detailed and delicate, though very clearly in a Roman tradition (cf. a bronze horse-head key-handle from Nijmegen, Jitta *et al.* 1973, no. 163), and the satyr is close to those on the Mildenhall silver (Painter 1977a, pl. 1–8). This satyr is part of a Bacchic theme which links the buckle with certain other items among the jewellery. Together with the other gold buckles discussed, the Thetford buckle represents one stylistic extreme for this class of object, at the opposite end of the scale from the 'Germanic' bronze buckles from sites such as Vermand (Eck 1891) and Lankhills (Clarke 1979).

Some interesting points are raised by the absence of other belt-fittings and by the composition of the buckle. The marked difference between the results of the original semi-quantitative analysis of the gold and the full quantitative analysis could be explained by the buckle having been subjected to a different burial environment from the other pieces of jewellery (see Table 5). If the buckle had already been mounted on leather, which would, of course, have decayed, and would not have been detected during the process of excavation by people untrained in recognising different colours and textures of soil, this could be the explanation of the effect on the surface of

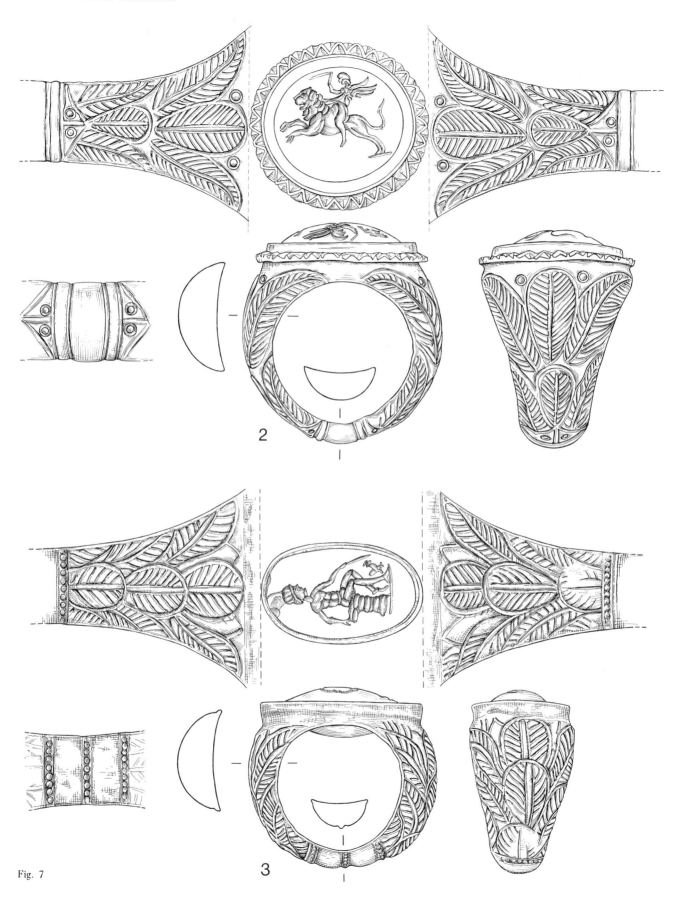

Fig. 7

80

the metal. The fact that the tongue and hinge-pin were not found is probably simply due to lack of care in excavation. It should be noted that the final analysis of the metal shows a composition similar to that of the necklaces **32** and **33** and the ring **23**, but unlike that of the other gold jewellery.

The above theory would suggest that the buckle was already attached to a leather belt before burial, and was perhaps enclosed in the middle of it. Against this is the fact that there are no other belt-fittings. It seems most unlikely that a buckle of this quality would have been the only metal fitting: had the belt been complete, even if unused, one would have expected at the very least a gold strap-end, if not additional plaques and stiffeners. Their absence implies that the buckle was a separate item, not yet placed in position on a belt, and this fits better with the supposition that the whole group of jewellery was as yet unsold. While a gold pin and even the buckle-tongue, could have been missed in excavation, it seems unlikely that a strap-end, which would have been as large as a buckle-plate, could have escaped notice.

These two conflicting theories are incapable of proof: the problem could only have been solved by trained observation at the time the material was unearthed.

2 Gold ring with engraved amethyst

Large gold ring with chased decoration on the hoop, set with an amethyst engraved with Cupid riding on a lion.
Measurements: Internal D 2.0 cm; bezel 2.4 × 2.2 cm; L of gem 1.8 cm; WT 15.5 g. Metal (QU): gold 95%, silver 3.4%, copper 1.1%

Description: The hoop is hollow, with a D-shaped cross-section; it expands evenly towards the shoulders. The large oval setting is surrounded by a border with dog-tooth ornament. The hoop is decorated with chased ornament in the form of pointed, heavily-veined leaves and small circles made with a ring-ended punch. The gem is a somewhat pale mauve amethyst with a convex surface, engraved with a leaping lion ridden by a Cupid who brandishes a whip. Traces of the sulphur backing can be seen through the translucent stone.

There is no evidence of wear on the ring.

Discussion: The gem, which is Severan in date, is discussed in Chapter 3. There is no close parallel for the leaf pattern on this ring, except on the other rings in the Thetford hoard, **3** and **4**, which are clearly by the same hand. Chased decoration on the hoop is not necessarily a late feature (cf. Marshall 1907, nos. 464 and 465), but it does accord with the tendency in the late-antique period to prefer textured metal surfaces to plain ones.

Marshall 1907, no. 505, from Egypt, is a related type, though the hoop is solid and the distinctive form of the gem suggests an earlier date than our ring. There is perhaps some comparison, too, with Henkel 1913, no. 204, which has chasing and granulation. There is no dating evidence for it, and Henkel's suggested second-century date may well be too early. There are four rings on display in the Musée des Beaux-Arts in Lyon which have fairly elaborate chased decoration on the

shoulders and are set with engraved gems; they are not dated or provenanced, but are perhaps most closely related to a ring from Sault-du-Rhone (Charvet 1863, no. 4), which is probably of third-century date.

The large bezel with its elaborate border is one of the features which sets this ring apart from these earlier types with decorated hoops: it is reminiscent of the bezel of a ring from the Vermand cemetery (Eck 1891, pl.xx, 4a and p.242), found in a grave with a coin of Valentinian I (AD 364–75). Another late ring which may be compared with ours because of the style of the decoration is one from Torriano (Peroni 1967, no. 75, pl. xvii): this has a raised bezel and the hoop is deeply chased or engraved with a vine-scroll and birds. The style is bolder than that of the Thetford pieces. There are two other rings known which are very like this one, Battke 1953, no. 45, set with an engraved emerald, and said to be from a Roman collection, and Dalton 1901, no. 44. All of these have been regarded as sixth-century in date.

The internal relationships of ring **2** in the assemblage are clearly primarily with **3** and **4**, which are decorated with incised leaves of precisely the same design. There are also links with other pieces based on the use of the small ring-ended punch. This was used on **2**, **4**, **9**, **28** and **29**. Its use is discussed in Chapter 9, Part 3 and Chapter 2.

Rings **3**, **4** and **5**, like the zoomorphic rings **5**, **6** and **7**, and also **9**, are in styles which cannot be properly paralleled elsewhere. They are typical of the work of the 'Thetford jeweller'.

3 Gold ring with engraved amethyst

Gold ring with chased decoration on the hoop, set with an amethyst engraved with a seated figure of Mercury.
Measurements: Internal D 1.8 cm; bezel (oval) 2.2 × 1.4 cm; WT 8.8 g. Metal (SQ): gold 96%, silver 3%, copper 1.1%

Description: The ring is closely similar in form and general style to **2**, with a hollow hoop decorated with deeply chased leaves. The gem, like that of **2**, is an amethyst, and is an elongated oval, engraved with Mercury seated on a rock and accompanied by a cockerel. The setting is completely plain. There is no wear on the ring.

Discussion: The gem is Severan; see Chapter 3. For parallels, none very close outside the Thetford hoard, see the discussion of ring **2**, to which this one is so closely related as to be identifiable beyond any reasonable doubt as the work of the same craftsman.

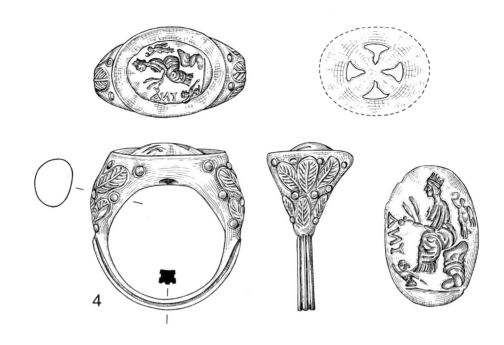

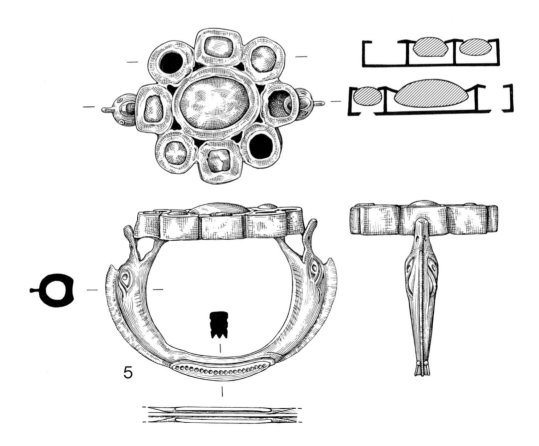

Fig. 8

4 Gold ring with engraved chalcedony

Gold ring with chased decoration on the hoop and a chalcedony gem engraved with a figure of the Tyche of Antioch.

Measurements: Internal D 1.6 cm; w of hoop 0.25 cm; gem (oval) 1.2 × 0.8 cm; WT 6.0 g. Metal (SQ): gold 94%, silver 5%, copper 0.7%

Description: The back of the hoop is solid, but the shoulders are hollow and are ornamented with chased leaves precisely like those on rings 2 and 3, though on a smaller scale. The back of the hoop is fluted. There is a plain oval bezel containing a small black chalcedony with a convex surface. At the back of the gem, the gold has been cut out in a quatrefoil pattern, making it possible to observe that the stone is yellow by transmitted light.

The engraving depicts the Tyche of Antioch seated on a rock and wearing a mural crown. She holds two ears of corn and a fruit. Behind her is a small winged Victory holding aloft a wreath, and at her feet is the small swimming figure which represents the river Orontes. In front of the Tyche are three neatly engraved Greek letters, ΔΝΓ (ΓΝΔ in an impression). There is no wear on the ring.

Discussion: The gem is the earliest and most competently engraved of the Thetford gems, dating to the first century. It is fully described and discussed in Chapter 3. The type of the seated Tyche is a well-known one, based on a famous statue of antiquity. It may be relevant to note the occurrence of the motif in late-Roman times, e.g. the Tyche of Antioch in a set of four silver-gilt city personifications in the Esquiline Treasure (Shelton 1981, no. 33).

The chased decoration on the shoulders is matched in 2 and 3, though the whole appearance of this ring, partly because of its smaller size and slenderer proportions, is far less flamboyant. This is one of the pieces on which a ring-ended punch was used (cf. 2, 9, 28, 29); this link is discussed in Chapter 2 and Chapter 9, Part 3.

5 Gold ring with zoomorphic ornament

Gold ring with shoulders in the form of dolphins, and a large flat bezel with settings for nine stones.

Measurements: Internal dimensions 2.0 × 1.6 cm; bezel 2.2 × 2.0 cm; WT 11.3 g. Metal (SQ): gold 93%, silver 6.1%, copper 0.9%

Description: The centre back of the hoop is solid and fluted, with a row of small incised dots on each side. The hoop expands to hollow shoulders, apparently containing some sulphur, which are modelled in the form of stylised dolphins with high crests, like boars, and elongated, beak-like jaws. Details of crests, eyes and fins are chased. The bodies of the animals coalesce in the rear of the hoop before the tail flukes are reached. The jaws of the dolphins grasp a large flat bezel embellished with an oval central box-setting containing a plain convex-surfaced amethyst, surrounded by eight cells which are alternately circular and sub-rectangular. The former con-

tain pointed conical garnets, of which two survive, and the latter emeralds, three of which are preserved. There is sulphur backing in the cells.

There is no detectable wear on the ring.

Discussion: Both the zoomorphic shoulders and the multiple gem setting on the large bezel are highly unusual features: the general appearance of the ring is far removed from that of the majority of rings of the Roman Imperial period. The use of multi-coloured settings is part of the more flamboyant taste of late-antique and barbaric art, and is paralleled within the Thetford assemblage itself in ring 8. Ward 1981, no. 97, an allegedly fourth to fifth-century ring from Syria, has a flat bezel with five cells with garnets, and is clearly a related type.

The zoomorphic shoulders, though rare, have a long history, cf. a sixth-century BC Etruscan ring (Ward 1981, no. 39) with lion shoulders. Within the Thetford group, the dolphins are precisely paralleled on ring 6, and the concept is slightly more generally echoed with the birds on ring 7.

Marshall 1907, no. 533 has lions on the shoulders: this is dated on stylistic grounds to the third century AD, which may well be correct. Another interesting parallel is a ring in the Walters Art Gallery, Baltimore (Catalogue 1979, no. 425 and Weitzmann 1979, no.78), which has a solid hoop supporting a pair of niello-spotted leopards which hold the bezel; the setting is a nicolo engraved with a winged Victory. The date now given for this ring, which is unprovenanced, is fourth-century: an earlier publication of the Walters Art Gallery dated it too late (fifth-sixth century), and while the present dating may well be correct, it is worth noting that the broad and very sharply angled form of the ring is directly derived from a very common third-century form. Ward 1981, no. 101 (= Dalton 1901, no. 210) is a ring from the Seine at Rouen, set with a gold coin of Marcian (AD 450–7) in a raised, pierced bezel, and a small purple garnet at the back of the hoop. The hollow shoulders are in the form of crouching hares or rabbits. This ring not only demonstrates a fifth-century use of the conceit of zoomorphic shoulders, but may hint at a Gaulish origin for the type.

These examples, especially this last, confirm the occasional use of zoomorphic ornament for ring shoulders in the later Roman period. The dolphins of our ring also deserve closer observation in their own right: they are so stylised as to be totally inaccurate representations of the animals intended, and their features correspond very closely indeed with the creatures to be found on many of the late-Roman bronze buckles, such as Eck 1891, pl. xv, 7 & 15 and pl. xvi, 11, from Vermand, or Clarke 1979, fig. 68, 92 from Lankhills. These dolphins have the same long beaks and boar-like crests as those on our ring, and this link provides additional confirmation of the late fourth-century date of the material. While this catalogue was in proof our attention was drawn to a dolphin-shouldered bronze ring from the latest Roman levels at the Marlowe Theatre site, Canterbury.

6 Gold ring with zoomorphic ornament

Gold ring with shoulders in the form of dolphins, set with an amethyst.

Measurements: Internal dimensions 1.6 × 1.4 cm; bezel (oval) 1.3 × 1.0 cm; gem 0.8 × 0.6 cm; WT 6.8 g. Metal (SQ): gold 94%, silver 5%, copper 1%

Description: The hoop is slender and square-sectioned, developing into shoulders in the form of stylised, crested dolphins like those on ring **5**. On each side of the hoop is a line of fine dots. The bezel is a plain box-setting containing a pale-coloured amethyst with a flat, undecorated surface and bevelled sides.

The ring shows no wear.

Discussion: For a discussion of the relationships of the dolphin shoulders, see ring **5**. Though smaller and simpler than **5**, this ring is extremely closely related to it, and must represent the work of the same craftsman.

The amethyst is of the same pale shade of mauve as the others in the group, i.e. in rings **2**, **3** and **5**.

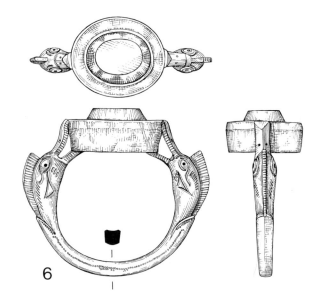

7 Gold ring with zoomorphic ornament

Gold ring with a raised bezel in the form of a vase, flanked by birds and containing a glass setting.

Measurements: Internal dimensions 1.8 × 1.4 cm; bezel: H 1.0 cm; w 1.3 cm; WT 8.4 g. Metal (SQ): gold 97%, silver 3.3%, copper 0.1%

Description: The hoop of the ring is narrow and rectangular in section. The shoulders are modelled as small birds with large heads and short tails, their plumage indicated by fine stippling, and their eyes by small punched circles. Between them rises the bezel in the form of a squat vase with reeded sides, a foot-ring, and a flat rim with a beaded border. This contains a square cushion-shaped setting in blue-green glass. The sulphur backing is visible, as the stone does not fit the circular opening of the bezel.

There is no trace of wear on the ring.

Discussion: The fine and detailed workmanship of the birds contrasts strangely with the use of a stone which is unsuitable both in size and shape for the setting in which it is placed. The square, blue-green glass gem is very similar to those in bracelet **27** and to that in the ring **17**, if the latter is correctly placed (see discussion of **17**). These glass gems must be from the same original source, whether their use in the Thetford jewellery is primary or secondary. Another internal link for this ring may be in the use of the ring-ended punch for the eyes of the birds. The same or a similar tool was used on several of the other rings.

The zoomorphic shoulders provide a link with the dolphin-shouldered rings **5** and **6**, and the parallels quoted in the discussion of **5** apply equally to this ring. In general, the motif of a cantharus or other vase flanked by birds is one which is widespread in Classical and early Christian iconography, though it has not been possible to parallel its use in this

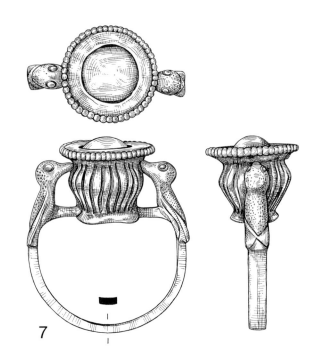

Fig. 9

fashion on a ring. Two late rings illustrated in Ward 1981 may demonstrate the idea persisting into periods after that of the Thetford Treasure; no. 91, identified as a seventh-century Merovingian piece, which has a high bezel in the form of a stylised but recognisable handled vase, and no. 105, a crude ring given the very broad dating sixth to tenth century AD, which has a confronted pair of birds in the round as its only decoration.

The precise appearance of the birds on our ring is of special interest: it may be unwise to attempt an identification of the species when the creature is modelled at such a tiny scale, little more than a centimetre in length, but the large heads and long beaks, with the diminutive bodies and short tails, do remind irresistibly of the proportions of a woodpecker. If the birds on Thetford ring **7** are woodpeckers, the implications are of importance to the interpretation of the treasure as a whole.

Birds were extremely important in Celtic religion and iconography, but there seems to have been no special significance attached to the woodpecker. In the Classical tradition, however, it was a different matter: the Latin for 'woodpecker' is *picus*, and this is also the name, in some sources, of the mythical king who was father of Faunus (Virgil, *Aeneid* 7, 48). The bird was also connected with Mars. It therefore seems that the choice of this species of bird is a subtle reference to the cult more explicitly indicated by the inscriptions on the silver spoons in the treasure. If so, it provides one link between the jewellery and the silver utensils.

One final point is that this ring is perhaps the least suitably designed for actual use of all the rings in the hoard: though the high projection of the bezel is a common enough feature of late-antique rings, inconvenient though it is in use, the broad D-shape of the hoop formed by the straight bar on which the bezel rests is particularly ill-adapted to fitting comfortably on the finger.

8 Gold ring with gems

Gold ring with settings for small gems all round the hoop and on the large flat bezel.

Measurements: Internal dimensions 1.9 × 1.3 cm; bezel 2.3 × 2.2 cm; centre gem in bezel 1.0 × 0.9 cm; WT 8.6 g. Metal (SQ): gold 96%, silver 3.4%, copper 0.8%

Description: The hoop is formed of nine small circular box-settings, with two additional, slightly smaller ones at each shoulder. The bezel has an almost square centre setting surrounded by eight small circular ones. There are traces of sulphur in some of the cells, but only two gems survive, both in the hoop; they are garnets of pointed form.

There is no wear on the ring.

Discussion: The multiple gem setting of the bezel is closely comparable with that of ring **5**, and it seems probable that it originally contained stones of different colours, perhaps the same combination of amethyst, garnet and emerald (mauve, dark red and bright green). The use of gem settings all round the hoop is a highly unusual feature: within the Thetford Treasure, the bracelet, **27**, is obviously related, but there is no other ring which is comparable. Two rings catalogued in Marshall 1907 have settings all round the hoop, though neither has a bezel at all. No. 856, an unprovenanced piece, has clearly separated cells, all containing conical garnets, while 858, said to be from Athens, has settings of irregular size and shape containing garnets, sapphires and green stones described as plasma, but far more likely to be emerald. This ring is also described and illustrated in Ward 1981, no. 66.

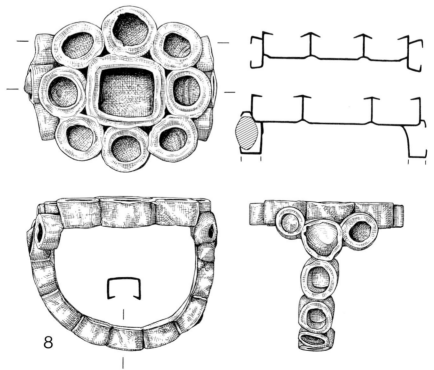

Fig. 10

8

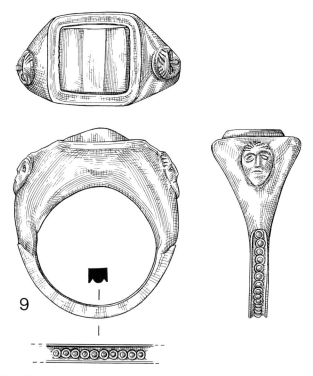

9

Fig. 11

9 Gold ring with human faces

Gold ring with human faces in relief on the shoulders, set with an emerald.

Measurements: Internal diameter 1.7 cm; w of hoop 0.25 cm; L of masks 0.7 cm; bezel 1.2 cm square; stone 0.9 cm square; WT 9.2 g. Metal (SQ): gold 97%, silver 2.7%, copper <0.1%

Description: The hoop is narrow and square-sectioned, expanding to heavy, smooth-surfaced shoulders, each ornamented with a small human face in relief. The faces have elliptical eyes, straight slit mouths and swept-back hair. The back of the hoop has neat beading, produced by the use of a small ring-ended punch. The plain square bezel contains an emerald which retains one of its natural rounded angles.

The ring is unworn.

Discussion: In both form and decoration, the ring appears to be completely unique. The form is superficially similar to that of many much earlier (Hellenistic and early Roman) rings, but the decoration of the hoop, though carried out in an unusual technique, seems stylistically entirely in the spirit of the fourth century. The shoulder decoration is the truly extraordinary feature: the zoomorphic shoulders of rings **5, 6** and **7** are very rare, but the human faces on **9** appear to be completely unparalleled. The face in the bezel of ring **23**, though equally extraordinary, is Roman in concept, but the faces on ring **9** display all the characteristics commonly attributed to 'Celtic' representations of the Roman and pre-Roman Iron Age, even to the brushed-back hair.

The pristine condition of the ring, the resemblance of the metal analysis to that of some of the other rings (**2, 3** and **4**), and the use of the same punch as that employed in the decoration of **2, 4, 7 28** and **29**, places the piece firmly within the 'Thetford workshop' (see Chapter 9, Part 3). That this was in a Celtic area of the Roman Empire seems in any case to be beyond reasonable doubt, but this hardly seems to account for the style of the masks at this late date. This ring must be regarded as one of the most interesting and puzzling pieces in the whole hoard.

10 Gold ring with filigree

Gold ring with filigree, 'basket' pattern, and clasped hands on bezel.

Measurements: Internal dimensions 1.8 × 1.5 cm; w of hoop 0.6 cm; bezel (oval) 1.4 × 1.7 cm; WT 6.6 g. Metal (SQ): gold 95%, silver 4%, copper 1.4%

Description: The hoop is a thin band of gold sheet, undulating and impressed to resemble basket-work. It is bordered on each side with beaded wire. The shoulders have neat, elaborate spirals in gold wire on a thin backing sheet. Surrounding the oval bezel is a roped flange, and within the setting is a gold plaque decorated in repoussé with a pair of clasped right hands (*dextrarum iunctio*) within a beaded border.

The ring shows no wear.

Discussion: The motif of clasped hands is common in Roman jewellery as a symbol of friendship or betrothal. Examples on late rings which are particularly close to ours are a ring from Richborough (Bushe-Fox 1949, pl. xxv, no. 93, p. 126) and one from Grovely Wood, Wiltshire, (Kent & Painter 1977, no. 140), which was found with a coin hoard deposited *c.* AD 395. The Richborough ring has beaded wire volutes, globules, and a roped border round the bezel, making it a very close parallel to the Thetford ring. The Grovely Wood ring is silver with a gold setting, and is simpler in form, possibly suggesting an earlier date of manufacture.

The applied wire forming filigree volutes on the shoulders is widely paralleled on late-Roman rings from many areas of the Empire. From Britain there is the Richborough ring mentioned above, and a ring from Havering, Essex (Henig 1978, 362 and Marshall 1907, no. 571); perhaps slightly less close, but still of the same general type, are two rings from Terling, Essex (Anon. 1841, 163), which are dated by the associated coin hoard to the early fifth century. The rings from New Grange, County Meath, Ireland, are also of this type (Kent and Painter 1977, nos 231 and 232).

From other parts of the Empire, one may compare Marshall 1907, no. 868, said to be from Rome, and an example from a late-Roman grave in Hungary (Vágó and Bóna 1976, Grave 19a, Taf. xxvi, 4a and 4b). The type also occurs at Trier (Henkel 1913, no. 284 and 285, and *Trierer Zeitschr.* 9. 1934, Abb. 26, p. 159).

Parallels for the 'basket' pattern naturally lead back to the bracelets, **24** and **25** in the Thetford Treasure itself, and thence to the Lyon bracelets which we have cited under those entries. There is, however, one parallel known to us for the use of this decoration on a ring: Catalogue 1911, no. 2105 is a double ring, said to be from Amrit in Syria. No dating

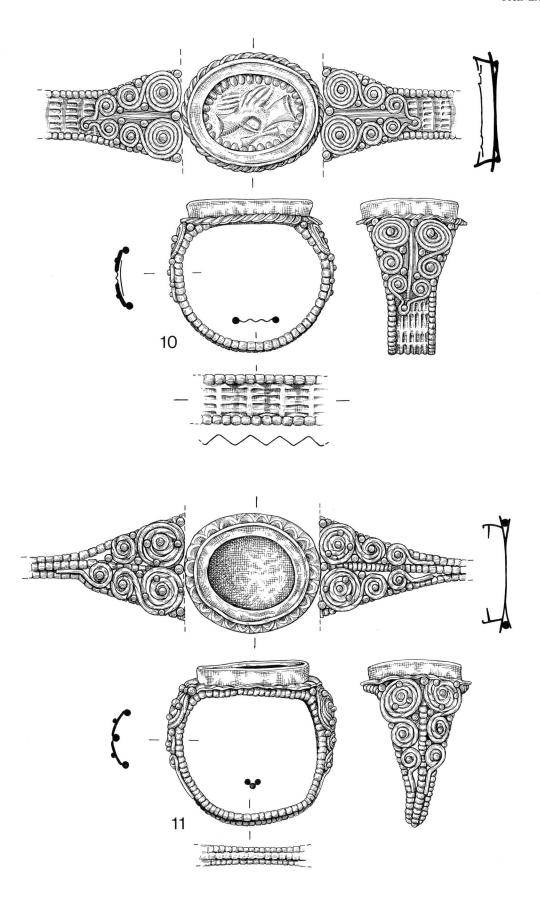

Fig. 12

evidence is quoted, but the square central bezel surrounded by a roped border and the small globules at its corners suggest a later date stylistically, perhaps in the fourth century. It is perhaps also worth citing a small ring in the British Museum collections, said to be from London (Marshall 1907, no. 821), the hoop of which is a thin ribbon of gold slightly ribbed lengthways, which is equivalent to the first stage of making the basket pattern strip. There is an extremely close parallel to this ring in Catalogue 1912, no. 362.

Ring 10 in the Thetford group is an important link in the hoard: the 'basket' pattern establishes the relationship with another ring, 12, and with the pair of bracelets, while the elaborate filigree provides a close comparison with several of the other rings, and most importantly, through dated external parallels, is stylistic confirmation of the late fourth-century date.

11   Filigree gold ring

Gold ring with decorated hoop and an empty oval box-setting.
Measurements: Internal D 1.8 cm; bezel (oval) 1.3 × 1.5 cm; WT 6.5 g. Metal (SQ): gold 94%, silver 5.2%, copper 1.3%

Description: The hoop and shoulders are formed of beaded and twisted wires used on their own, without a backing plate. The shoulders have spirals in twisted wire, with the addition of small gold globules. The oval box-setting is surrounded by a flange which is decorated in dog-tooth ornament, and the cell itself is empty. The bevelled collar which should hold the stone in position is present.

There are slight traces of wear on the hoop and the bezel.

Discussion: Several of the parallels quoted for ring 10 apply equally here. The presence or absence of a backing plate for the filigree is probably of little significance.

12   Gold filigree ring

Gold ring with filigree, 'basket' pattern and empty box setting.
Measurements: Internal dimensions 1.9 × 1.6 cm; w of hoop 0.5 cm; bezel (oval) 1.3 × 1.2 cm; WT 4.9 g. Metal (QU): gold 96%, silver 3.7%, copper 0.3%

Description: Though differing a little in size, proportion and weight, this is essentially a pair to ring 10, with its 'basket' pattern hoop, filigree spirals and a roped flange round the oval bezel. The setting, like that of 11, is empty of any decorative element, but it contains a loose plain oval piece of gold sheet, the function of which is not clear. There may be some slight wear on the hoop.

Discussion: For parallels, see the discussion of 10. The presence of the loose slip of gold in the setting is difficult to explain. While there is no evidence for the type of setting which the ring contained, we may perhaps speculate that it was a gold plate rather than a stone. There is no sulphur in the setting.

13   Gold ring with engraved gem

Gold ring, set with a gem engraved with a figure of Abrasax.
Measurements: Internal dimensions 2.0 × 1.5 cm; setting (oval) 1.5 × 1.8 cm; w of hoop 0.6 cm; WT 8.7 g. Metal (SQ): gold 94%, silver 5%, copper 1.3%

Description: The hoop is flat with three finely beaded or milled wires and two twisted, roped ones. There are three gold globules at the shoulders (two are lost on one side) and a raised oval box-setting surrounded by a roped flange. Held loosely within the setting by a gold strip forming a bevelled rim is a worn engraved gem, a brownish chalcedony (jasper). The design is of a cock-headed, snake-legged deity wearing a short tunic and carrying a scourge and a shield on which are the Greek letters IAΩ. On removal from the setting, the back of the gem, which is relatively unworn, was found to be engraved with the names ΑΒΡΑΣΑΣCΑΒΑΩΘ in Greek.

There is no wear on the gold.

Discussion: The gem, of second- to third-century date, is discussed fully in Chapter 3. The form of the ring may be compared with that of 15, though the spiral terminals of the bordering wires are omitted. The parallels cited under 15 are relevant.

14   Gold ring with triple setting

Gold ring with filigree decoration and triple green glass setting.
Measurements: Internal D 1.8 cm; w of hoop (back) 0.25 cm; w at bezel 2.0 cm; box-settings 0.6 cm D and 0.6 cm square; WT 6.4 g. Metal (SQ): gold 94%, silver 4.2%, copper 1.9%

Description: The hoop is flat, narrow at the back and expanding to a broad area on which the three box-settings are placed. Three twisted or roped wires are applied to the hoop, and develop into spirals at the shoulders, five on each side. There are numerous small gold globules attached on and around the spirals. The three box-settings in line on the bezel all contain green glass; the centre cell is square and the gem flat, and the flanking cells circular, with pointed, conical stones.

No wear of the metal is evident. One of the glass settings is damaged.

Discussion: The ring is the only example of its type in the hoard, and its baroque appearance seems typically late-antique. No close parallels have been found, but two rings illustrated in Henkel have some features in common with it. Henkel 1913 no. 267, from Wiesbaden, has two conical garnets and two small sapphires on the shoulders, while no. 268, from Nancy, has a similar double setting from which the stones have been lost.

Both of these rings are decorated on the expanded area of the shoulders with patterns composed of small globules — a coarse form of granulation, in fact. Though the design on our ring depends on the wire to produce the pattern, there is a particularly lavish use of the small gold beads compared with most of the other Thetford rings on which they occur. Henkel dates his nos 267 and 268 to the fourth century.

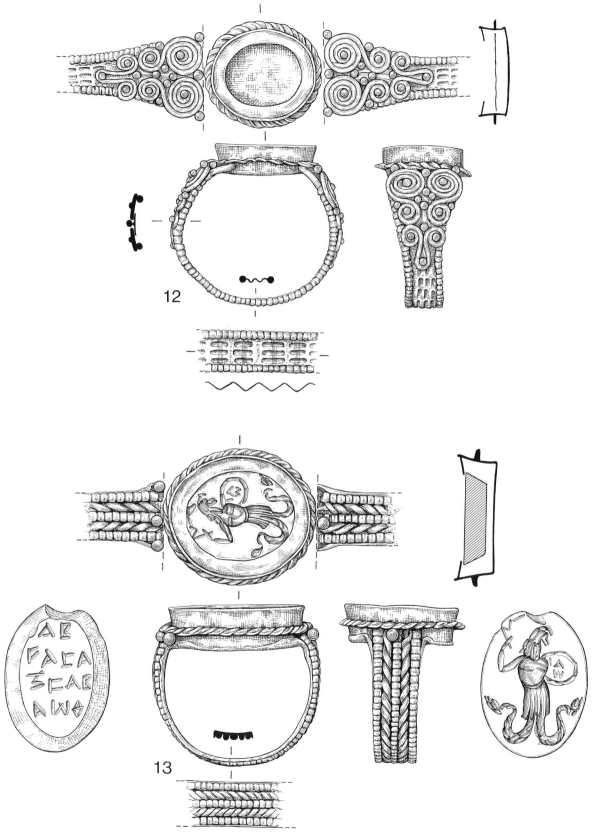

12

13

Fig. 13

Fig. 14

Ward 1981, no. 65 is a parallel for the use of three small gems in line. It is unprovenanced, and looks later than the suggested third-century date.

15   Gold ring with rectangular bezel

Gold ring with decorated hoop and a rectangular setting containing green glass.
Measurements: Internal dimensions 1.8 × 1.6 cm; w of hoop 0.5 cm; bezel 1.3 × 1.2 cm; WT 7.4 g. Metal (QU): gold 92.5%, silver 5.2%, copper 2.3%

Description: The hoop is flat and of constant width. Applied to it are two twisted, roped wires, producing a plaited effect, bordered on each side by finely milled wires which turn outwards at the shoulders to form spirals, each with a central gold globule. There are three further globules in a row at the junction of hoop and bezel. The almost square box setting has high, thin sides, and a surrounding roped flange. It contains a flat darkish green glass gem, now cracked across.

The ring displays extensive wear which is undoubtedly the result of use; the milled wire at the sides of the hoop is worn almost completely smooth in places.

Discussion: There is a fairly close parallel for this ring in the Canterbury hoard (Painter 1965, no. 15). This has a rectangular bezel somewhat lower than ours, also set with green glass, and a hoop ornamented with a finer and more elaborate plaited pattern in applied wire. Perhaps even closer to the Thetford ring in its bolder treatment of the hoop, and the extension of the milled borders into spirals, is a silver ring, now very damaged, from the Whorlton, (Yorks) coin hoard, found in 1810 (Burnett & Johns 1979, p. 114, no. 9). The Whorlton ring was set with an oval dark blue glass. An unprovenanced parallel, possibly from Italy, is Marshall 1907, no. 515, but in this, the plaited and milled wire is used alone, not applied to a plain gold band.

The date of deposition of the Canterbury hoard is accepted as being shortly after AD 400, while the coins in the Whorlton hoard give a date-range for burial of AD 410–25.

The noticeably worn condition of this ring is in marked contrast to the other twenty-one, which range from pristine condition to very faint traces of use.

16   Gold ring with engraved gem

Large plain gold ring, set with an onyx engraved with a figure of Mars.
Measurements: Internal dimensions 2.5 × 2.0 cm; w of hoop 0.45 cm; bezel (oval) 2.1 × 1.8 cm; WT 19.7 g. Metal (SQ): gold 98%, silver 1.8%, copper <0.1%

Description: The hoop is plain, flat and of equal width throughout. The oval bezel has slightly flared sides in profile, and contains a flat, bevelled blue-grey onyx (chalcedony), engraved with a standing Mars with spear and shield. Six small gold globules are attached on each side where the hoop meets the bezel.

There is no visible wear on the metal.

Discussion: For comments on the gem, which is of second- to third-century date, see Chapter 3. The form of the ring is very close indeed to Henkel 1913, no. 272, from Mainz: Henkel dates this to the fourth century. Another parallel is Henig 1978, no. 581, from Tuddenham, Suffolk. This was associated with a hoard of *siliquae* with a date-range from Constantius II to Honorius, and therefore confirms the type as current in the later part of the fourth century.

This ring is notable in the Thetford Treasure as the only one which is of really large size: even as a thumb ring, it would fit very few women.

17   Gold ring with filigree

A small gold ring with expanded shoulders decorated with filigree and with a glass setting.
Measurements: Internal D 1.5 cm; w of hoop (back) 0.2 cm; D of bezel 0.7 cm; WT 2.6 g. Metal (SQ): gold 95%, silver 3.4%, copper 1.8%

Description: The hoop is flattened at the back, and expands to smooth shoulders which bear an undulating pattern in applied plain wire filigree, further ornamented with numerous small gold globules. The setting is circular, and now contains a square, cushion-shaped blue-green glass setting. There is no evidence of wear, but the stone has been set, or reset, in the ring between the time of finding and the arrival of the jewellery in the British Museum.

Discussion: The filigree decoration links the ring with several others in the hoard, e.g. 10–12 and 14, while the ill-fitting square blue-green glass stone is itself like those in the bracelet, 27, and the ring, 7. Scientific examination (see Chapter 9) revealed that the backing material in the setting of ring 17 included cotton and modern adhesive, and that therefore the stone has been inserted into the cell since finding. It is impossible to tell whether the stone originally belonged in this ring or not: if it did, and was merely reset by the finders there is a link between rings 7 and 17 in the use of very similar square glass gems in unsuitable circular settings.

No close parallel has been found for the form, though the filigree is perhaps very slightly reminiscent of that on the shoulders of a larger ring from Vermand (Eck 1891, pl. xx, 4a), which is from a grave containing a coin of Valentinian I (AD 364–75).

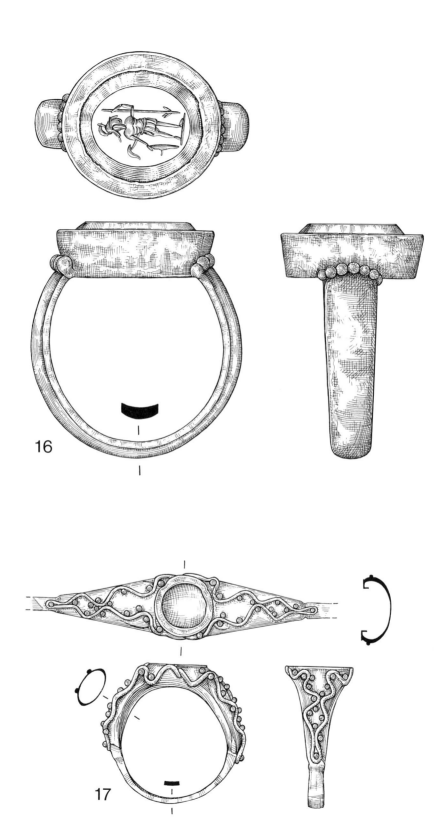

16

17

Fig. 15

18 Gold openwork ring

Small gold ring with openwork hoop and a garnet setting.
Measurements: Internal D 1.4 cm; w of hoop 0.25 cm; D of bezel 0.6 cm; WT 2.0 g. Metal (SQ): gold 94%, silver 4.2%, copper 2.1%

Description: The hoop of the ring consists of a zig-zag gold wire between borders of plain rectangular-sectioned gold. The gem setting is circular, and there are four small globules of gold at each shoulder, where the hoop and bezel meet. The stone is a conical garnet.

There seem to be very slight traces of wear on the hoop and the gem setting.

Discussion: There are other examples of rings with an openwork hoop in a zig-zag pattern, but none is from a dated association. There are several in the British Museum collections, one of which (Marshall 1907, no. 817) is from Britain (Brough, Westmorland). Others include Marshall 558, 816 and 818. No. 558 is said to be from Athens; it has a raised bezel with an earlier engraved gem, cut down to fit. Marshall dates this ring 'late Roman or possibly Merovingian', but there seems to be no specific reason for the suggestion that it could be post-Roman. No. 816 is a little more elaborate than our piece, and 818 is a distant parallel, with a double row of zig-zag and an elaborate and rather clumsy multiple gem setting; it is from Egypt.

The garnet setting may be compared with the gems in rings 22 and 23.

19 Plain gold ring with glass setting

A small plain gold ring with a green glass stone.
Measurements: Internal D 1.5 cm; w of hoop 0.15 cm; D of bezel 0.7 cm; WT 2.5 g. Metal (SQ): gold 96%, silver 2.5%, copper 1.8%

Description: The hoop is slender and rectangular in cross-section at the back, and expands into simply faceted shoulders. The shoulders are hollow (perhaps packed with sulphur). The bezel is flat and circular, and contains a plain green glass stone. The ring shows no signs of wear.

Discussion: Though very plain, the form of the ring is quite distinctive. It is not easy to parallel. One ring in the British Museum collections (Marshall 1907, no. 774), from Syria, is not dissimilar, but its form is more angled than ours, and therefore perhaps more closely related to the common third-century form with sharp and facetted shoulders.

20 Plain gold ring with emerald

A small plain ring with a raised rectangular setting containing an emerald.
Measurements: Internal D 1.4 cm; w of hoop 0.1 cm; bezel 5 × 3 cm; WT 1.2 g. Metal (SQ): gold 95%, silver 4.5%, copper 0.2%

Description: The plain, narrow hoop supports a small rectangular box-setting. The tiny emerald which it contains is damaged, so that it is uncertain whether it originally had a flat or a convex surface.

There is no visible wear.

Discussion: The form, simple though it is, seems to be uncommon. Marshall 1907 no. 785, set with a diamond of pyramidal form, is fairly close but undated; it is from Syria.

21 Gold ring with inlaid gem

Small gold ring, set with a glass gem inlaid with gold.
Measurements: Internal D 1.5 cm; bezel: D 0.8 cm; H 0.3 cm; WT 2.3 g. Metal (SQ): gold 96%, silver 3.8%, copper 0.5%

Description: The hoop is formed of beaded wire with two gold globules at the shoulders. The gem setting is plain and circular, and contains a flat green glass inlaid in fine gold wire with a pattern of four outward-facing peltae. A tiny depression in the centre implies a central dot of gold which is now lost.

There may be slight traces of wear on the outside of the hoop.

Discussion: The most striking feature of this ring is the gold-inlaid glass of the setting, which is extremely closely paralleled in the Thetford assemblage itself by the slightly more elaborate inlaid dark blue glass set in the base of the pendant, 28. A similar gem is illustrated but not described in Catalogue 1761, pl. XCIV, 2, but the type is undoubtedly extremely rare. The method of manufacture is described in Chapter 9. The gems of 21 and 28 must surely emanate from the same source, but we cannot say whether their use here is primary or secondary.

A distant parallel for the gem is the use of a cloissoné rosette pattern in a ring illustrated by Greifenhagen 1975, pl. 64, 15/16, dated to the fifth century, but unprovenanced.

There are numerous parallels for the simple beaded hoop, e.g. Marshall 1907, 560, 862, 863, 864 and Henkel 1913, 278 and 279.

22 Small gold ring with three garnets

Small gold ring with 'plaited' hoop, set with one round and two oval garnets.
Measurements: Internal D 1.4 cm; w of hoop 0.15 cm; WT 2.2 g. Metal (SQ): gold 95%, silver 4.4%, copper 0.5%

Description: The hoop is formed of the loop-in-loop or 'plaited' gold cord often found as a flexible chain in necklaces. At each shoulder are three gold globules. There is a central circular gem setting, and above it are two oval cells set at 60° angles, producing an effect like a small animal face with large pointed ears. All the settings contain garnets with a pointed or keeled surface.

There is no wear.

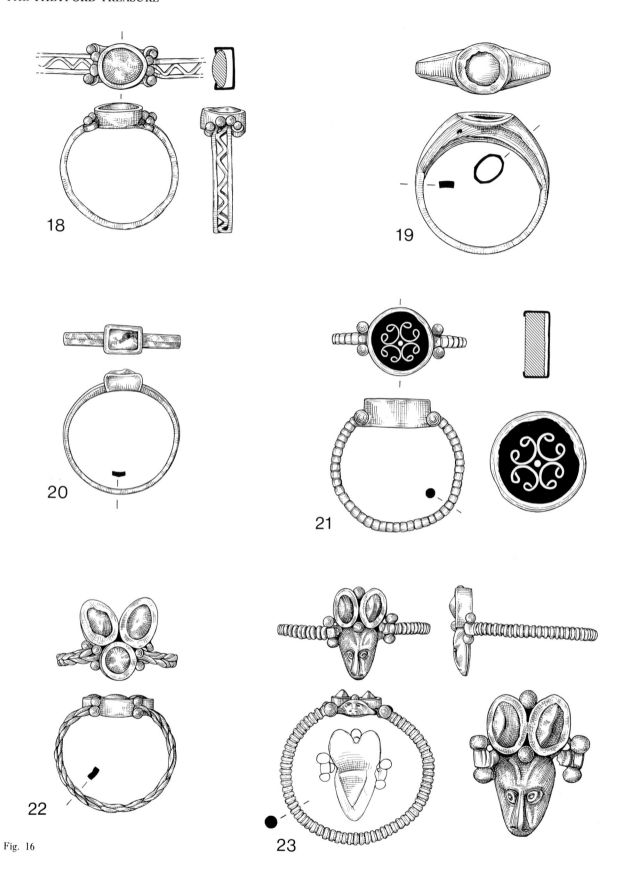

Fig. 16

Discussion: No close parallel has been found. Within the hoard ring **23** is the closest comparison. For the 'plaited' hoop, see Pollak 1903, no. 443, said to be from Constantinople.

Marshall 1907, no. 821, probably from London, is a related type; though it has a ribbed hoop, approaching the technique of the 'basket' pattern gold strip, the garnet-set bezel in the form of a small handled vase is in the same taste as ring **22**.

23 Gold ring with face of Pan

Gold ring with a head of Pan and two garnets.
Measurements: Internal D 1.8 cm; L of face 0.7 cm; w of hoop *c.* 0.2 cm; WT 2.8 g. Metal (SQ): gold 90%, silver 9.7%, copper 0.7%

Description: The hoop is of latitudinally ribbed wire, and there are two gold globules at each shoulder. The bezel is flat at the back, hollow, and modelled in relief at the front. The back has an angled cut which can be raised to give access to the interior; the cavity contains fragments of sulphur. The front of the bezel is modelled with a face surmounted by short horns: above the head are two small oval settings containing garnets.

There is no wear.

Discussion: The ring is unparalleled. Rings with human figures or heads are extremely rare, and though there is one other (**9**) in the Thetford group itself, the heads are very different in style. The faces on ring **9** have all the standard 'Celtic' characteristics, while the horned head on **23** appears to be entirely Roman. It must be identified as Pan himself, or a faun or satyr — in any case, a Bacchic personage. As such, this ring provides the most clear and explicit link between the religious connections revealed in the inscriptions on the silver objects, and the jewellery. The woodpeckers on ring **7** are a hint in this direction, but at most a subtle one; this ring seems to make a more positive statement that there is some link between the gold and silver objects in the hoard.

24, 25 Pair of gold bracelets

Pair of gold bracelets decorated with 'basket' pattern.
Measurements: External D *c.* 6.5 cm (some distortion); w (overall) 1.4 cm; patterned strip 1.2 cm; WT (**24**) 26.8 g, (**25**) 25.9 g; Metal: **24** (QU): gold 96.1%, silver 3.1%, copper 0.8%; **25** (SQ): gold 94.0%, silver 5.5%, copper 0.4%

Description: The bracelets are an exactly matching pair. They are complete circular hoops, formed of a strip of thin gold sheet, ridged and impressed to resemble basket-work (cf. rings **10** and **12**). They are bordered on each side by a plain rectangular-sectioned gold flange. The ends of the strip or ribbon are simply overlapped, and are held in position only by this edging.

The bracelets show no trace of wear of any kind, the slight physical deformation clearly being the result of pressure during burial. The surface of the metal appears pristine.

Discussion: The form of these bracelets is highly distinctive, and there is a close parallel in the matching pair of bracelets from a third-century hoard found at Lyon in 1841 (Comarmond 1844, pl.2, 3 & 4). These are of exactly the same type, differing only in having additional small relief-decorated plaques attached. There is no sign of such a feature on the Thetford pair. The only other item of Roman jewellery known to the authors with this 'basket' pattern finish is a double finger-ring (see under discussion of ring **10**).

The earlier date of the Lyon group as a whole is a problem, but it seems possible that the link between the Thetford and Lyon bracelets is a geographical rather than a chronological one, and that the use of this rare and umistakeable form of decoration is a hint of a source for the Thetford jewellery in this area of France.

The obvious relationship of bracelets **24** and **25** with the rings **10** and **12** is yet another demonstration of homogeneity within the Thetford hoard itself, and incidentally refutes any suggestion that the bracelets, as parallels to the Lyon pieces, might be earlier than late fourth-century, since there is no doubt about the late date of the rings. The bracelets cannot have been old when buried; they are among the most obviously new items in the hoard in terms of their condition.

26 Twisted gold bracelet

Heavy twisted gold bracelet with stud and loop fastening.
Measurements: Overall D (open) *c.* 7.0 cm; broadest point (back) *c.* 1.0. cm; D of loop or eye 1.2 cm; WT 108.1 g. Metal (SQ): gold 95%, silver 4.3%, copper 0.5%.

Description: The bracelet is formed of two thick gold rods twisted together, each tapering from its thickest point at the back to a smaller diameter near the fastening. The latter is in the form of a stud and loop, the loop being circular with an applied decorative 'plait' of gold wire.

There are very minor traces or wear on the body of the bracelet and on the surfaces of the clasp which would come into contact when closed, but these seem too slight to indicate any extensive use.

Discussion: The bracelet belongs to a known Roman type, though it is thicker and heavier than any other extant example. Two bracelets of the same type occur in the New Grange find (Kent & Painter 1977, nos 233 and 234), where they are associated with rings of undoubtedly late-Roman form (cf. parallels for ring **10**), while the Ténès Treasure provides further parallels (Heurgon 1958, pl. v, 3 and 4). Another example, without any history, but said to be from Sussex, was acquired by the British Museum in the Payne Knight bequest in 1824. Bronze bracelets of a similar form are also known. While there is too little evidence to say that these bracelets are restricted to the later Roman period, their presence at New Grange and Ténès confirms that they were in fashion in the fourth century, and had a wide distribution in the Empire.

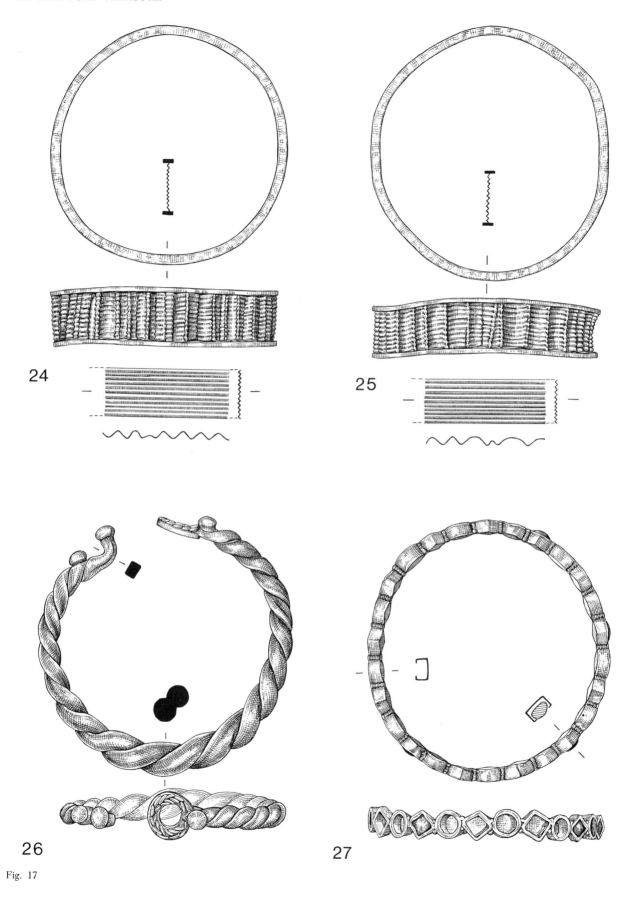

24

25

26

27

Fig. 17

27 Gold and gem bracelet

Gold bracelet with box-settings for stones.
Measurements: D (external) 6.8 cm; (internal) 6.2 cm; D of circular settings 0.8 cm; lozenge settings, sides 0.6 cm; WT 17.8 g. Metal (SQ): gold 92%, silver 7.5%, copper 0.3%

Description: The bracelet is a complete circle, broken in one place when found, consisting of twenty-six box-settings, alternately round and lozenge-shaped. Between each pair of cells are rows of small gold globules. All but four of the stones are missing: the survivors, all from lozenge-shaped settings, are of blue-green glass. The circular settings would probably have contained gems of a contrasting colour, perhaps garnets. Sulphur was used as a backing material for the gems, and is present in a number of the settings.

There is no trace of wear on the bracelet.

Discussion: The hoop composed entirely of settings for coloured stones is reminiscent of one of the rings in the Thetford hoard, (8) and the surviving green glass gems are close to those in ring 7 and 17, if the latter originally contained this stone. The only comparatively close parallel for the bracelet is from the Ténès Treasure (Heurgon 1958, pl. v, 2). This is about the same size as the Thetford example, and has twenty-six settings containing garnets and emeralds. The form is not quite the same as ours, as the settings are all circular, and are set on alternate sides of a gold wire which is shaped to an undulating line. Another bracelet of the same general type, set with twenty garnets, comes from a rich late third-century burial at Cologne (Peter La Baume and Elisabeth Nuber, *Kölner Jahrbuch* 12 (1971), pp. 80).

28 Gold pendant

Gold pendant in the form of a club of Hercules, with a gold-inlaid gem in the base.
Measurements: L (incl. loop) 3.6 cm; D of base 1.3 cm; WT 10.5 g. Metal (SQ): gold 94%, silver 4.5%, copper 1.8%

Description: The pendant is of slender conical form, and represents a stylised club of Hercules, the knobs on the sides indicated by engraved lines and tiny circular punch-marks. The surface of the suspension ring is fluted. Around the top of the pendant, and again 7mm further down, the object is encircled with beaded gold wire. Set into the base is a flat dark blue glass gem, inlaid in gold with four outward-facing peltae and a small central cross. A shallow circular channel remains around this motif where further gold inlay has probably been lost.

The pendant shows slight traces of wear of the internal surface of the loop, the beaded wire, and the base of the body.

Discussion: Ear-rings in the form of a club of Hercules are quite common in Roman jewellery; they are widespread geographically, and range in date from the first to the fourth century AD. There are at least three examples from Britain, probably all of first- or second-century date, from the Walbrook, Birdoswald and Ashtead, Surrey (Charlesworth

1977). A number from the Rhineland include an unprovenanced piece in the Trier Museum (Schindler 1977, Taf. 241), another unprovenanced example in Bonn (Catalogue 1963, Abb. 41), and one from a late third-century woman's grave in Bonn (Haberey 1960). Perhaps one of the best parallels for the Thetford pieces is from Romania (Simion 1977, pl. x, 7): this is a large specimen, described as an amulet-pendant rather than an ear-ring. A lost example from the Beaurains Treasure was also quite large (Bastien & Metzger 1977, B.20). There are more than a dozen pendants of this form in the British Museum collections, nearly all unprovenanced and undated.

It seems likely that both the Thetford examples, 28 and 29, were intended to be worn as necklace-pendants rather than ear-rings, since they are comparatively large and heavy, though use as ear-rings, like most of the other objects of this form, remains perfectly feasible.

The only satisfactory parallel for the inlaid glass setting is to be found within the Thetford hoard itself, in ring 21, while a further link with other items in the treasure is provided by the small circular punch-marks, precisely similar to those on rings 2, 4 and 9, and pendant 29, and almost certainly made with the same tool. The method of manufacture of the inlaid gem is described in Chapter 9. A similar inlaid gem is published in an eighteenth-century source, but without any description (Catalogue 1761, pl. xCIV, no. 2).

The slight wear on this pendant and on 29 poses something of a problem. The wear within the suspension loop is not sufficient to indicate that the object was suspended on a gold chain, yet this is the way in which one would have expected it to be used; a leather thong or a cord seems far less likely. If used as an ear-ring, it would have depended from a gold wire. It is hard to envisage some form of use other than these which could have resulted in surface wear, and the matter must remain an open one for the present.

29 Gold pendant

Gold pendant in the form of a club of Hercules, with green glass and garnet settings.
Measurements: Overall L 4.1 cm; D of gem in base 1.2 cm; WT 10.6 g. Metal (SQ): gold 95%, silver 3.5%, copper 1%

Description: The pendant is of precisely the same form as 28, with a suspension loop, beaded gold wire, stylised knobs, and a gem set in the base. The knobs have, in addition to the engraved lines, small round settings containing green glass and garnets. The gem in the base is a plain, convex-surfaced garnet.

The pendant shows the same type and extent of wear as 28, namely on the inside of the suspension loop, the encircling beaded wire, and the case of the body.

Discussion: See 28 for parallels.

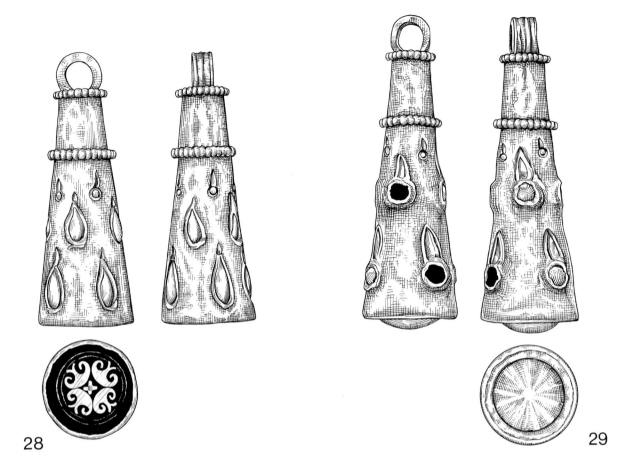

28

29

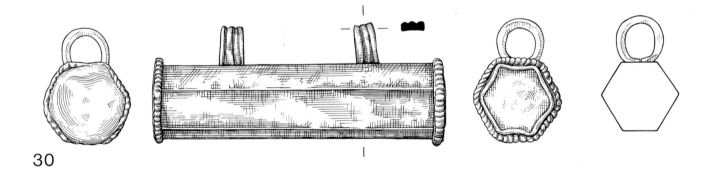

30

Fig. 18

30　Gold amulet

Gold amulet in the form of a hexagonal-sectioned tube with two suspension rings.
Measurements: L 3.9 cm; w 1.0 cm; wt (with contents) 13.3 g.
Metal (QU): gold 92.5%, silver 4.5%, copper 3.1%

Description: The object is a hollow gold tube of regular hexagonal cross-section, with two reeded suspension rings attached to one side. Each end is decorated with a border of beaded wire. One end is soldered closed while the other is sealed with a thick hexagonal plate of gold, held in position by the turned-over edges of the tube.

When opened, the case proved to be tightly packed with sulphur.

There is some wear on the rings and on the beaded wire.

Discussion: Tubular gold amulet cases, designed to contain some substance or object of religious or magical significance, have a very long history. Examples which are of essentially the same form as ours, though made to be suspended vertically rather than horizontally, are known from Egypt (Catalogue 1976, no. 342a, of Middle Kingdom date). Other examples which illustrate the wide range, geographically and chronologically, of the type are numbers 378 and 379 in the same catalogue, both decorated horizontally-hung tubes, the first of second to third century AD date from Gandhara, the second from Persia and of the twelfth to thirteenth century AD. Within the Roman period, the type is normally of cylindrical or or polygonal cross-section, designed to hang horizontally (often with three or four suspension loops, in spite of the relatively light weight), and with varying decoration.

The Ténès Treasure provides two parallels in the same date-range as Thetford (Heurgon 1958, pl. v., 5 and 6). Heurgon has a general discussion of the type on pages 57–9. The larger of the Ténès pieces, no. 5, is very large, with flared ends, and lions' masks in relief on the end-plates. The smaller is somewhat closer in form to our rather simple example. Two other cases with decorated end-plates (one with the clasped-hands motif) occur in the treasure of Planche (Poncet, 1889): this is a small hoard, probably deposited early in the fourth century. The Planche amulets also have a zig-zag pattern in relief along the sides. There are several examples of the type, most of them unprovenanced, in the British Museum collections (Marshall 1911, nos 2981 and 3155 are of particular interest), while a pair quite close in appearance to ours exists on an allegedly sixth to seventh century necklace in the Burton C. Berry collection (Rudolph, 1973, no. 193.). Apparently the only parallel known from Britain is a fairly recent find from York (MacGregor 1976, fig. 8, 72, p.10–11).

Several of these cases have been opened. Some contain odd items such as small fragments of earth (e.g. the smaller Ténès amulet), but more, including the Thetford piece, contain sulphur, and some enclose a thin slip of gold inscribed, usually in Greek, with a magical or gnostic message. Marshall 2981 contained sulphur and a fragment of white silk thread; the thread is significant since the concepts of making spells and of binding are related, cf. the Greek verb καταδεσμεώ, to bind, literally, or to control by means of enchantments. Marshall 3155, from southern Italy, is one of the cases which

contains an inscription, in this instance seemingly considerably earlier than the container itself.

The significance of the sulphur as an apotropaic substance seems obscure, though Pliny records its use in a religious context, for purification (see Chapter 2). It is noteworthy that several of the items of jewellery in the Thetford Treasure incorporate sulphur, evidently used as an adhesive and as a packing for hollow shells of gold; while its practical usefulness seems certain, we should not overlook the possibility that the sulphur may have been chosen because of its magical significance as well. Note that the oracle of Faunus was probably in a region of sulphurous springs (see Chapter 7).

31　Gold necklace with beads

Gold chain necklace with green beads.
Measurements: L 40.0 cm; w 18.4 g. Metal (SQ): gold 95%, silver 4.7%, copper 0.3%

Description: The chain is of the loop-in-loop ('plaited') type, and has a plain hook-and-eye clasp. The chain is four-sided in section. There were originally five beads, threaded on straight sections of very slender gold wire. Four survive; they are hexagonal in cross-section, and three of them are of marbled green-and-yellow glass, somewhat decayed on the surface. The other, which is damaged, is an emerald. The glass beads and the emerald are of exactly the same type as the loose beads, 42–46.

As on all the chain necklaces, there is some wear on the wire links where they rub against each other, and also a little wear on the surfaces of the clasp which are in contact. It is difficult to judge whether this implies actual use as jewellery, or whether it could simply result from handling.

Discussion: Roman necklaces with green beads, either glass or emerald, or sometimes, as in this case, both, are fairly common and have a very long chronological range. In Britain, fragments are now known from London, Canterbury and Wincle (Johns 1976, 1979a, 1979b, Johns *et al.* 1980). Probably the best parallel for our necklace is from the Beaurains Treasure (Bastien & Metzger 1977, B.I.). The form is precisely like ours, but the workmanship is finer and neater, lacking the slight irregularity of the links seen in the Thetford example.

The loop-in-loop cord chain has an extremely long history from Egyptian, Greek and Hellenistic examples down to Byzantine jewellery. The technique of manufacture is illustrated in an article of Roman jewellery technique by Reynold Higgins (Higgins 1976, 56–9).

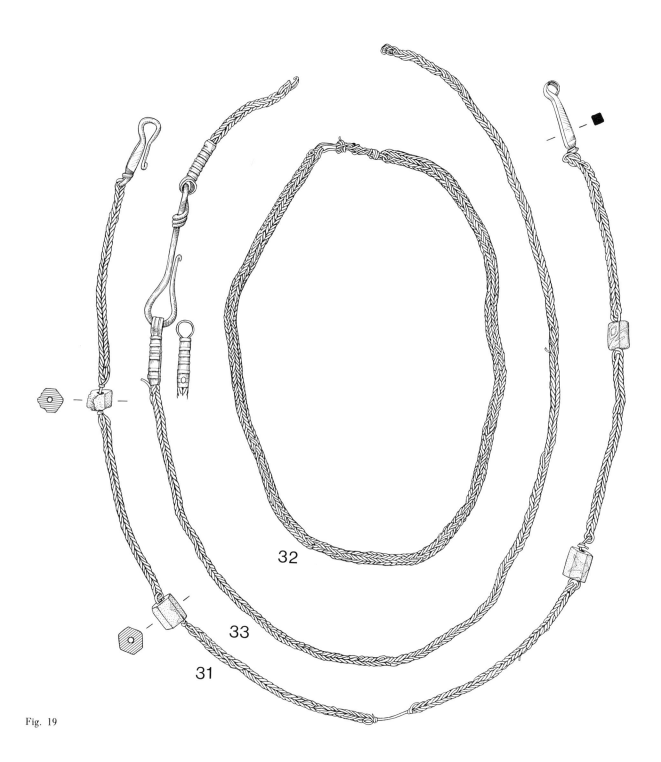

32

33

31

Fig. 19

32 Gold necklace

Plain necklace of 'plaited' gold wire.
Measurements: L *c.* 30.8 cm; D of cross-section *c.* 0.35 cm; WT 19.5 g. Metal (SQ): gold 89%, silver 10.2%, copper 0.6%

Description: A plain chain of loop-in-loop ('plaited') gold wire, of six-sided section. No clasp is fitted, and the end loops are held together with crudely twisted strands of wire.

The links show slight wear at contact points, from the movement of the flexible chain.

Discussion: This type of 'plaited' chain is common not only throughout the whole of the Roman period, but for centuries earlier and later (see references in discussion of **31**). The interesting feature of this example is the rough joining together of the ends; clearly the object cannot be worn in this condition, and it is tempting to suppose that it is unfinished, and awaits the addition of a suitable fastener. There are two unattached clasps in the hoard, **37** and **38**. We should also remember, however, that the objects were not seen by competent observers immediately they were found, and therefore the supposition that the chain is incomplete is not totally certain. In its present state, the necklace looks too small to be worn around the neck. However, the addition of a clasp about 5 cm long, similar to **37** and **38**, would bring it to a length that would be adequate on the average female neck. It may have been intended to be worn on its own, or to have been used with a pendant.

The composition of the metal is strikingly close to that of necklace **33**, ring **23**, and the buckle, **1**. These four pieces all have a noticeably higher silver content than any of the other items of jewellery.

33 Gold necklace

Necklace of plain 'plaited' gold wire.
Measurements: Total L 40.3 cm; WT 17.2 g. Metal (SQ): gold 89%, silver 10.5%, copper 0.5%

Description: The necklace is of 'plaited' or loop-in-loop gold cord (four-sided), and has a simple and undecorated hook-and-eye clasp. There is slight wear from the rubbing together of the links.

Discussion: This chain is complete, unlike **32**, and may also have been intended for use with a pendant. The composition of the metal is almost identical to that of **32**, and it therefore seems likely that the same batch of metal was used to make both chains. The gold of the buckle, **1**, and the ring **23** is also very similar.

34 Gold necklace

Gold necklace of interlocking beads, with hollow gold beads as pendants or fasteners.
Measurements: Surviving L *c.* 25.6 cm; L (oval bead) 1.3 cm;
L ('vase' beads) 2.2 cm; D of interlocking beads *c.* 0.4 cm; WT 9.8 g. Metal (SQ): gold 92%, silver 6.6%, copper 1%

Description: Part of a necklace made of tiny hub- or spindle-shaped beads which interlock to form a flexible, ribbed chain. There is one hollow bead of oval form and two larger ones which are shaped somewhat like vases, with a longitudinally reeded surface and a ring at one end. All these large beads are severely damaged and distorted. The 'vase' beads could be pendants or part of the fastening assembly. There is no certainty that the three larger beads belong with the small interlocking ones, though it seems likely that they do.

Discussion: The chain is clearly not complete, and it may confidently be assumed that many of the tiny gold beads were overlooked during the recovery of the hoard. The finder stated that this necklace was one of the pieces found inside the shale box; if this was so, then all the beads ought to be present, but there is some doubt about the accuracy of the finder's recollection on this point.

The interlocking spindle-shaped beads are highly unusual and seem to be paralleled only, and not very closely, in another hoard of jewellery from Britain, that from Wincle, Cheshire (Johns *et al.* 1980, pl. I, b, fig.4). The beads in the Wincle hoard are much larger than those from Thetford, though the form is close. The Wincle hoard is of third-century date.

The point has been made in Chapter 2 that beads of this type and size are unlikely to have survived in most cases, and the paucity of parallels is therefore not surprising.

The larger beads are quite well paralleled in at least three necklaces now in Namur Museum, from late-Roman cemeteries in that area of Belgium. In particular, eight longitudinally reeded beads from a necklace found in Grave 9 in the late-Roman and Frankish cemetery at Samson are clearly related to the Thetford examples (Dasnoy 1968, 292–3, fig. 9, 5): this grave contained a *siliqua* of Jovinus (AD 411–13).

35/36 Gold necklace

Plain necklace of 'plaited' gold wire, the clasp ornamented with snakes' heads.
Measurements: Chain: L 30.9 cm; D 0.3 cm; L of clasp 6.8 cm; WT (chain) 23.1 g, (clasp) 5.5 g. Metal (SQ): gold 94%, silver 4.8%, copper 0.9%

Description: The necklace is a six-sided 'plaited' (loop-in-loop) chain. The ends fit neatly into the collars of the clasp, and though separate when found, there is no doubt that the two elements belong together. Both the ends of the chain and the tubular collars have holes which indicate the position of small gold rivets or pins which would have attached the clasp to the chain. The collars are encircled at each end with beaded wire, and the actual terminals are modelled in the form of snakes' heads, their eyes set with dark blue glass (one only survives). The snakes are relatively crudely modelled, and are decorated on the upper surface of the heads with fine stippling.

There are slight traces of wear among the links of the chain and also on the beaded wire and the surfaces of the hook-and-eye fastening which come into contact.

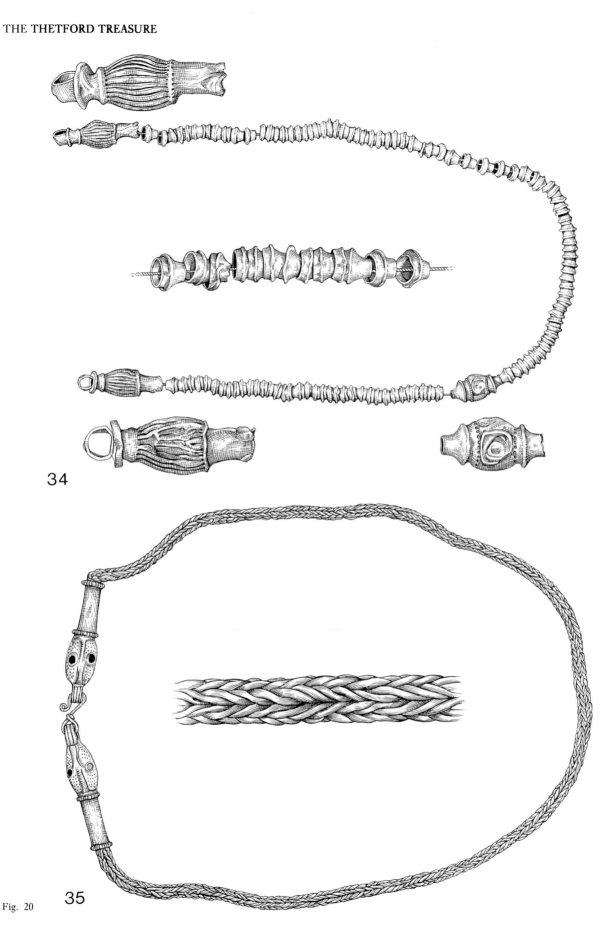

34

35

Fig. 20

102

Discussion: The necklace as a whole has no intrinsically datable features, since the type of chain was used throughout antiquity, and snakes as decorative motifs in jewellery were also very widespread indeed. A necklace very similar to this one (Greifenhagen 1975, Taf. 26, 5) is dated first century BC/first AD, though there appears to be no real dating evidence.

Snakes occur more frequently as motifs in rings and bracelets than in necklaces. Earlier examples, including ones found in Britain (e.g. Dolaucothi — Brailsford 1964, 13, 2) display a very realistic and detailed treatment of the reptiles compared with the somewhat cursory rendering in the Thetford necklace.

37   Gold necklace-clasp

Gold hook-and-eye clasp for a necklace.
Measurements: L 6.2 cm; WT 4.4 g. Metal (SQ): gold 93%, silver 6.2%, copper 0.9%

Description: A plain gold hook-and-eye fastener. The main elements are of slender pyramidal form, each of the four flat sides decorated with a raised zig-zag in narrow gold strip. The workmanship, especially at the base of the pyramids where the attachment rings are soldered on, is fairly rough. There is slight wear on the fastening loop and hook and on the decoration, but it seems possible that this could have been caused by handling and movement rather than use as a necklace fastener.

Discussion: The slender pyramid form is matched within the Thetford hoard in **38**. The gold necklace-clasp from the Canterbury Treasure (Painter 1965, no. 16) is rectangular in section, and though not as developed as the Thetford examples, is clearly related, as, indeed, is the simple clasp of Thetford **33**.

The raised zig-zag decoration has not been found on other necklace-clasps, but it is paralleled on other items of third and fourth century jewellery, such as the amulet cases from the Planche Treasure (Poncet 1889) and the collars or spacers from the medallion necklaces of Beaurains and Naix (Bastien & Metzger 1977, B. 23 and pl.B) and L'Houmeau (Flouret *et al.* 1981, 93, 3).

38   Gold necklace-clasp

Gold hook-and-eye clasp for a necklace.
Measurements: L 5.1 cm; WT 3.8 g. Metal (SQ): gold 94.7%, silver 5.2%, copper 0.1%

Description: Gold hook-and-eye fastener, the terminals being of pyramidical form like **37**, but without decoration.

Discussion: See comments on **37**.

39   Cameo pendant

Irregular oval onyx cameo of a lion, mounted in gold as a pendant.
Measurements: L 2.0 cm; H 1.6 cm; H (including ring) 2.0 cm; WT 3.9 g. Metal (SQ): gold 94%, silver 5.3%, copper 1.2%

Description: The gem is an onyx (chalcedony), varying in colour from dark blue to a light blue-grey, with a small area of brown. It is carved in cameo with a lion walking to the left. The gem is very rough and irregular on the back, and cutting down for reuse has also damaged the front, removing part of the tail and the near hind leg of the lion. The gem is enclosed in a plain gold frame which follows its irregular contours. There is a small suspension loop.

The stone itself shows considerable wear, particularly on the face of the lion. The wear on the gold mount is very slight.

Discussion: For a detailed discussion of the gem, see Chapter 3. It is probably of Severan date, and would appear to be reused for the *second* time in this mount, since the cutting which has damaged the tail and leg of the lion is in no way necessary for fitting the stone into the present mount, and presumably reflects an earlier frame.

40   Pendant with engraved gem

Oval chalcedony engraved with Diana Venatrix, mounted in gold as a pendant.
Measurements: Overall H 2.3 cm; overall W 1.8 cm; Gem: H 1.8 cm; W 1.4 cm; WT 3.3 g. Metal (SQ): gold 94%, silver 5%, copper 1.4%

Description: The stone is a milky, translucent chalcedony with a faint brownish streak. Both faces are flat, with a bevelled edge at the back. The engraving represents Diana as huntress, in short tunic and boots, with bow and quiver, and accompanied by a small hound. The outer border of the gold frame is in a rather crude roped pattern, and there is a small suspension loop.

There are apparently slight traces of wear on the gold.

Discussion: The gem is discussed fully in Chapter 3. The roped border is widely paralleled, both for pendant-mounts and ring-bezels. An example in the Beaurains Treasure is typical (Bastien & Metzger 1977, B 17). The style is too widespread to have any chronological significance.

36

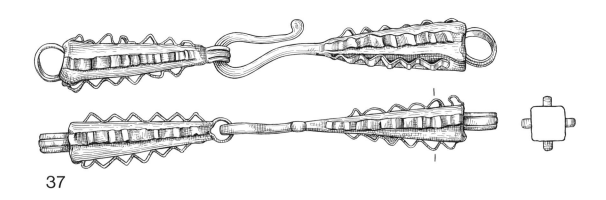

37

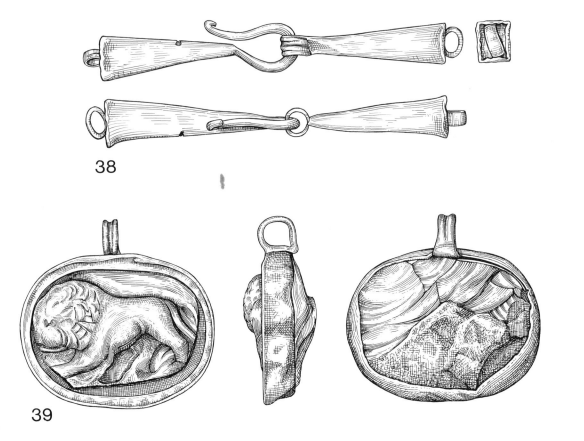

38

39

Fig. 21

40

41

Fig. 22

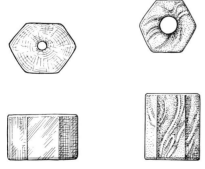

42–46

Fig. 23

41 Unmounted gem

A rectangular gem with slightly curved sides, engraved with Venus and Cupid.
Measurements: L 2.2 cm; w 1.7 cm; wt 4.9 g.

Description: The stone is a slightly translucent orange-red cornelian (chalcedony). The engraved decoration is of Venus, naked apart from some drapery over her arm, seen in three-quarter back view. A large circular shield rests on the ground beside her, and she holds a sword and two spears. In front of her is Cupid, holding up a small helmet.

The gem has been cut down, probably from an originally elongated oval form. The present upper and lower edges of the stone closely skim the engraving.

Discussion: See Chapter 3; the gem is of Severan date. It has been removed from an earlier setting, preparatory to reuse as a ring or pendant, perhaps more likely the latter in view of its large size.

42 Bead

Hexagonal-sectioned green bead.
Measurements: L 0.6 cm; Max. w 0.8 cm

Description: A bead of slightly rounded hexagonal section in polished bright green stone: beryl (emerald).

Discussion: This is the type of bead used in necklace **31**. Though there is one bead missing in that chain, the presence of four extra beads implies existence of a longer beaded necklace. It is possible that the green beads, emerald and glass, like so many other gems in the treasure, were reused, and their original gold mounts and settings fashioned into new jewellery.

43–46 3 Beads

Hexagonal-sectioned bead.
Measurements: L 0.7 cm; Max. w 0.7 cm.

Description: Beads of hexagonal cross-section in marbled green-and-yellow glass. The surface of **43** is somewhat decayed and pitted.

Discussion: The beads match those in necklace **31**. See remarks on **42**.

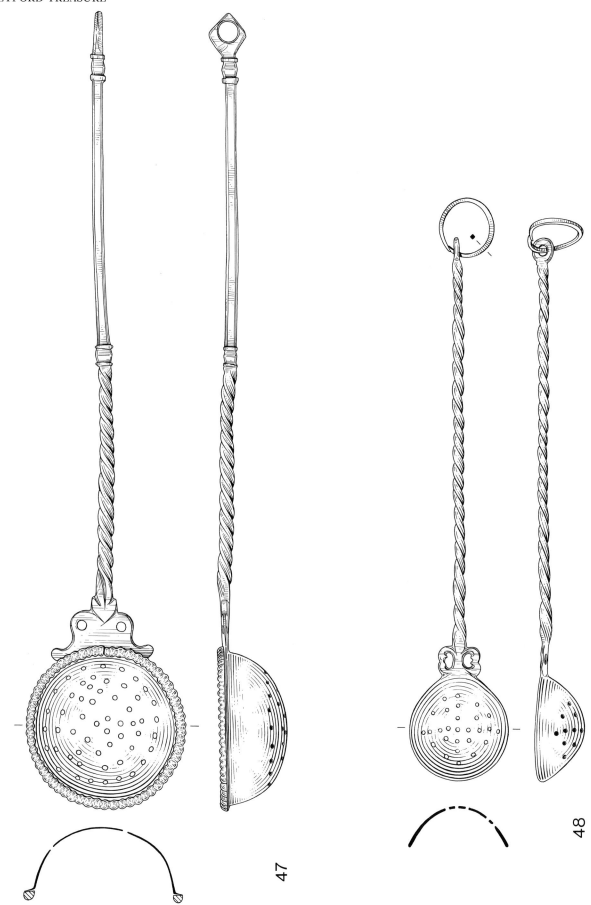

Fig. 24

106

47

48

47 Silver strainer

Silver strainer with long handle.
Measurements: Total L 21.2 cm; D of bowl 4.3 cm; WT 33.2 g.
Metal (SQ): gold 0.8%, silver 96%, copper 2.7%, lead 0.5%,
zinc <0.1%

Description: The strainer has a deep circular bowl with a boldly
beaded rim, separately made and soldered on. The strainer
holes are *c.* 1 mm in diameter, and they do not form a pattern.
The handle attachment is very stylised, but probably based
on a bird's head form, pierced with two holes. The first section
of the handle is twisted, the end, separated by a baluster
moulding, is square-sectioned, terminating in another moulding and a flat lozenge-shaped point at 90° to the plane of the
bowl. There is a hole in the centre of this lozenge, perhaps
intended for a suspension ring.

Discussion: The strainer belongs to a type which is well known
in late-Roman hoards, and continues to occur as grave-
furniture in the post-Roman period. One of the best parallels
is the large silver strainer from the Water Newton hoard
(Painter 1977b, no. 7), which has a separately made beaded
rim and a similar stylised zoomorphic handle-attachment.
The Water Newton strainer is in a Christian group of material,
and is decorated on the handle-terminal with a Chi-Rho
monogram. There is a small strainer with a comma-shaped
terminal, like **49**, from a late context at Richborough
(Bushe-Fox 1949, pl. xxxvii, 126), which has a twisted handle,
a feature which is, of course, paralleled many times in the
other strainers and the spoons within the Thetford assemblage
itself (**48, 49, 69, 73, 74, 81**). Similar strainers also occur
in the Kaiseraugst and Traprain Law Treasures (Laur-Belart
1963, Abb. 20; Curle 1923, no. 111). More distant parallels
for the type are noted in Chapter 8.

48 Silver strainer

Silver strainer with ring at handle terminal.
Measurements: L 14.3 cm; D of bowl 2.7 cm; D of ring 1.5 cm;
WT 12.8 g. Metal (SQ): gold 0.9%, silver 96%, copper 3.0%

Description: The small circular bowl is pierced with holes in
a cross pattern, each quadrant containing three additional
holes. The handle attachment is in double-pelta form. The
handle is of twisted square-sectioned rod with a small pierced
disc at the end. Attached to this is a silver ring.

Discussion: Most of the parallels cited in the discussion of **47**
apply equally to this strainer. Points to note in **48** include the
suspension ring at the end of the handle, and the fact that
the piercing of the bowl forms a perceptible pattern; this is
in fact more usual than the haphazard distribution of the holes
in **47**. The weight is close to half an ounce.

49 Silver strainer

Implement with a small strainer bowl and a comma-shaped
terminal.
Measurements: L 15 cm; D of bowl 1.5 cm; WT 10.3 g. Metal
(SQ): gold 1%, silver 96%, copper 2.8%

Description: The implement has a very small strainer bowl with
a large central hole and a ring of smaller perforations around
it. A small segment of the bowl is missing. The handle attachment is in the form of a decorative baluster moulding, while
the handle itself has a plain square-sectioned portion and a
twisted one, demarcated by further mouldings. The terminal
is flat and in the shape of an elongated comma, placed at 90°
to the plane of the bowl. It is pierced with two circular holes
and one roughly following the external outline.

Discussion: Silver implements with the distinctive comma-
shaped terminal are well known and have been widely discussed, though there is as yet no real consensus about their
function. The matter is considered fully in Chapter 8. The
characteristic terminal prong is found in combination with
various types of implement; the combination with a strainer
occurs at Kaiseraugst and Richborough (Laur-Belart 1963,
Abb. 20, Bushe-Fox 1949, pl. xxxvii, 126). Other types
include a small disc-shaped implement set at an angle to the
handle, found at both Kaiseraugst and Richborough, and the
long narrow ligula-spoon bowl.

Variants of the comma-shaped prong continue to occur on
objects of the post-Roman period, notably in the well-known
example from the St Ninian's Isle Treasure (Wilson 1973, also
Richardson 1980, 95f.). Comparison with the Richborough
strainer/pronged implement suggests that one of the holes
in the terminal of our example may well have been intended
for the attachment of a suspension ring. Note that a ring is
present on strainer **48**.

50 The Triton spoon

Silver spoon with duck handle and parcel-gilt decoration in
the bowl depicting a Triton and a dolphin. In the bowl is the
inscription DEINARI.
Measurements: Total L 10.2 cm; Bowl: 7.3 cm, W 4.6 cm; WT
25.4 g. Metal (QU): *bowl* gold 0.5%, silver 95.8%, copper
3.1%, lead 0.7%, zinc <0.1%; (QU): *handle* gold 0.6%, silver
94.7%, copper 3.9%, lead 0.8%, zinc <0.1%

Description: The bowl of the spoon is oval with a slightly
pointed tip, and it is decorated with a Triton, chased and
picked out in gilding. He is blowing a horn which he holds
in his right hand, and has a steering-oar in his left. There
is a dolphin in front of him and a rosette behind. Below the
figure is the inscription DEINARI. Further gilding is applied in
a band around the inner rim of the bowl, and there is also
some on the bird's head. This faces away from the bowl, and
details such as the eyes and the line of the beak are indicated
with chasing and punching.

Discussion: Large spoons furnished with short, coiled or
recurved handles terminating in the head of a duck or swan

49

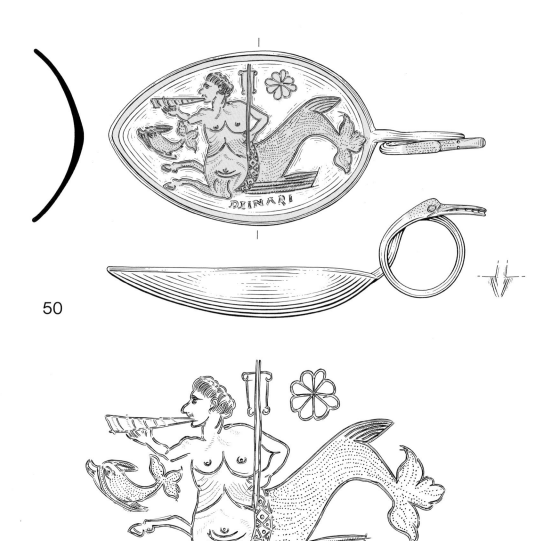

50

Fig. 25

are a standard late-Roman type, found in a number of hoards of this period, such as Kaiseraugst, Traprain Law and Canterbury (Laur-Belart 1963, Abb. 21; Curle 1923, pl. XXVI. 102, 103; Painter 1965, pl. III). The usual handle forms are a sideways curving one in which the bird's head is almost in contact with the side of the bowl (represented at Kaiseraugst), and a simple upright s-curve (represented at Canterbury); the complete coil above the bowl, as in all the Thetford examples with the exception of **56**, seems to be exceptional, though the original form of one of the Traprain Law spoons could possibly have followed this pattern. The typology of the handles is discussed more fully in Chapter 5.

Within the Thetford treasure, spoon **50** is extremely closely related to the long-handled Panther spoon (**66**): the figural decoration and the parcel-gilding is in the same style, the slightly pointed oval bowls are identical in form (and unlike the other spoons in the treasure), and the inscriptions are clearly linked, reading DEINARI and DEIIFAVNINARI respectively. Though the inscriptions provide several repetitions of names and epithets between duck-handled and long-handled spoons, the only demonstrable stylistic link between the two groups is in the relationship between **50** and **66**.

The parcel-gilding is not in itself very unusual on late-Roman silverware. It can be found, for example, on items in the Kaiseraugst Treasure (Laur-Belart 1963), the Traprain Law Hoard (Curle 1923), the Esquiline Treasure (Shelton 1981), and on a very few pieces in the Mildenhall Treasure (Painter 1977a, 12 and 18–26). On spoons specifically, it is not common: the Helpston spoon (Johns, 1982) is of earlier date, and better parallels are provided by an unprovenanced long-handled spoon with a gilded fish in the bowl (Potter, *forthcoming*) and in particular by a large unprovenanced duck-handled spoon in the Cleveland Museum of Art (Weitzmann 1979, no. 316), decorated with a figure of a muscular young man. This spoon, thought to have been found in Syria, has the sideways-curving handle and a somewhat long and narrow bowl like those of the Kaiseraugst spoons.

The weights of the spoons are fully discussed in Chapter 5, but we may note here that **50** is a one-ounce spoon. Interestingly, the Cleveland parallel cited above weighs 52.5 g, and is therefore to be regarded as a two-ounce spoon.

The choice of decorative motif is in accord with the Bacchic theme seen elsewhere in the Thetford hoard, since Tritons are found in some types of Bacchic decoration. In particular, we should note the sea-thiasos occupying the inner frieze of decoration on the Mildenhall great dish.

The inscription is discussed in Chapter 6.

51   Inscribed silver spoon

Duck-handled silver spoon with niello inscription DEIIFAVNINARI in the bowl.
Measurements: L 12.6 cm; bowl: L 9.3 cm; W 5.0 cm; WT 45.5 g.
Metal (QU): *bowl* gold 0.6%, silver 97.2%, copper 1.8%, lead 0.5%, zinc <0.1%; (QU): *handle* gold 0.5%, silver 97.2%, copper 1.9%, lead 0.5%, zinc <0.1%

Description: Oval, slightly keeled bowl with a coiled handle, its duck-headed terminal facing inwards. The inscription in the bowl, in niello, reads DEIIFAVNINARI.

Discussion: General parallels are cited under **50** and in Chapter 5. The inscription is discussed in Chapter 6: it is the same as that on **66** and related to the inscription on **50**. This spoon is the heaviest in the whole group.

52   Inscribed silver spoon

Duck-handled spoon with niello inscription DEIFAVNI ⊄ GRANI in the bowl.
Measurements: L 9.2 cm; bowl: L 7.6 cm; W 4.5 cm; WT 27.3 g.
Metal (SQ): *handle* gold 0.8%, silver 98%, copper 1.5%

Description: Oval bowl, the coiled handle with its duck-head facing outwards. The eye of the duck is finely chased, and the bird holds a cake or fruit in its beak. The niello inscription in the bowl reads DEIFAVNI ⊄ GRANI.

Discussion: General parallels are cited under no. **50** and in Chapter 5. The inscription is discussed in Chapter 6, and is linked with the inscriptions on the long-handled spoons **74** and **82**.

The cake held in the bird's beak is a feature which is quite often found in Roman and perhaps some Iron-Age bronzes: see the discussion in Chapter 5. It occurs in five of the Thetford duck-handles, all of them outward-facing ducks, namely **52** to **56**.

53   Inscribed silver spoon

Duck-handled silver spoon with niello inscription DEIFAVANDICROSE in the bowl.
Measurements: L 9.8 cm; bowl L 7.5 cm, W 4.6 cm; WT 27.4 g.
Metal (SQ): *handle* gold 0.8%, silver 97%, copper 1.7%

Description: Oval bowl with a coiled handle, the duck-head facing outwards and holding a cake in its beak. The niello inscription in the bowl reads DEIFAVANDICROSE.

Discussion: General parallels are cited under **50** and in Chapter 5. The inscription is discussed in Chapter 6; it is the only one with the CROSE element.

Nos **52–56** are cake-holding ducks; this feature is also discussed in Chapter 5.

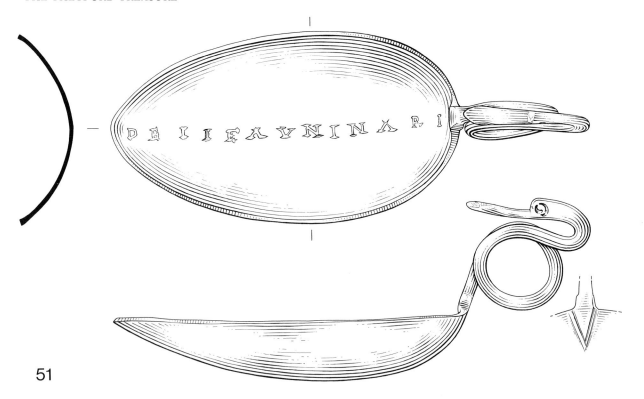

51

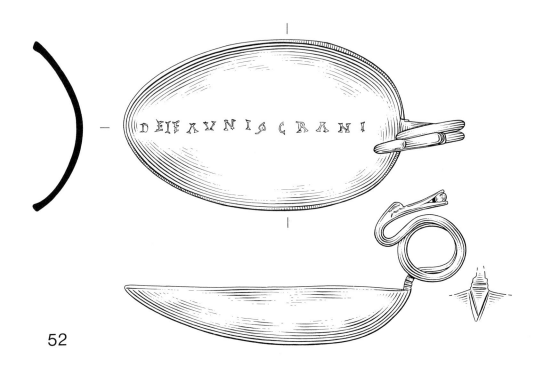

52

Fig. 26

110

53

DEIFAVANDICROSE

54

DEIFAVMEDVGENI

Fig. 27

55

DEI FAVNIAVSECI

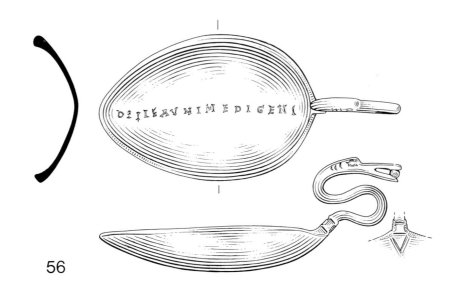

56

DEIIFAVNIMEDIGENI

Fig. 28

112

54 Inscribed silver spoon

Duck-handled silver spoon with niello inscription
DEIFAVMEDVGENI in the bowl.
Measurements: L 10.4 cm; bowl L 7.1 cm; w 4.8 cm; wt 26.7 g.
Metal (SQ): *handle* gold 1.2%, silver 97%, copper 1.5%

Description: Oval, slightly keeled bowl with a coiled handled
and a duck-head facing outwards, a cake in its beak. The head
is well modelled, with neatly drawn eyes. The niello inscription in the bowl reads DEIFAVMEDVGENI.

Discussion: General parallels are cited under **50** and in Chapter
5. The inscription is discussed in Chapter 6; versions of the
name Medugenus are found on spoons **56**, **71** and **79**.

  Nos **52–56** are cake-holding ducks; the feature is discussed
in Chapter 5.

55 Inscribed silver spoon

Duck-handled silver spoon with niello inscription
DEIFAVNIAVSECI in the bowl.
Measurements: L 9.4 cm; bowl L 7.5 cm; w 4.6 cm; wt 27.3 g.
Metal (SQ): *handle* gold 0.9%, silver 98%, copper 1.3%

Description: Oval bowl with a coiled handle and an outward-
facing duck-head holding a cake in its beak. Within the bowl
is the niello inscription DEIFAVNIAVSECI.

Discussion: General parallels are cited under **50** and in Chapter
5. The inscription is discussed in Chapter 6. There is a similar
inscription on the long-handed spoon **73**.

  Nos **52–56** are cake-holding ducks; the feature is discussed
in Chapter 5.

56 Inscribed silver spoon

Duck-handled silver spoon with niello inscription
DEIIFAVNIMEDIGENI in the bowl.
Measurements: L 8.5 cm; bowl L 6.3 cm, w 4.1 cm; wt 26.3 g.
Metal (QU): *bowl* gold 0.6%, silver 96.3%, copper 2.8%, lead
0.3%, zinc <0.1%; (QU): *handle* gold 0.7%, silver 95.9%,
copper 3.2% lead 0.3%, zinc <0.1%

Description: An oval, keeled bowl, with an s-shaped handle, the
duck's head facing outwards and holding a cake in its beak.
The niello inscription in the bowl is neatly lettered, and reads
DEIIFAVNIMEDIGENI.

Discussion: General parallels are cited under **50** and in Chapter
5. The inscription is discussed in Chapter 6. Versions of the
name Medugenus are also found on **54**, **71**, and **79**. Nos **52**,
53, **54** and **55** also have ducks holding cakes in their beaks,
a feature discussed further in Chapter 5.

  This spoon is the only one amongst the Thetford duck-
handled spoons which has a simple s-shaped handle rather
than the fully coiled form. The bowl is slightly more pointed
and tapered than any of the others.

57 Inscribed silver spoon

Duck-handled silver spoon with niello inscription
DEIFAVBLOTVGI in the bowl.
Measurements: L 9.2 cm; bowl L 7.0 cm; w 4.6 cm; wt 28.9 g.
Metal (SQ): *handle* gold 0.8%, silver 98%, copper 1.7%

Description: Oval, very slightly keeled bowl with a coiled
handle and an outward-facing duck-head. The latter has a
slender upcurved beak. The niello inscription in the bowl
reads DEIFAVBLOTVGI.

Discussion: General parallels are cited under **50** and in Chapter
5. The inscription is discussed in Chapter 6. There are several
related inscriptions in the hoard, on spoons **64**, **75**, **78** and
80.

58 Inscribed silver spoon

Duck-handled silver spoon with niello inscription
DEOFAVNISATERNIO in the bowl.
Measurements: L 9.5 cm; bowl L 7.4 cm; w 4.5 cm; wt 25.2 g.
Metal (SQ): *handle* gold 0.9%, silver 98%, copper 1.2%

Description: Oval, keeled bowl, the coiled handle having a
duck-head facing inwards. The inscription in the bowl reads
DEOFAVNISATERNIO.

Discussion: General parallels are cited under **50** and in Chapter
5. The inscription is discussed in Chapter 6. It is not closely
related to any of the other inscriptions.

59 Inscribed silver spoon

Duck-handled silver spoon with the inscription VTI ⊄ FELIX in
the bowl.
Measurements: L 11.5 cm; bowl L 7.6 cm; w 4.4 cm; ;wt 41.3 g.
Metal (SQ): *bowl* gold 0.5%, silver 95%, copper 3.5%; (SQ)
handle gold 0.5%, silver 97%, copper 1.9%

Description: Oval, shallow, keeled bowl with a coiled handle
and a long duck-head terminal facing inwards. No niello now
remains in the inscription, which reads VTI ⊄ FELIX.

Discussion: General parallels are cited under **50** and in Chapter
5. The inscription is discussed in Chapter 6; it is a unique
one in the group.

  This is one of the three largest and heaviest spoons in the
treasure, and the modelling of the duck's head is unusually
bold.

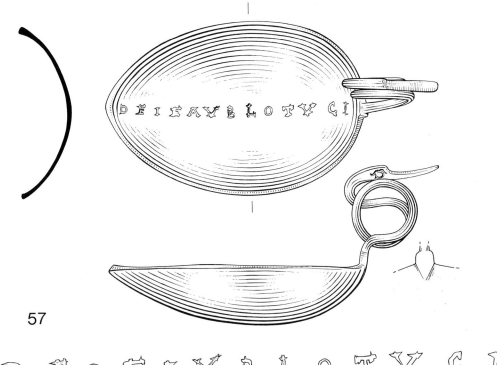

57

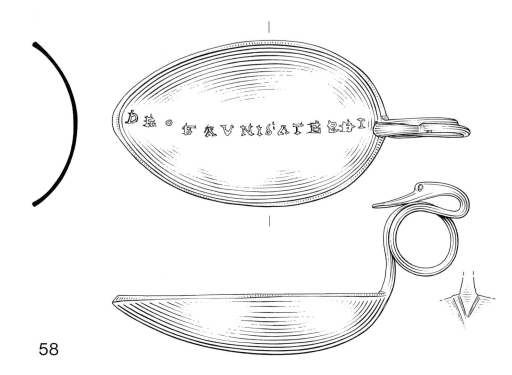

58

Fig. 29

114

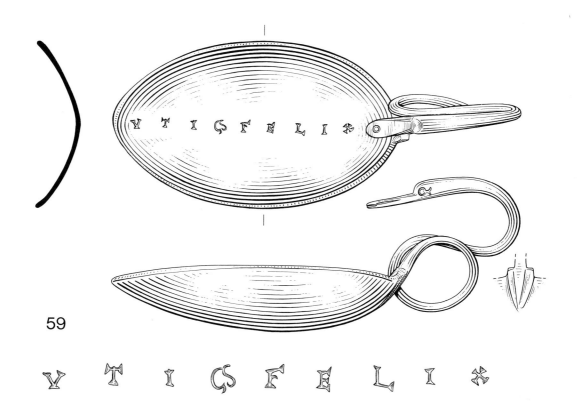

59

V T I Ç F E L I ✱

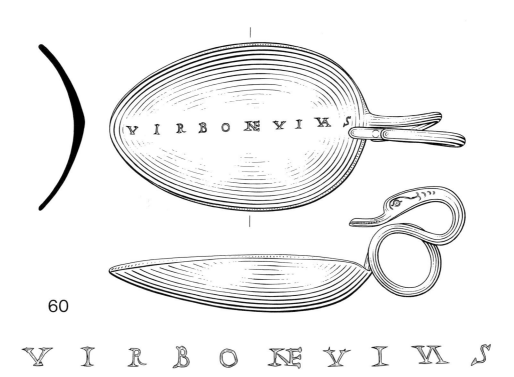

60

V I R B O N E V I V S

Fig. 30

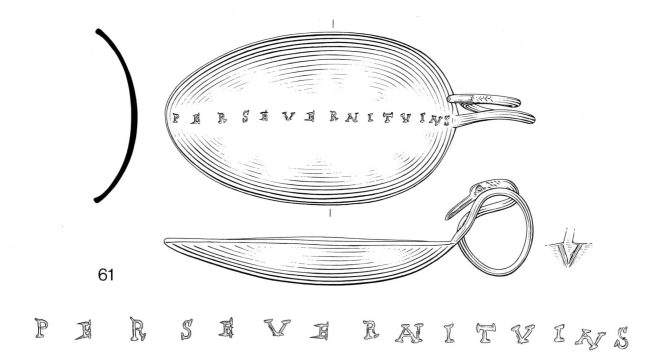

61

PERSEVERAITVIAS

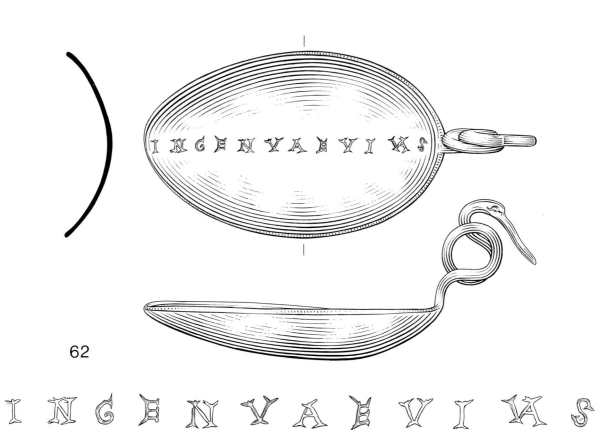

62

INGENVAEVIAS

Fig. 31

60 Inscribed silver spoon

Duck-handled silver spoon with the inscription VIRBONEVIVAS in the bowl.
Measurements: L 9.8 cm; bowl L 7.0 cm, w 4.5 cm; WT 37.5 g.
Metal (SQ): *handle* gold 0.5%, silver 97%, copper 2.0%

Description: Oval, keeled bowl with an elegantly coiled handle and an inward-facing duck's-head terminal. The head is particularly skillfully modelled, with teeth, 'eyebrows' and other details picked out in niello, and the beak given an upward curve. The inscription, which has lost its niello infill, is also very neatly lettered. It reads VIRBONEVIVAS.

Discussion: General parallels are cited under 50 and in Chapter 5. The inscription is discussed in Chapter 6: it has no parallel in the Thetford hoard. Though not as heavy as some of the spoons, 60 is well above the one-ounce standard of most of the duck-handled spoons, and is remarkable for its attractive workmanship, especially in the rendering of the bird's head.

61 Inscribed silver spoon

Duck-handled silver spoon with niello inscription PERSEVERAVITVIVAS in the bowl.
Measurements: L 10.2 cm; L 8.1 cm; w 4.6 cm; WT 26.1 g. Metal (SQ): *handle* gold 0.9%, silver 96%, copper 3.0%

Description: Oval bowl, the handle thin, slightly distorted and coiled, with an inward-facing duck-head. Details of the head are lightly incised. The niello inscription in the bowl reads PERSEVERAVITVIVAS.

Discussion: General parallels are cited under 50 and in Chapter 5. The inscription, which is a unique one, is discussed in Chapter 6.

The bird's head on this spoon has a drooping beak, very unlike, for example, 57 and 60.

62 Inscribed silver spoon

Duck-handled silver spoon with the niello inscription INGENVAEVIVAS in the bowl.
Measurements: L 11.0 cm; bowl L 8.3 cm; w 5.0 cm; WT 41.7 g.
Metal (SQ): *handle* gold 0.8%, silver 99%, copper 0.6%

Description: An oval bowl with a tightly-coiled handle terminating in an outward-facing duck-head whose beak appears to be slightly bent and damaged. The eye is deeply incised. The niello inscription in the bowl, in a florid style, reads INGENVAEVIVAS.

Discussion: General parallels are cited under 50 and in Chapter 5. The inscription is discussed in Chapter 6. This spoon is another of the three heavy examples in the hoard.

63 Inscribed silver spoon

Duck-handled silver spoon with niello inscription PRIMIGENIAVIVAS in the bowl.
Measurements: L 9.7 cm; bowl L 6.6 cm; w 4.5 cm; WT 27.4 g.
Metal (SQ): *bowl* gold 0.6%, silver 95%, copper 4.0%; (SQ): *handle* gold 0.6%, silver 96%, copper 3.3%

Description: Oval bowl and coiled handle with an outward-facing duck-head. The bird has a straight beak. The niello inscription, in a style similar to that of 62, reads PRIMIGENIAVIVAS.

Discussion: General parallels are cited under 50 and in Chapter 5. The inscription is discussed in Chapter 6; it is the only one in the hoard with this name.

64 Inscribed silver spoon

Duck-handled silver spoon with the niello inscription BLO on the handle.
Measurements: L 10.0 cm; bowl L 7.8 cm; w 4.8 cm; WT 27.2 g.
Metal (SQ): *bowl* gold 0.6%, silver 98%, copper 1.6% (SQ): *handle* gold 0.8%, silver 97%, copper 1.4%

Description: The oval bowl is slightly keeled, and the coiled handle has a leaf motif modelled where it joins the bowl. The duck-head terminal, facing outwards, is well modelled, with details inlaid in niello, and the beak curving upwards, though the head itself looks down a little. On the left side of the bird's head behind the eye is an inscription inlaid in niello, BLO, retrograde, and upside-down in relation to the bird.

Discussion: General paralles are cited under 50 and in Chapter 5. The inscription is discussed in Chapter 6. It relates to the 'Blotugus' inscriptions also found on spoons 57, 75, 78 and 80.

This spoon is remarkable in being the only one of the duck-handled type which is inscribed on the handle. Handle inscriptions occur on several of the long-handled spoons, but their form is better suited to this placing of the inscription. It is also noteworthy that the inscription on 64 is the only one written in reverse, though it is impossible to judge whether this has any significance.

65 Silver spoon

Duck-handled silver spoon.
Measurements: L 9.5 cm; bowl L 7.6 cm; w 5.1 cm; WT 36.3 g.
Metal (SQ): *handle* gold 0.8%, silver 98%, copper 1.5%

Description: A keeled, broad oval bowl with a coiled handle and an inward-facing duck-head. The bird's beak is bent down. There is no inscription on the spoon.

Discussion: General parallels are cited under 50 and in Chapter 5. This spoon is the only uninscribed specimen amongst the duck-handled type. One of the long-handled spoons, 67, also lacks an inscription, though it has incised decoration.

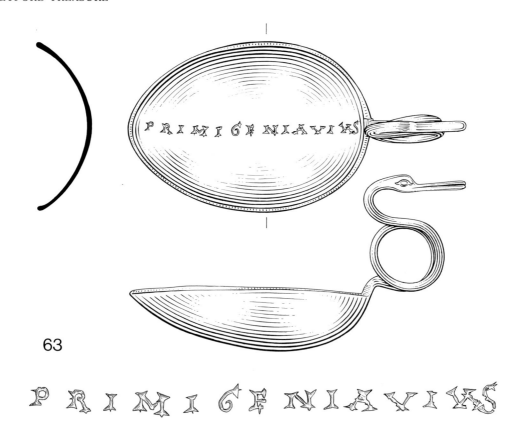

63

PRIMIGENIAVINS

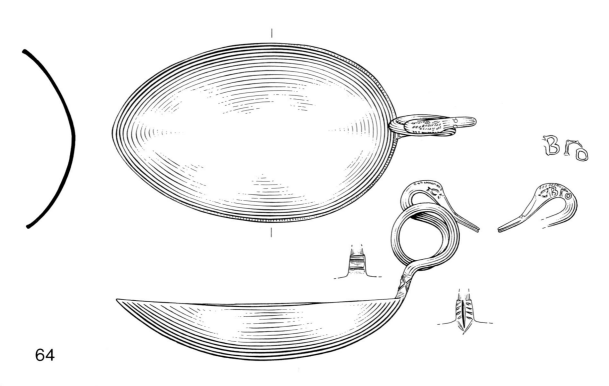

64

Fig. 32

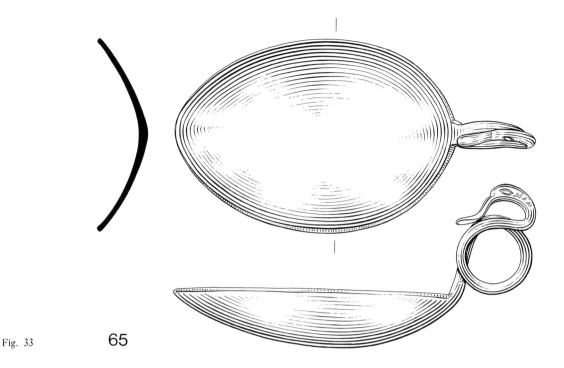

Fig. 33   **65**

66   The Panther spoon

Long-handled silver spoon with parcel-gilt decoration in the bowl depicting a panther, and an inscription in niello on the handle reading DEIIFAVNINARI.
Measurements: L 17.7 cm; bowl L 5.2 cm; w 3.3 cm; wт 22.3 g. Metal (QU): *bowl* gold 0.9%, silver 96.9%, copper 1.8%, lead 0.4%, zinc < 0.1%; (QU): *handle* gold 0.6%, silver 95.2%, copper 3.9%, lead 0.4%, zinc < 0.1%

Description: The bowl is a slightly pointed oval, keeled on the underside. It is decorated with a panther springing to the left, executed in gilding and fine surface chasing. Behind the panther is small three-branched tree, and round the rim of the bowl is a narrow gilt border. The handle offset is a simple scroll, and the handle itself, tapering to a point, is square-sectioned nearest the bowl and bevelled towards the tip. On its upper surface is the niello inscription DEIIFAVNINARI.

Discussion: Spoons of this size with oval or pear-shaped bowls and long tapering handles, attached by decorative offsets, are the standard Roman spoon type of the fourth century. In Britain alone, they occur in numerous hoards, sometimes associated with the duck-handled large spoons, sometimes alone. General parallels and typology are discussed in Chapter 5. For the Thetford spoons, the best parallels are found in the Canterbury hoard (Painter 1965), the Dorchester-on-Thames hoard (Kent and Painter 1977, nos 109–113), the Dorchester (Dorset) group (Dalton 1922) and the Little Horwood spoon (Waugh 1966).

Within the Thetford Treasure, the obvious and outstanding parallel for **66** is the Triton spoon, **50**. Not only is the bowl shape the same, albeit smaller, but the inscription is closely related, DEINARI on **50** and DEIIFAVNINARI on **66**, and the decorative style of the gilded decoration is the same, including the border of gilding around the rim of the bowl. The stylistic link between these two spoons brings the duck-handled and long-handled spoons in the Thetford assemblage together.

Parallels for gilded spoons are quoted in the discussion of spoon **50**. We do not know of another long-handled fourth-century spoon with such elaborate parcel-gilt ornament as this one. In contrast to the very detailed decoration, the form of **66** is relatively plain, with a simple scroll offset and a plain handle without mouldings or twisted effects. The pair of spoons inscribed RESTITVTI (**77** and **78**) are of virtually the same form, apart from the tip of the bowl. The panther motif must be regarded as overtly Bacchic, since this animal is so closely associated with the god. The inscription includes the name of Faunus, and this spoon is therefore part of the evidence for seeing the Faunus cult in the fourth century as a part of the broader Bacchic one. The inscription is fully discussed in Chapter 6.

67   The Fish spoon

Silver spoon decorated in the bowl with a fish and a plant.
Measurements: L 17.8 cm; bowl L 5.0 cm; w 3.7 cm; wт 24.3 g. Metal (SQ): *bowl* gold 0.3%, silver 98%, copper 1%; (SQ): *handle* gold 0.4%, silver 98%, copper 0.8%

Description: The bowl is a broad and shallow oval with a 'rat-tail' on the underside. The handle offset is a simple scroll which is open, and the handle is plain. Within the bowl is incised a fish approaching a feathery plant-like motif. The

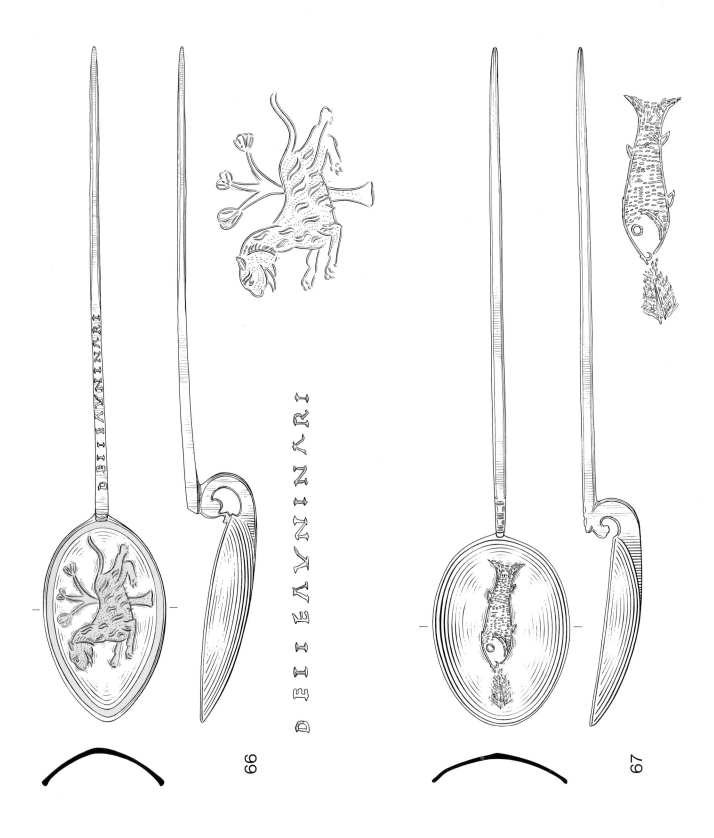

Fig. 34

scales of the fish are depicted, as are its gill-cover, two dorsal fins (or a dorsal and adipose), and a ventral or pectoral and anal fin.

Discussion: For a general discussion of the typology of spoons, see Chapter 5. Within the Thetford Treasure, this spoon stands out in several respects. It is one of only two spoons without an inscription (the other is the duck-handled spoon **65**); its decoration, though depicting an animal, is not in a very similar style to the decoration of the other 'picture' spoons, **50** and **66**; and its form is unique, particularly the bowl, which is noticeably broader and shallower than any other spoon in the assemblage.

Fishes are found as decorative motifs on several Roman spoons, e.g. one from Dorchester (Dorset), Traprain Law, Loché, and Canoscio (all illustrated in Milojčić 1968, Abb. 9) and on an unprovenanced spoon which is parcel-gilt (Potter, *forthcoming*). The fish on **67** is depicted with greater care and realism than any of these. Naturally, it has been assumed that the fish is intended as a Christian symbol where it occurs on spoons, but while this may sometimes be the case, there is no reason to suppose it was invariably so, and in the present instance, it is exceedingly unlikely. We do not have any suggestions for the significance of the plant, which is also paralleled on the last-mentioned unprovenanced spoon. There seems to be some slight evidence that the open scroll offset is an earlier form than the fully closed one, since it is merely a development from the open offset of pre-fourth-century types. Certainly it is not a characteristically late form like the zoomorphic offset seen in six of the Thetford spoons.

68   Inscribed silver spoon

Silver spoon inscribed SILVIOLAVIVAS in the bowl.

Measurements: L 18. cm; bowl L 5.3 cm; w 3.3 cm; wT 25.0 g. Metal (sQ) *handle* gold 0.7%, silver 98%, copper 1.6%

Description: Oval, keeled bowl, inscribed SILVIOLAVIVAS. Niello seems to have been lost from the inscription. The handle offset is in the form of a small, well-modelled animal head, probably feline. The main part of the handle is incised in a lattice pattern on a basically square-sectioned rod, to produce a chip-carved effect. The tapering tip of the handle is plain, and the different areas are demarcated by baluster mouldings.

Discussion: For general parallels, see Chapter 5 and **66**. The inscription is discussed in Chapter 6: it is virtually the same as that on **69**, but in form the spoon is a pair to **72**.

The zoomorphic handle offset relates this spoon to **69**, **70**, **71**, **72** and **75**. The style of these animal heads is rather more accomplished and realistic than that of the comparable examples from Canterbury, Dorchester-on-Thames and other sites.

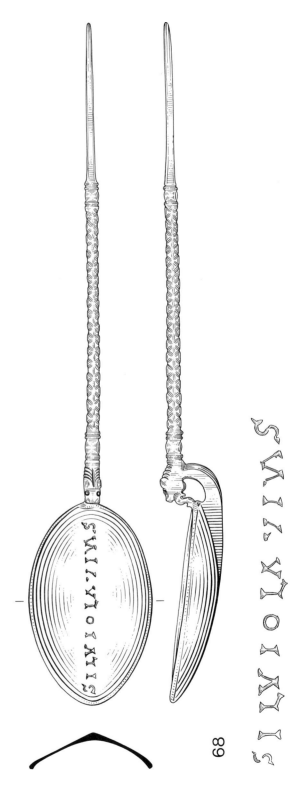

Fig. 35

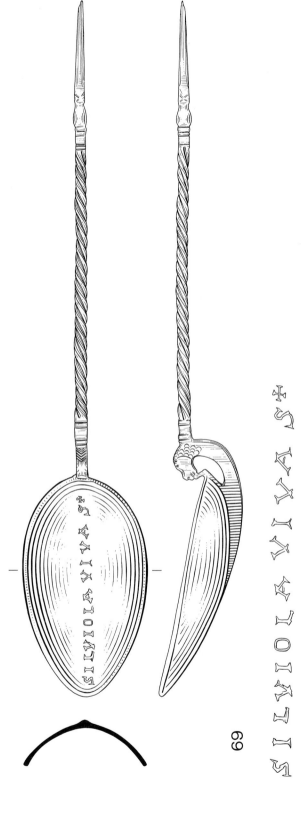

Fig. 36

69 Inscribed silver spoon

Silver spoon with niello inscription in the bowl reading SILVIOLAVIVAS +.
Measurements: L 18.4 cm; bowl L 5.8 cm; W 3.4 cm; WT 26.2 g.
Metal (SQ): *handle* gold 1.3%, silver 98%, copper 0.6%

Description: A narrow oval bowl with a 'rat-tail' on the underside. The niello inscription reads SILVIOAVIVAS +. The handle offset is in the form of a horse's head, and the main part of the handle is a twisted rod, divided by baluster mouldings from the plain tapered tip.

Discussion: For general parallels, see Chapter 5 and **66**, and for the inscription, Chapter 6. No.**69** has a very similar inscription. The animal heads are found on five other spoons (see **68** for details).

70 Inscribed silver spoon

Silver spoon inscribed AVSPICIVIVAS in the bowl.
Measurements: L 14.5 cm; bowl L 4.5 cm; W 3.0 cm; WT 18.1 g.
Metal (SQ): *handle* gold 1.8%, silver 96%, copper 2.3%

Description: A small oval bowl, with the inscription AVSPICIVIVAS. The niello inlay is lost. The handle offset is in the form of a simple and stylised animal head, without any incised detail, and the main part of the handle is in the 'chip-carved' style: the tapered tip of the handle is broken, making this spoon shorter and lighter than the others in the treasure.

Discussion: For general parallels, see Chapter 5 and **66**. The inscription is discussed in Chapter 6. The other spoons with zoomorphic offset are listed under **68**.

71 Inscribed silver spoon

Silver spoon with niello inscription in the bowl, reading DEIFAVMEDIGENI.
Measurements: L 17.3 cm; bowl L 5.0 cm; W 3.3 cm; WT 24.2 g.
Metal (SQ): *bowl* gold 0.5%, silver 98%, copper 1.4%; (SQ): *handle* gold 0.8%, silver 98%, copper 0.3%

Description: Oval bowl with a 'rat-tail' on the underside. The niello inscription reads DEIFAVMEDIGENI. The handle offset is a zoomorphic one, and the handle is in the 'chip-carved' style.

Discussion: For general parallels, see Chapter 5 and **66**. The inscription is discussed in Chapter 6: it is related to the other Medugenus inscriptions in the group, on spoons **5**, **56** and **79**, and is in fact identical with that on **56**.
    The other spoons with zoomorphic offsets are listed in the dicussion of **68**.

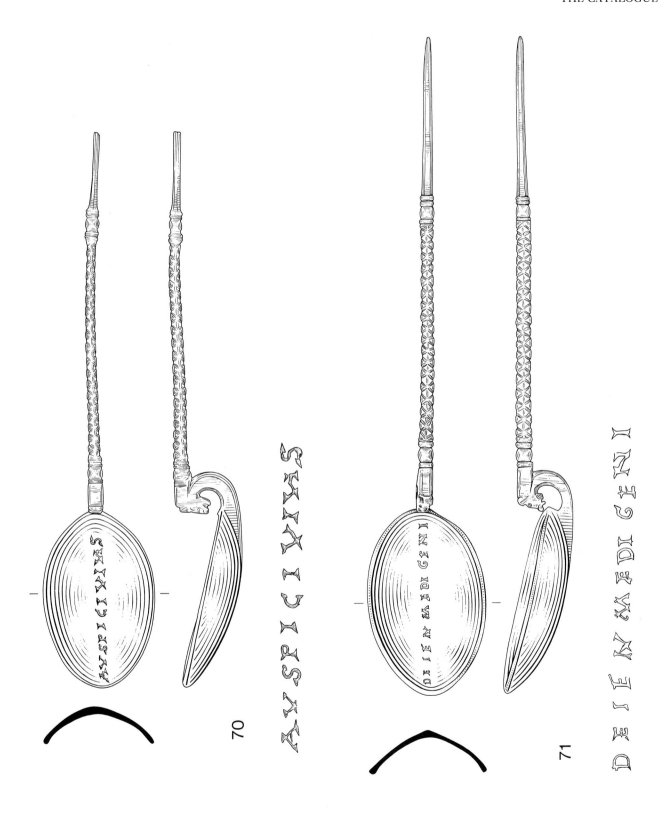

Fig. 37

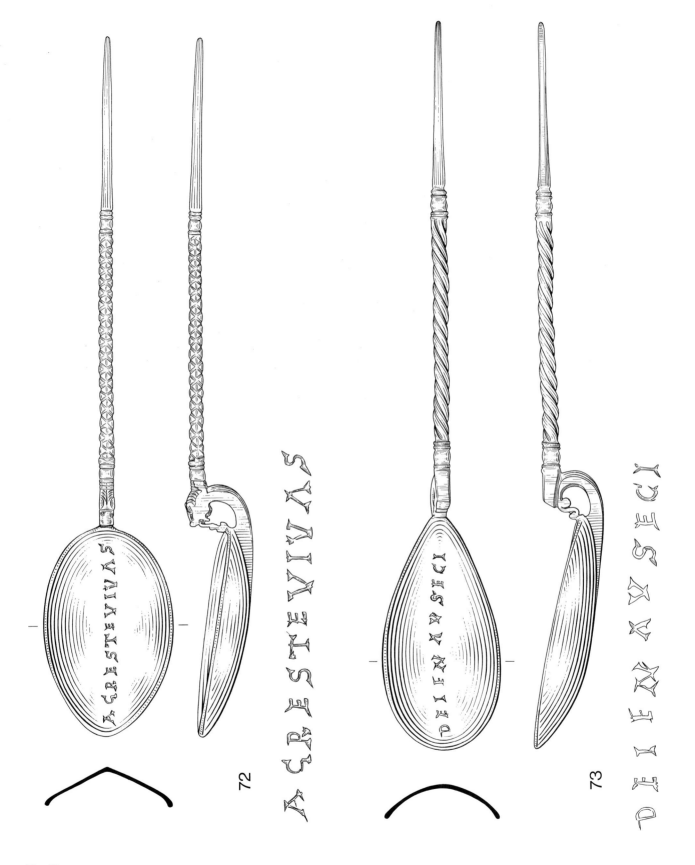

Fig. 38

72   Inscribed silver spoons

Silver spoon inscribed AGRESTEVIVAS in the bowl.
Measurements: L 18.3 cm; bowl L 5.3 cm; w 3.5 cm; WT 24.2 g.
Metal (SQ): *handle* gold 0.8%, silver 97%, copper 2.2%

Description: An oval bowl with a 'rat-tail' beneath, inscribed
AGRESTEVIVAS. The zoomorphic offset is of the same form as
that on spoon **68**, and the handle has 'chip-carved' ornament,
with a plain tapered tip.

Discussion: For general parallels, see Chapter 5 and **66**, and
for the inscription, see Chapter 6. Though the inscription is
different, this spoon may be regarded as a pair to **68**. The
animal heads are discussed under **68**.

73   Inscribed silver spoon

Silver spoon with niello inscription in the bowl reading
DEIFAVAVSECI.
Measurements: L 19.3 cm; bowl L 6.1 cm; w 3.2 cm; WT 27.7 g.
Metal (SQ): *handle* gold 0.7%, silver 97%, copper 1.7%

Description: A narrow pear-shaped bowl with a 'rat-tail' on the
underside. The niello inscription reads DEIFAVAVSECI, and the
handle offset is of a simple scroll form. The main part of the
handle is twisted.

Discussion: For general parallels see Chapter 5 and **66**. The
inscription is discussed in Chapter 6. This spoon may be
regarded as a pair in its form to **74**; the handle twists in the
opposite direction, but the shape and the dimensions and
weight are extremely close. The metal composition is also
almost identical.

74   Inscribed silver spoon

Silver spoon with niello inscription in the bowl reading
DEIFAVNI ♭ CRANI.
Measurements: L 19.5 cm; bowl L 6.0 cm; w 3.2 cm; WT 27.1 g.
Metal (SQ): *handle* gold 0.9%, silver 97%, copper 1.7%

Description: A narrow pear-shaped bowl with a marked keel.
The niello inscription reads DEIFAVNI ♭ CRANI. The handle offset is a simple scroll, and the main part of the handle is
twisted.

Discussion: For general parallels, see Chapter 5 and **66**. The
inscription is discussed in Chapter 6; it is the same as that
on spoon **52**, and probably also connected with that on **82**.
In form, size and metal composition, this spoon is clearly a
pair to **73**.

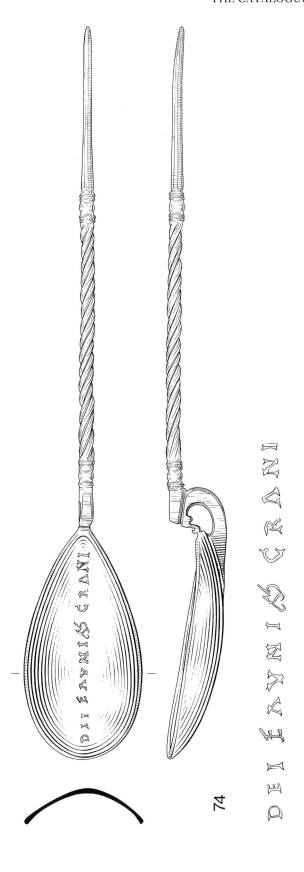

Fig. 39

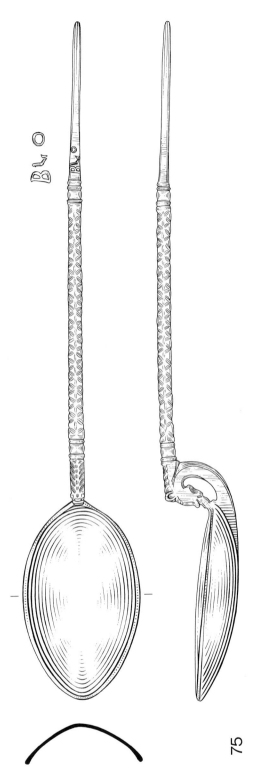

Fig. 40

75 Inscribed silver spoon

Silver spoon with the inscription BLO on the tapered end of the handle.
Measurements: L 18.0 cm; bowl L 5.2 cm; w 3.2 cm; WT 25.6 g.
Metal (QU): *bowl* gold 0.5%, silver 97.2%, copper 2.0%, lead 0.3%, zinc <0.1%: (QU): *handle* gold 0.7%, silver 97.3%, copper 1.7%, lead 0.3%, zinc <0.1%

Description: A slightly pointed oval bowl, keeled on the underside. The handle offset is a zoomorphic one, a horse-head, and the handle decorated in 'chip-carving'. The inscription, inlaid in niello, is on the plain tapered handle terminal nearest the decorated section; it reads BLO.

Discussion: For general parallels, see Chapter 5 and **66**. The inscription is discussed in Chapter 6; it is the same as that on spoons **64** and **80**, and the name concerned is obviously Blotugus, versions of which also appear on spoons **57** and **78**. The horse-head offset is similar to that on **69**.

76 Inscribed silver spoon

Plain silver spoon with the inscription RESTITVTI in niello on the handle.
Measurements: L 17.3 cm; bowl L 5.1 cm; w 3.4 cm; WT 25.9 g.
Metal (SQ): *handle* gold 1.3%, silver 97%, copper 1.3%

Description: A plain oval bowl with a 'rat-tail' beneath. The handle offset is a simple scroll, and the handle is plain and tapered, with a niello inscription near the bowl reading RESTITVTI. There is a small modern break in the bowl.

Discussion: For general parallels, see Chapter 5 and **66**. The inscription is discussed in Chapter 6. It is the same as that on **77**, to which this spoon is in every respect a pair.

77 Inscribed silver spoon

Plain silver spoon with the inscription RESTITVTI in niello on the handle.
Measurements: L 17.1 cm; bowl L 5.2 cm; w 3.3 cm; WT 27.0 g.
Metal (SQ): *handle* gold 0.6%, silver 98%, copper 1.2%

Description: As for **76**, except that this spoon is undamaged.

Discussion: This spoon is a pair to **76**.

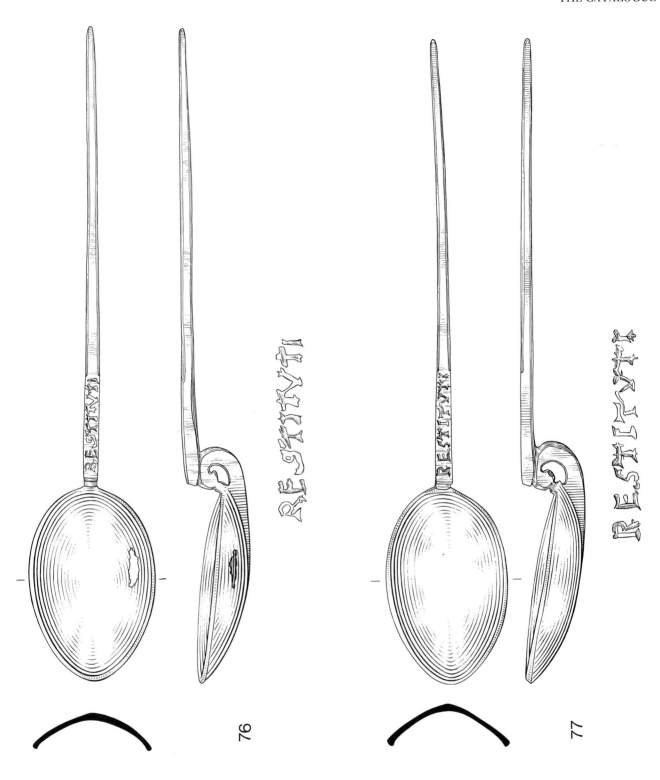

Fig. 41

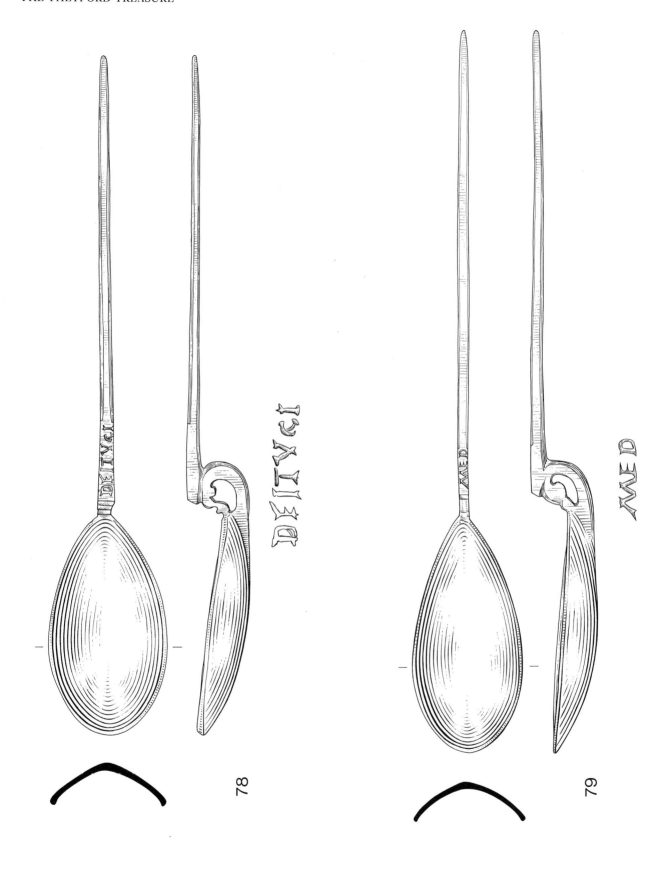

Fig. 42

78   Inscribed silver spoon

Silver spoon with a niello inscription on the handle reading
DEITVCI.
Measurements: L 18.1 cm; bowl L 5.8 cm; W 3.2 cm; WT 25.8 g.
Metal (SQ): *handle* gold 0.8%, silver 97%, copper 1.7%

Description: The bowl is pear-shaped with a 'rat-tail' on the
underside. The handle offset is in the form of a scroll, and
the tapered handle is plain, inscribed in niello near the bowl
DEITVCI.

Discussion: For general parallels, see Chapter 5 and **66**. The
inscription is discussed in Chapter 6; the spoons with versions
of the name Blotugus are listed under **57**. Nos **79** and **80** are
of the same form as this spoon, with pear-shaped bowls and
plain handles.

79   Inscribed silver spoon

Silver spoon inscribed MED on the handle.
Measurements: L 19.2 cm; bowl L 6.2 cm; W 3.0 cm; WT 26.0 g.
Metal (SQ): *handle* gold 0.8%, silver 97.5%, copper 1.8%

Description: A keeled, pear-shaped bowl, with a plain scroll
handle offset and an undecorated tapered handle. The inscription is on the handle near the bowl, and reads MED.

Discussion: For general parallels, see Chapter 5 and **66**, and
for the inscription, see Chapter 6. The inscription belongs to
the Medugenus group, which also includes **54**, **56**, and **71**.
The form of the spoon is close to **78** and **80**.

80   Inscribed silver spoon

Silver spoon with the niello inscription BLO on the handle.
Measurements: L 17.7 cm; bowl L 5.8 cm; W 3.0 cm; WT 24.5 g.
Metal (QU): *bowl* gold 0.5%, silver 96.6%, copper 2.6%, lead
0.3%, zinc <0.1%; (QU): *handle* gold 0.5%, silver 96.8%,
copper 2.3%, lead 0.3%, zinc <0.1%

Description: A pear-shaped bowl with a simple scroll offset and
a plain tapered handle, inscribed in niello near the bowl with
BLO.

Discussion: For general parallels, see Chapter 5 and **66**. The
inscription is discussed in Chapter 6; the inscriptions referring
to the name Blotugus are listed under **57**, and two other
spoons, **6** and **75** are inscribed BLO. The form of the spoon
is like that of **78** and **79**.

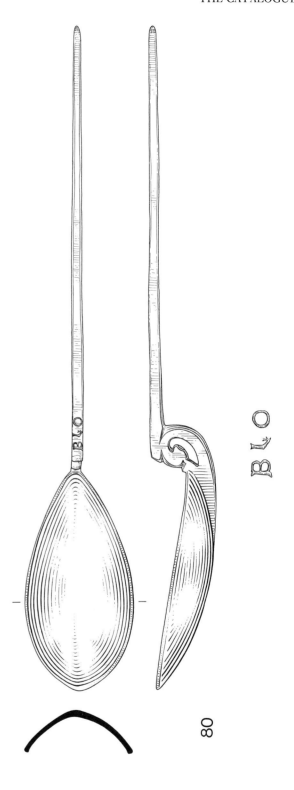

Fig. 43

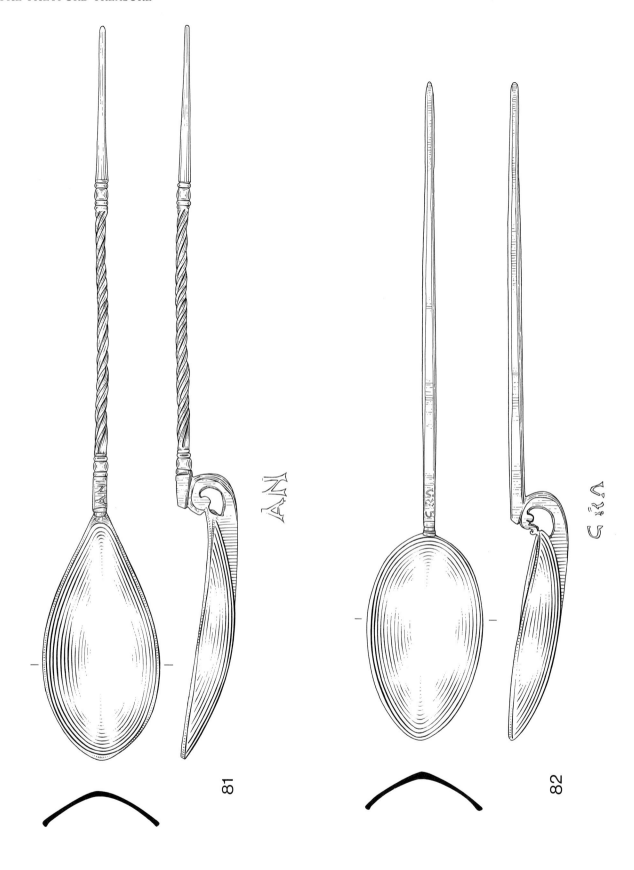

Fig. 44

81 Inscribed silver spoon

Silver spoon with the inscription AN in niello on the handle.
Measurements: L 19.4 cm; bowl L 6.5 cm; W 3.2 cm; WT 24.8 g.
Metal (SQ): *handle* gold 1.1%, silver 97%, copper 1.4%

Description: The bowl is pear-shaped, with a 'rat-tail' beneath.
The handle offset is a scroll, and the main part of the handle
is twisted, with the usual mouldings and pointed tip. The
niello inscription is on the small flat area which is the upper
section of the offset, and reads AN.

Discussion: For general parallels, see Chapter 5 and **66**. The
inscription is discussed in Chapter 6. The form of the spoon
is like that of **73** and **74**, but they are inscribed in the bowl.

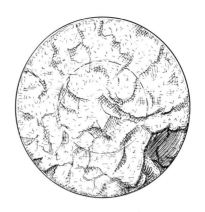

82 Inscribed silver spoon

Silver spoon with niello inscription GRA on the handle.
Measurements: L 17.2 cm; bowl L 5.5 cm; W 3.2 cm; WT 25.3 g.
Metal (SQ): *handle* gold 1.1%, silver 97%, copper 2.3%

Description: The bowl is oval with a 'rat-tail' beneath. The offset is a scroll, and the handle is plain and tapered, inscribed
in niello nearest the bowl with GRA.

Discussion: For general parallels see Chapter 5 and **66**; it is
connected with the inscriptions on **52** and **74**. The form of
the spoon matches the pair **76** and **77**.

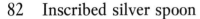

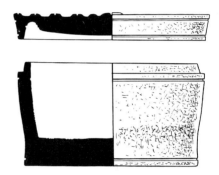

83 Shale box

Round shale box with lid.
Measurements: D (base) 9.7 cm; D (rim) 10.0 cm; D (lid)
10.5 cm; H of box 4.8 cm; H with lid 6.2 cm; average thickness
c. 0.6 cm; depth (interior) *c.* 3.5 cm.

Description: Turned circular shale box with a raised lid-seating.
The sides of the box are very slightly waisted. On the
base, the flaking of the surface has revealed part of a fossil
impression, an ammonite, while the interior base shows slight
turning grooves. The lid is ornamented with turned decoration
consisting of concentric ridges and grooves (six ridges).

Discussion: The only British parallel appears to be from Verulamium, from a context dated AD 350–41 + (Frere 1972,
fig. 57, no. 228). See full discussion, Chapter 4.

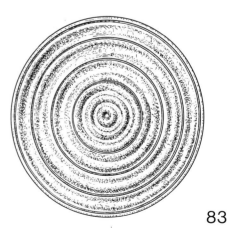

83

Fig. 45

Bibliography

ANASTASIADIS, E. 1950. Bronze welding, riveting and wiremaking by the Ancient Greeks', *Metal Progress,* Sept. 1950, pp. 322–4.

ANON. 1846. *Arch. Journal* 3, pp. 162–3.

ARCHER, S. 1979. 'Late Roman gold and silver coin hoards in Britain: a gazetteer', in *The End of Roman Britain* (ed. P. J. Casey), British Archaeological Reports 71, pp. 29–64.

ARRHENIUS, B. 1971. 'Granatschmuck und Gemmen aus nordischen Funden des frühen Mittelalters', *Acta Universitas Stockholmiensis,* Studies in North European Archaeology, Series B, Stockholm.

BARATTE, F. 1979. 'La Plaque de Ceinture du Coudray', *Monuments et Mémoires,* Fondation Eugene Piot, 62, p. 43.

BASTIEN, PIERRE AND METZGER, CATHERINE. 1977. *Le Trésor de Beaurains,* Wetteren.

BATESON, J. D. 1973. 'Roman material from Ireland: a reconsideration', *Proc. Royal Irish Acad.* 73, pp. 21–97.

BATHURST, W. H. 1879. *Roman Antiquities at Lydney Park,* London.

BATTKE, HEINZ. 1953 *Geschichte des Ringes,* Baden-Baden.

BOARDMAN, JOHN 1964. *Greek Art,* Oxford.

BÖHME H. W. 1970. 'Löffelbeigabe in spätrömischen Gräbern nördlich der Alpen', *Jahrb. des römisch-germanisches Zentralmuseum, Mainz* 17, pp. 172–200.

BONNER, C. 1950. *Studies in Magical Amulets, chiefly Graeco-Egyptian,* Ann Arbor.

BRAILSFORD, J. 1964. *Guide of the Antiquities of Roman Britain,* London.

BRAILSFORD, J. 1975. *Early Celtic Masterpieces from Britain in the British Museum,* London.

BRAY, W. 1978. *The Gold of El Dorado,* London.

BULLINGER, HERMANN. 1969. *Spätantike Gurtelbeschläge, Typen, Herstellung, Trageweise und Datierung,* Brugge.

BURNETT, ANDREW and JOHNS, CATHERINE. 1979. 'The Whorlton (Yorks) Hoard in *Recent Coin Hoards from Roman Britain* (ed. R. A. G. Carson and A. M. Burnett), British Museum Occ. Pap. 5, London.

BUSHE-FOX, J. P. 1915. *Excavations at Hengistbury Head, in 1911–12,* Soc. of Ants. Res. Report 3.

BUSHE-FOXE, J. P. 1949. *Fourth Report on the Excavations of the Roman Fort at Richborough, Kent,* Soc. of Ants. Res. Report 16.

CABROL, F. and LECLERQ, H. 1914. *Dictionnaire d'archéologie chrétienne et de liturgie* 3, 3175–6 (S. V. *cuiller*).

CALEY, E. R. 1950. 'Fineness of gold coins of the Roman Empire', *The Numismatist* 63, Series 2, pp. 66–70.

CARROL, D. L. 1972. 'Wire drawing in antiquity', *American Journ. of Arch.* 76, pp. 321–79.

CARSON, R. A. G. 1976. 'Gold and silver coin hoards and the end of Roman Britain', in *The Classical Tradition: British Museum Yearbook I,* London, pp. 67–81.

CARSON, R. A. G. 1979. 'The Water Newton Hoard, 1974', in *Recent Coin Hoards from Roman Britain* (ed. R. A. G. Carson and A. M. Burnett), British Museum Occ. Pap. 5, London.

CASEY, P. J. 1979. 'Magnus Maximus in Britain', in *The End of Roman Britain,* (ed P. J. Casey), B. A. R. 71, pp. 66–79.

CATALOGUE. 1761. *Recueil d'Antiquités Egyptiennes, Étrusques, Grèques et Romaines,* Paris.

CATALOGUE 1911. *Collection De Clercq, Vol. 7: Les Bijoux et les Pierres Gravées* by A. de Ridder, Paris.

CATALOGUE 1912. *Catalogue of a Collection of Ancient Rings formed by the late E. Guilhou,* Paris.

CATALOGUE. 1947. *Early Christian and Byzantine Art,* Baltimore.

CATALOGUE. 1963. *Aus rheinischer Kunst und Kultur,* Bonn.

CATALOGUE. 1976. *Jewellery through 7000 Years,* London.

CATALOGUE. 1979, *Jewellery, Ancient to Modern,* Baltimore.

CHARLESWORTH, D. 1977. 'A Roman gold earring from Birdoswald', *Ant. J.* 57, p. 323.

CHARVET, J. 1863. *Notice sur des Monnaires et Bijoux antiques,* Paris.

CLARKE, G. 1979. *The Roman Cemetery at Lankhills,* Winchester Studies 3.

CLUTTERBUCK, J. C. 1870–3. *Proc. Soc. Ant.* 2nd Series (5), p. 321.

COMARMOND, A. 1844. *Description de l'Ecrin d'une Dame Romaine trouvé à Lyon en 1841,* Lyon.

COWELL, M. R. 1977. 'Energy dispersive X-ray fluorescence analysis of ancient gold alloys', *PACT* 1, pp. 76–85.

CUNLIFFE, B. 1964. *Winchester Excavations 1949–1960,* Winchester.

CUNLIFFE, B. 1971. *Excavations at Fishbourne, 1961–1969,* Soc. of Ants. Res. Report 26.

CURLE, A. O. 1923. *The Treasure of Traprain,* Glasgow.

DALTON, O. M. 1900. 'A Byzantine silver treasure from the district of Kerynia, Cyprus, now preserved in the British Museum', *Archaeologia* 57, pp. 159–74.

DALTON, O. M. 1901. *Catalogue of the Early Christian Antiquities and objects from the Christian East in the Department of British and Medieval Antiquities and Ethnography of the British Museum,* London.

DALTON, O. M. 1922. 'Roman spoons from Dorchester', *Ant. J.* 2, pp. 89–92.

DALTON, O. M. 1964. *The Treasure of the Oxus with other Examples of Early Oriental Metal-work (3rd edn),* London.

DASNOY, ANDRÉ 1968. La nécropole de Samson (IVe–VIe siècles)', *Annales de la Société Archéologique de Namur* 54, pp. 277–334.

DAVIES, H. F. 1936. 'The shale industries of Kimmeridge, Dorset' *Arch. J.* 93, pp. 200–19.

DOPPELFELD, O. 1960. 'Das fränkische Frauengrab unter dem Chor des Kölner Domes', *Germania* 38, pp. 89–113.

ECK, THEOPHILE. 1891. *Les deux Cimetières Gallo-romains de Vermand et de Saint-Quentin,* Paris.

EPPRECHT, W, and MUTZ, A. 1974/5. 'Gezogener römischer Draht', *Jahrb. der Schweiz. Gesellschaft für Ur- u. Frühgeschichte* 58, pp. 157–61.

EVANS, D. Ellis. 1967. *Gaulish Personal Names,* Oxford.

FLOURET, J., NICOLINI G., and METZGER C. 1981. Les Bijoux d'or Gallo-romains de l'Houmeau (Charente-Maritime)', *Gallia* 39, pp. 85–101.

FOLTZ, E. 1979. 'Einige Beobachtungen zu antiken Gold- und Silberschmiedetechniken', *Arch. Korrespondenzblatt* 9 (2), pp. 215–322.

FORTUM, C. DRURY. 1869. On some finger-rings of the Early Christian period', *Arch. J.* 26, pp. 137–48.

FORTNUM, C. DRURY. 1871. 'On Finger-rings of the Early Christian period', *Arch. J.* 28, pp. 266–92.

FORTNUM, C. DRURY. 1880, 'Notes on some of the Antique and Renaissance Gems and Jewels in Her Majesty's Collection at Windsor Castle', *Archaeologia* 45, pp. 1–28.

FRERE, S. S. 1972. *Verlamium Excavations, Vol. I,* Soc. of Ants. Res. Report 28.

FRERE, SHEPPARD. 1978. *Britannia: A History of Roman Britain* (2nd, revised, edn), London.

FURGER–GUNTI, A. 1978. 'Gezogener Draht an keltischen Fibeln des 1 Jahr. v Chr.', *Draht* 29(12), pp. 727–30.

GHIRSHMAN, R. 1969. *Sept Mille Ans d'Art en Iran,* Paris.

GIOVAGNOLI, D. E. 1935. 'Una collezione de vasi eucaristici scoperti a Canoscio', *Rivista di Archeologia Cristiana* 12, pp. 313–28.

GOUGH, R. 1789. *Britannia: or, A chorographical description of the flourishing kingdoms of England, Scotland, and Ireland, and the islands adjacent.* by W. Camden. Translated from the edition published in 1607, enlarged by the latest discoveries, London.

GREEN, B. 1979. 'Roman Coin Hoard from Thetford', *Norfolk Archaeology* 37, part 2, pp. 221–3.

GREIFENHAGEN, A. 1970. *Schmuckarbeiten in Edelmetall. Band I,* Berlin.

GREIFENHAGEN A. 1975. *Schmuckarbeiten in Edelmetall. Band II (Einzelstücke),* Berlin.

GRIERSON, P. 1964. 'Weights and Coinage', *Num. Chron.* Ser. 7 (4), pp.i–xvii.

GRÜNHAGEN, W. 1954. *Der Schatzfund von Gross Bodungen,* Römisch-germanische Forschungen Band 21, Berlin.

HABEREY, W. 1960. 'Römische Brandgräbergruppe an der Ecke Adolfstrasse/im Krausfeld zu Bonn', *Bonner Jahrb.* 160, p. 285.

HASSALL, MARK. 1981. 'Roman Britain in 1980; inscriptions' *Britannia* 12, pp. 389–93.

HAVERFIELD, F. 1914. 'Roman Silver in Northumberland', *J. R. S.* 4, pp. 1–12.

HAWKES, SONIA C., and DUNNING, G. C. 1961. 'Solders and Settlers in Britain, Fourth to Fifth Century', *Med. Arch.* 5, pp. 1–70.

HENIG, M. 1970. 'A new cameo from Lincolnshire', *Ant. J.* 50, part 2, p. 338.

HENIG, M. 1977. 'Death and the maiden: funerary symbolism in daily life', in *Roman Life and Art in Britain,* British Archaeological Reports 41, London, pp. 347–66.

HENIG, M. 1978. *A Corpus of Roman Engraved Gemstones from British Sites* (2nd edn) British Archaeological Reports 8, Oxford (1st edn 1974).

HENIG, M. 1981. 'Continuity and change in the design of Roman jewellery', in *The Roman West in the Third Century* (ed. A. King and M. Henig), British Archaelogical Reports, S. 109, pp. 127–43.

HENKEL, FRIEDRICH. 1913. *Die römischen Fingerringe der Rheinlande und der benachbarten Gebiete,* Berlin.

HEURGON, JACQUES. 1958. *Le Trésor de Ténès,* Paris.

HIGGINS, R. 1976. 'Jewellery', in *Roman Crafts* (ed. David Brown and Donald Strong), London.

HIGGINS, R. 1979. *The Aegina Treasure: an Archaelogical Mystery,* London.

HOLDER, A. 1891. *Alt-celtischer Sprachschatz,* vol. 1, A–H, Leipzig.

HOLDER, A. 1904. *Alt-celtischer Sprachschatz,* vol. 2, I–T, Leipzig.

HOLDER, A. 1907. *Alt-celtischer Sprachschatz,* vol. 3, U–V, Leipzig.

HUGHES, M. R. and HALL, J. A. 1979. 'X-ray fluorescence analysis of late Roman and Sassanian plate', *Journ. of Arch. Science* 6, pp. 321–44.

JACOBI, G. 1979. 'Drahtzieheisen der Latènezeit', *Germania* 57, pp. 111–15.

JITTA, A. N. Z–J., Peters, W. J. T., and Witteveen, A. M. 1973. *Description of the Collections in the Rijksmuseum G. M. Kam at Nijmegen; VII, The Figural Bronzes,* Nijmegen.

JOHNS, C. M. 1976. 'A Roman gold and emerald necklace from Cannon Street, London', *Ant. J.* 56, p. 247.

JOHNS, C. M. 1979a. Note on Roman necklace in A. Boddington and M. Rhodes, *Excavations at 48–50 Cannon Street, City of London, 1975',* London and Middx. Arch. Soc. Trans. 30 (1979), p. 22.

JOHNS, C. M. 1979b. 'Fragments of two Roman necklaces from Canterbury', *Ant. J.* 59, pp. 420–21.

JOHNS, C. M. 1981a. The Thetford Treasure; a major find of late Roman gold and silver', *Gold Bulletin* 14 (4), pp. 169–70.

JOHNS, C. M. 1981b. 'The Risley Park Silver Lanx: a lost antiquity from Roman Britain', *Ant. J.* 61 [1981], pp. 53–72.

JOHNS, C. M. 1982. 'A Roman spoon from Helpston, Cambridgeshire', *Britannia* 13, p. 309.

JOHNS, C. M., THOMPSON, F. H., and WAGSTAFF, P. 1980. 'The Wincle, Cheshire, hoard of Roman gold jewellery', *Ant. J.* 60, pp. 48–58.

JONES, A. H. M. 1964. *The Later Roman Empire,* Oxford.

KENT, J. P. C. 1956. 'Gold coinage in the later Roman Empire', in *Essays in Roman Coinage* (ed. R. A. G. Carson and C. H. V. Sutherland), pp. 190–204.

KENT, J. P. C., and PAINTER, K. S. 1977. *Wealth of the Roman World,* London.

KRUG, A. 1980. 'Antike Gemmen im Römisch-Germanischen Museum köln, *'Bericht der Römisch-Germanischen Kommission* 61, pp. 151–260.

LAUR-BELART, R. 1963. *Der spätrömische Silberschatz von Kaiseraugst,* Basel.

LAWSON, A. J. 1976. 'Shale and jet objects from Silchester', *Archaeologia* 105, pp. 241–76.

LE CLAY, MARCEL. 1981. 'Abraxas', *Lexicon Iconographicum Mythologiae Classicae* 1, Zürich and Munich, pp. 2–7, pls 6–14.

LINS, P. A. and ODDY, W. A. 1975. 'The origins of mercury gilding', *Journ. of Arch. Science* 2, pp. 365–73.

MAASKANT–KLEIBRINK, MARIANNE. 1978. *Catalogue of the Engraved Gems in the Royal Coin Cabinet, the Hague. The Greek, Etruscan and Roman Collections,* the Hague and Wiesbaden.

MACALISTER, R. A. S. 1945. *Corpus Inscriptionum Insularum Celticarum* vol. 1, Dublin.

MACGREGOR, A. 1976. *Finds from a Roman sewer system and an adjacent building in Church Street,* York Arch. Trust/CBA, York.

MCKERRELL, H. and STEVENSON, R. B. K. 1972. 'Some analyses of Anglo-Saxon and associated oriental silver coinage', in *Methods of Chemical and Metallurgical Investigation of Ancient Coinage* (ed. E. T. Hall and D. M. Metcalfe).

MCROBERTS, DAVID. 1965. 'The Ecclesiastical Character of the St Ninian's Isle Treasure', *The Fourth Viking Congress,* A. Small (ed), Aberdeen.

MARSHALL, F. H. 1907. *Catalogue of the Finger Rings, Greek, Etruscan and Roman, in the Departments of Antiquities, British Museum,* London (reprint 1968).

MARSHALL, F. H. 1911. *Catalogue of the Jewellery, Greek, Etruscan and Roman, in the Departments of Antiquities, British Museum,* London (reprint 1969).

MARTIN, M. 1976. 'Römische und frühmittelalterliche Zahnstocher', *Germania* 54, pp. 456–60.

MARYON, H., and PLENDERLEITH, H. J. 1954. 'Fine Metal-work', in *A History of Technology,* vol. 1 (ed. Singer *et al.*), Oxford, pp. 623–62.

MATTINGLY, H. 1922. 'Find of siliquae at Dorchester, Dorset', *Num. Chron.* Series 5, pp. 134–9.

MATTINGLY, H., PEARCE, J., and KENDRICK, T. D. 1933. 'The Coleraine Hoard', *Antiquity* 11, pp. 39–45.

MEEKS, N. D. and TITE, M. S. 1980. 'An analysis of platinum-group element inclusions in gold antiquities', *Journ. of Arch. Science* 7, pp. 267–75.

MELLOR, J. 1930. *Comprehensive Treatise on Inorganic and Theoretical Chemistry* vol. 10. London.

MILOJČIĆ V. 1968. Zu den spätkaiserzeitlichen und merowingischen Silberlöffeln, *B. R. G. K.* 49, pp. 111–52.

ODDY, W. A. 1977. 'The production of gold wire in antiquity', *Gold Bulletin* 10 (3), pp. 79–87.

ODDY, W. A. 1979. 'Hand-made wire in antiquity; a correction', *MASCA Journal* 1 (2), pp. 44–5.

ODDY, W. A. 1980. 'Swaged wire from the Bronze Age?', *MASCA Journal* 1 (4), pp. 110–11.

ODDY, W. A. 1981. 'Gilding through the Ages', *Gold Bulletin* 14(2), pp. 75–80.

ODDY, W. A., *forthcoming*. Report on the wire artefacts from Timna site 200, in B. Rothenburg *et al.*

OGDEN, J. 1981. 'The Thetford Treasure', *Society of Jewellery Historians* 11, June 1981.

PAINTER, K. S. 1965. 'A Roman silver treasure from Canterbury', *Journ. of the Brit. Arch. Assoc.* 28, pp. 1–15.

PAINTER, K. S. 1972. 'A late-Roman silver ingot from Kent', *Ant. J.* 52, pp. 84–92.

PAINTER, K. S. 1975. 'A Roman Christian silver treasure from Biddulph, Staffordshire', *Ant. J.* 55, pp. 62–9.

PAINTER, K. S. 1977a. *The Mildenhall Treasure*, London.

PAINTER, K. S. 1977b. *The Water Newton Early Christian Silver*, London.

PERONI, A. 1967. *Oreficiere e Metalli Lavorati tardoantichi e altomedievali del territorio de Pavia*, Spoleto.

POKORNY, J. 1918. *Zeitschrift für celtische Philologie* 12, p. 424.

POKORNY, J. 1948. *Indogermanisches etymologisches Wörterbuch*, Bern.

POLLACK, Ludwig. 1903. *Klassisch-Antike Goldschmiedearbeiten im Besitze Sr. Excellenz A. J. von Nelidow*, Leipzig.

POTTER, T. W. *forthcoming*. 'A fourth-century silver spoon', *Ant. J.*

POTTER, T. W., and JOHNS, C. M. 1981. 'The Thetford Treasure', *Illustrated London News*, April 1981.

PONCET, E. 1889. 'Le Trésor de Planche', *Révue Numismatique* 3. série (7) pp. 514–38.

RAUB, C. J. 1977. 'Technologische Untersuchung einer römischen Goldkette aus Aalen', *Fundberichte aus Baden-Wurttemberg* 3, pp. 388–401

RAUB, C. J. 1981. 'Technologische Untersuchung einer römischen Silberkette aus Buch, Ostalbkreis', *Fundberrichte aus Baden-Wurttemberg* 6, pp. 529–40.

RAVEN, S. 1981. 'The future of the past', *Sunday Times Colour Supplement,* 29 March, 1981, pp. 42–6.

REIFFERSCHEID, A. 1866. 'Sulle imagini del dio Silvano e del dio Fauno', *Annali dell' Instituto di Corrispondenza archeologica* 38, pp. 210–27.

RICHARDSON, H. 1980. 'Derrynavlan and other early Church treasures', *Journ. Roy. Soc. of Antiq. of Ireland* 110, pp. 92–115.

RICHTER, GISELA. 1959. *Handbook of Greek Art,* London.

RICHTER, GISELA. 1971. *Engraved Gems of the Romans,* London.

RIVET. A. F. L. 1970. 'The British Section of the Antonine Itinerary', *Britannia* 1, pp. 34–82.

ROSCHER, W. H. *et al.* 1886–90. *Ausführliches Lexikon der griechischen und römischen Mythologie*, Bd. 1 (2), Leipzig.

ROSS, MARVIN C. 1965. *Catalogue of the Byzantine and early Medieval Antiquities in the Dumbarton Oaks Collection*, vol. 2, Washington.

RUDOLPH, W., and RUDOLPH, E. 1973. *Ancient Jewellery from the Collection of Burton Y. Berry*, Indiana.

RUMP, P. 1967. 'Nagel- oder Zieheisen?', *Draht-Welt* 53 (6), pp. 393–7.

RUMP, P. 1968. 'Beitrag zur Geschichte des Drahtzieheisens', *Stahl und Eisen* 88 (2), pp. 53–7.

SÁGI, KÁROLY. 1981. *Das römische Gräberfeld von Keszthely-Dobogó*, Budapest.

SALOMONSON, J. W. 1961. 'Zwei spätrömische Geschenk-Silberbarren mit eingestempelten Inschriften in Leiden', *Oudheidkundige Mededelingen* 42, pp. 63–77.

SALWAY, P. 1981. *Roman Britain,* Oxford.

SCHINDLER, R. 1977. *Führer durch das Landesmuseum Trier,* Trier.

SCHMIDT. 1957. *Zeitschrift für celtische Philologie* 24, p. 151.

SHELTON, KATHLEEN. 1981. *The Esquiline Treasure,* London.

SHERLOCK, D. 1973. 'Zu einer Fundliste antike Silberlöffel', *B. R. G. K.* 54, pp. 203–11.

SHERLOCK, D. 1976. 'The Roman Christian silver treasure from Biddulph', *Ant. J.* 56, pp. 235–7.

SIMION, G. 1977. 'Descoperiri noi pe teritoriul Noviodunensis', *Peuce* 7, Tulcea, pp. 130–1, pl. X, 7.

SMITS, ELISABETH C. H. 1946. *Faunus,* Leiden.

SPRATLING, M. G. 1980. 'The Sutton Hoo Purse: analysing the weights of its contents', in *Anglo-Saxon Cemeteries* (ed. P. Rahtz, T. Dickinson and L. Watts), B. A. R. 88, pp. 363–9.

STRONG, D. E. 1966. *Greek and Roman Gold and Silver Plate,* London.

THOMAS, CHARLES. 1981. *Christianity in Roman Britain to AD 500,* London.

THOUVENIN, A. 1971. 'La Fabrication des fils et des filigranes de metaux précieux chez les anciens', *Révue d'Histoire des Mines et de la Metallurgie*, 3.

TOYNBEE, J. M. C. 1962. *Art in Roman Britain,* London.

TOYNBEE, J. M. C. 1963. *A silver casket and strainer from the Walbrook Mithraeum in the City of London,* Leiden.

TOYNBEE, J. M. C. 1964. *Art in Britain under the Romans,* Oxford.

VÁGÓ, ESZTER B., and BÓNA, ISTVÁN, 1976. *Die Gräberfelder von Intercisa: der spätrömische Südostfriedhof,* Budapest.

WALTERS, H. B. 1926. *Catalogue of the Engraved Gems and Cameos, Greek, Etruscan and Roman, in the British Museum,* London.

WARD, ANNE. 1981. 'The rings of antiquity', in *The Ring, from Antiquity to the 20th Century,* Ward *et al.*, London.

WARDE FOWLER, W. 1899. *The Roman Festivals of the Period of the Republic.* London.

WATERBOLK, H. T. and GLASBERGEN, W. 1957. Der spätrömische Goldschatz von Beilen', *Palaeohistoria* 4.

WATKINS. 1955. *Language* 31, p. 17.

WAUGH, H. 1966. 'The hoard of Roman silver from Great Horwood, Buckinghamshire' *Ant. J.* 46. pp. 60–71.

WEBSTER, JANET. 1975. 'Objects of shale', in B. Cunliffe, *Excavations at Portchester Castle,* Soc. of Ants. Research Report 32, pp. 226–30.

WEITZMANN, KURT. 1979. *Age of Spirituality: late Antique and Early Christian Art, Third to Seventh Century,* New York.

WHATMOUGH, J. 1970. *The Dialects of Ancient Gaul,* Cambridge, Mass.

WILLIAMS, C. R. 1924. *Catalogue of Egyptian Antiquities: Gold and Silver Jewellery and Related Objects,* New York.

WILSON, D. M. 1973, 'The treasure', in A. Small, C. Thomas, and D. M. Wilson, *St Ninian's Isle and its Treasure,* Oxford, pp. 45–148.

WOOLLEY, C. L. 1934. *Ur Excavations II: the Royal Cemetery,* London and Philadelphia.

ZIEGLER, K., and SONTHEIMER, W. 1967. *Der Kleine Pauly. Lexikon der Antike,* vol. 2, Stuttgart.

ZIEGLER, K. and SONTHEIMER, W. 1969. *Der Kleine Pauly, Lexikon der Antike,* vol. 3, Stuttgart.

Index

The figures in italic refer to pages on which the line drawings appear; those in bold refer to catalogue numbers.

Abergele 53
Abraxas (Abrasax) 21, 28, 30, 31, 32, 88
Aegina Treasure 64
Alexander the Great 79
Alexandria 43, 73
Amesbury 69
Amethyst 20, 22, 30, 31, 59, 60, 81, 83, 84, 85
Albunea 50
Alcester 70
Allington 70
Ammianus Marcellinus 43
Ammonite 33, 131
Amrit, Syria 25, 86
Anastasiadis, E. 62
Antioch 20, 28, 43, 83
Apollo Grannus 46
Aquamarine 30
Arcadius 39
Arnobius of Sicca 44, 50, 51, 74
Asclepius 50
Ashtead 25, 97
Athens 85, 93

Bacchic cult/motifs 28, 29, 31, 47, 49, 51, 52, 74, 79, 95, 109, 119
Bacchus 31, 40, 79
Backworth Treasure 64
Bailey, D. M. 9
Balinrees, see Coleraine
Balline Treasure 68
'Basket' pattern 22, 24, 25, 86, 88, 95
Bath, Avon 74
Beads, biconical gold; 26, 66, 101
Beaurains Treasure 25, 26, 28, 30, 31, 69, 97, 99, 103
Benseddik, N. 10
Bentley Priory coin hoard 24
Berlin 79
Beryl, see emerald
Biddulph Treasure 43, 44, 68
Birdoswald 25, 97
Birds 21, 24, 65, 84, 85
Bloodstone, see jasper
Boars 83
Bona Dea 49
Bonn 25, 97
Boon, G. C. 9
Bowley, V. 9
Brading 32
Brittan, L. 14
Brooks, A. & Mrs G. 13, 14, 15
Brough 64, 93
Buckles, zoomorphic 24, 79–81, 83

Caley, E. R. 59
Campus Martius 51
Canoscio 37, 68, 121
Canterbury Treasure 37, 38, 39, 44, 54, 59, 69, 72, 91, 99, 103, 109, 119
Caracalla 31
Carleton St Peter, Norfolk 70

Carson, R. A. G. 69
Carthage 43, 68
Celtic design 22, 24, 86, 95; language 46–48, 51, 71; religion 46–48, 51, 85
Chain, loop-in-loop 26, 66, 99, 101
Chalcedony 20, 26, 30, 31, 59, 60, 83, 88, 91, 103, 105
Chaourse Treasure 53
Chelmsford 70
Christianity 28, 40, 50, 51, 53, 54, 68, 71, 73, 74, 84, 107, 121
Cleeve Prior coin hoard 27, 69, 73
Cockerel 81
Coins/coin hoards 15, 16–17, 18–19, 24–25, 27, 39, 43, 69, 86, 91
Colchester 74
Coleraine Treasure 68
Cologne 53, 54
Compton, P. 9
Constantine the Great 43, 68
Constantinople 43, 95
Constantius II 25, 32n, 68, 91
Corbridge, coin hoard 27, 69; Lanx 35; Treasure 68
Cornelian 20, 22, 30, 31, 60, 105
Crete 64
Cupid 20, 23, 28, 30, 31, 81, 105
Cybele 31
Cyprus 34, 64

Dalton, O. M. 34
Decorative techniques, chasing 22, 24, 81, 83; filigree 20, 21, 24, 26, 59, 65, 86, 88, 91; granulation 20, 21, 24, 59, 65, 81, 88, 91; piercing 20, 65
Derrynavlan 53
Diamond 93
Diana 26, 30, 31, 71, 103
Dogs 51, 103
Dolaucothi 64, 103
Dolphins 21, 24, 28, 53, 65, 83, 84, 107
Dorchester, Dorset 38, 39, 44, 54, 69, 72, 119, 121
Dorchester-on-Thames 33, 35, 38, 39, 41, 119
Dove, S. 19n
Dreams 49, 50
Ducks 23–24, 37, 79, 107; with objects in beaks 37, 79, 109, 113

East Harptree 69
Egypt 25, 64, 81, 93, 99
Emerald 20, 23, 25, 26, 30, 59, 60, 83, 85, 86, 93, 97, 105
Enkomi, Cyprus 64
Epidauros 50
Epprecht, W. 62
Esquiline Hill 51; Treasure 43–44, 68, 83, 109
Ethiopia 31
Eugenius 19, 70, 72, 73

Evans, D. Ellis 47, 48n
Eye, Suffolk 69, 73

Fairies 50
Faunus 10, 11, 26, 28, 29, 31–32, 34, 40, 44, 46, 49–52, 54, 70–71, 73, 74, 85, 99, 119
Fenland 13, 15, 74
Fish 38, 40, 71, 109, 119
Foederati 79
Fox, M 10
Furies 50

Gallows Hill, Thetford 9, 13, 15–19, 34, 73
Gandhara 99
Garnet 20, 23, 25, 30, 59, 60, 79, 83, 85, 88, 93, 95, 97
Gaul 11, 24, 26, 39, 44, 70, 83
Gelasius I 51
Gems, reuse in jewellery 20, 22, 30, 60, 103, 105
Gilding 36, 44, 58, 59–60, 65, 107–109, 119
Glass ('gems') 20, 23, 26, 30, 59, 60, 84, 88, 91, 93, 97, 101, 105; gold-inlaid 23, 25, 93, 97
Goats 49, 51
Goths 73
Gratian 39
Great Horwood Treasure 44
Gregory, A. 10, 13, 15
Gross Bodungen Treasure 68
Grovely Wood, Wilts 69, 86
Guisborough 70

Hacksilber 34, 68, 69, 70
Hala Sultan Tekke 64
Hall, J. A. 58
Hama, Syria 34
Hares 83
Hassall, M. 9, 48n, 71
Havering, Essex 86
Heliodorus; 30, 31
Heliotrope, see jasper
Helpston 86, 109
Hengistbury Head 33
Henig, M. 9, 71, 73
Herculaneum 53
Hercules club 25, 97
Higgins, R. 26, 99
Hockwold, Norfolk 9
Hof Iben, Mainz 37, 43
Holmes, R. 9
Honorius 24, 25, 39, 68, 91
Horace 49, 52, 71
Horse-heads 24, 79, 122, 126
Hostentorp, Denmark 68
L'Houmeau, France 26, 103
Howletts, Kent 64
Hughes, M. R. 58
Human faces (as decoration) 22, 86, 95

Iao, see Abraxas
Icklingham 70
Icknield Way 15–16
Incubus 49, 50
India 31
Ingots, silver 36, 43, 68, 69, 72
Inuus 50, 51
Ipswich torcs 13

Jackson, K. H. 9
Jacobi, G. 62
Jasper 30, 60, 88
Jerusalem; 73, 74
Johns, C. M. 10
Jones, A. H. M. 73
Jovinus 101
Julian the Apostate 19, 39, 43, 68, 70, 72

Kaiseraugst Treasure 34, 37, 39, 43, 53, 54, 68, 72, 107, 109
Kimmeridge 33
Kells, book of 53
Kent, J. P. C. 68, 72
Kertch, Crimea 39, 54
Kerynia, see Cyprus
Kinnes, I. A. 45n
Köln-Müngersdorf 39
Kyngadle 53

Lankhills 79, 83
Latinus 50
Latium 49, 50, 52
Lawson, A. 18
Leaf decoration 22, 24, 81, 83
Leopards 83
Lions 26, 28, 30, 31, 81, 83, 103
Littlecote, Wilts 32
Littledale, H. A. P. 65
Little Horwood, Bucks 39, 119
Livy; 50
Loché 121
London 88, 95, 99
Longworth, I. H. 10
Low Ham 51
Lupercalia 50, 51; Lupercal cave 51
Lupicinus 68
Lydney 54
Lyon 25, 30, 43, 70, 81, 86, 95

Maaskant-Kleibrink, M. 30
McKerrell, H. 58
Magnus Maximus 15, 19, 70, 72, 73
Maiden Castle 70
Mainz 91
Malachite 65
Marcian 24, 83
Mars 28, 31, 32, 50, 71, 91
Mercury 28, 30, 31, 81
Milan 43
Mildenhall Treasure 13, 24, 28, 35, 37, 38, 39, 44, 58, 68, 79, 109
Milojčić, V. 34, 54
Mithraism 53

Moylarg, Ireland 53
'Munich' Treasure 43
Mutz, A. 62

Naix, France 26, 103
Namur 101
Nancy, France 88
New Grange 24, 25, 28, 64, 69, 86, 95
Newton, Carlisle 63
Nicodemia 43
Nicolo 30, 31, 83
Niello 36, 44, 59, 65, 83, 109, 113, 117, 119, 121, 122, 125, 126, 129, 131
Nightmares 50
Nijmegen 79
Niš, Yugoslavia 43
Numa 5

Oddy, W. A. 9
Ogden, J. 15
Onyx 20, 26, 30, 60, 91, 103
Ovid 44, 51
Oxus Treasure 64

Painter, K. S. 9, 36, 39, 43, 68, 71
Palatine Hill 51
Palestine 79
Pan 28, 47, 49, 51, 52, 74, 95
Panthers 28, 40, 52, 58, 71, 79, 109, 119
Parabiago 44
Parcel-gilding, see gilding
Pengelly, R. 9
Persia 25, 99
Picus 28, 50, 71, 85
Planche, France 26, 99, 103
Plasma 30, 31, 85
Platinum 59
Pliny the Elder 26, 65, 99
Pompeii 30, 53
Priscillian 74
Proiecta 43
Protarchos 31

Quartz 20, 60

Raub, C. J. 64
Ravenna 43
Reading 70
Reculver 36
Reedie, K. 44n
Rhayader 64
Richborough 24, 31, 53, 54, 64, 79, 86, 107
Risley Park lanx 68
Romania 25, 97
Rome 39, 43, 86
Romulus 51
Rouen 83
Rump, P. 62

Sabaoth 30–31
St Ninian's Isle Treasure 54, 107
Saint-Quentin, France 39
Samson, Belgium 101
Sapphire 85, 88
Sardonyx 30, 31
Saturn 47, 50
Satyrs 24, 49, 51, 52, 71, 74, 79, 95
Sault-du-Rhone 81
Serapis 31
Shapwick, Dorset 70
Shelton, K. 43, 44
Sherlock, D. 9, 34
Silchester 30, 43
Sileni 49

Siliquae 15, 18–19, 24–25, 70, 72, 91, 101
Silvanus 49, 51
Snakes 26, 28, 101, 103
Snettisham Treasure 13, 62
Soldering 65–66
Solidi 15, 24, 27, 43, 59, 68, 69, 72
South Shields 31
Spencer, B. 19n
Sphinx 31
Spratling, M. G. 75n
Springhead, Kent 70
Stevenson, R. B. K. 58
Stilicho 73
Strap-ends 81
Strong, D. E. 53
Sturmer, Essex 70
Sully Moors, Cardiff 69
Sul Minerva 74
Sulphur 21, 25–26, 50, 60, 66, 77, 81, 83, 84, 85, 88, 93, 95, 97, 99
Sutton Hoo Treasure 13, 60
Syria 25, 34, 83, 86, 93, 109

Ténès Treasure (Algeria) 10, 24, 25, 26, 27, 28, 30, 69, 71, 72, 79, 95, 97, 99
Terling, Essex 24, 69, 72, 86
Theodosius I 39, 73
Thetford Treasure
  contents
  amulet-case 30 21, 25, 26, 61, 65–66, 71, 99; 98
  beads 42–46 14, 15, 19n, 23, 77, 105; 105
  bracelet 24 20, 21, 25, 27, 59, 61, 65, 72, 86, 95; 96
  bracelet 25 20, 21, 25, 27, 61, 65, 72, 86, 95; 96
  bracelet 26 13, 20, 21, 24, 25, 27, 59, 60, 61, 63, 72, 95; 96
  bracelet 27 22, 23, 25, 61, 63, 66, 84, 85, 91, 97; 96
  buckle 1 15, 21, 22, 23, 27, 59, 61, 65, 77, 79–80, 101; 78
  cameo pendant 39 22, 26, 27, 30, 31, 61, 103; 104
  gem 41 14, 19n, 20, 22, 23, 26, 31, 105; 105
  necklace 31 23, 25, 60, 61, 63, 99, 101, 105; 100
  necklace 32 22, 23, 25, 27, 61, 63, 81, 101; 100
  necklace 33 22, 25, 27, 61, 63, 81, 101, 103; 100
  necklace 34 26, 61, 66, 101; 102
  necklace 35/36 25, 61, 63, 77, 101–103; 102
  necklace-clasp 37 26, 61, 101, 103; 104
  necklace-clasp 38 26, 61, 63, 101, 103; 104
  pendant 28 21, 22, 23, 25, 60, 61, 63, 65, 66, 81, 83, 86, 93, 97; 98
  pendant 29 21, 22, 25, 61, 63, 65, 66, 81, 83, 86, 97; 98
  pendant 40 26, 27, 30, 31, 61, 103; 105
  ring 2 20, 22, 24, 28, 30, 31, 60, 61, 65, 66, 67, 81, 83, 84, 86, 97; 80
  ring 3 20, 22, 24, 28, 30, 31, 61, 81, 83, 84, 86; 80
  ring 4 20, 22, 24, 28, 30, 31, 61, 65, 66, 67, 81, 83, 86, 97; 82
  ring 5 21, 24, 61, 65, 66, 81, 83, 84, 85, 86; 82
  ring 6 20, 21, 24, 28, 61, 65, 72, 81, 83, 84, 86; 84

ring 7 20, 21, 22, 23, 28, 61, 65, 66, 71, 72, 81, 83, 84–85, 86, 91, 95, 97; 84
ring 8 22, 23, 24, 61, 83, 85, 97; 85
ring 9 22, ;24, 61, 65, 66, 67, 81, 83, 86, 95, 97; 86
ring 10 20, 22, 24, 25, 26, 28, 59, 61, 63, 65, 77, 86–88, 91, 95; 87
ring 11 20, 23, 24, 28, 59, 61, 63, 88; 87
ring 12 20, 21, 22, 23, 24, 25, 26, 59, 61, 63, 65, 72, 77, 88, 91, 95; 89
ring 13 21, 26, 30, 31, 59, 61, 63, 88; 89
ring 14 20, 24, 28, 59, 61, 63, 72, 88, 91; 90
ring 15 21, 24, 26, 59, 60, 61, 63, 70, 71, 73, 74, 88, 91; 90
ring 16 24, 31, 59, 61, 70, 71, 72, 91; 92
ring 17 23, 28, 61, 63, 84, 91, 97; 92
ring 18 28, 61, 93; 94
ring 19 25, 28, 61, 66, 93; 94
ring 20 25, 61, 93; 94
ring 21 23, 28, 60, 61, 63, 93, 97; 94
ring 22 28, 61, 63, 93–95; 94
ring 23 22, 25, 27, 28, 44, 52, 61, 63, 66, 86, 93, 95, 101; 94
shale box 83 13, 14, 33, 77, 131; 131
spoon 50 (Triton spoon) 28, 35, 40, 42, 44, 47, 52, 56, 58, 65, 71, 77, 107–109, 113, 117, 119, 121; 108
spoon 51 36, 37, 46, 47, 56, 59, 109; 110
spoon 52 37, 46, 47, 48, 109, 125, 131; 110
spoon 53 37, 46, 47, 109; 111
spoon 54 37, 46, 113, 129; 111
spoon 55 37, 46, 47, 113; 112
spoon 56 37, 46, 47, 109, 113, 122, 129; 112
spoon 57 46, 47, 113, 117, 126, 129; 114
spoon 58 37, 46, 47, 59, 113; 114
spoon 59 46, 113; 115
spoon 60 37, 117; 115
spoon 61 35, 37, 46, 117; 116
spoon 62 35, 37, 46, 117; 116
spoon 63 37, 46, 117; 118
spoon 64 35, 37, 47, 113, 117, 126, 129; 118
spoon 65 35, 37, 117, 121; 119
spoon 66 (Panther spoon) 28, 36, 40, 41, 42, 46, 47, 52, 56, 58, 65, 71, 109, 119, 121, 122, 125, 126, 129, 131; 120
spoon 67 (fish spoon) 38, 40, 65, 71, 117, 119–121, 120
spoon 68 38, 39, 46, 51, 121, 125; 121
spoon 69 38, 39, 46, 51, 71, 107, 121, 122, 122
spoon 70 15, 38, 39, 41, 46, 121, 122, 123
spoon 71 38, 39, 41, 47, 113, 121, 122, 129; 123
spoon 72 38, 39, 41, 46, 51, 65, 121, 125; 124
spoon 73 38, 39, 41, 47, 59, 65, 107, 125, 131; 124
spoon 74 39, 41, 46, 47, 48, 65, 107, 109, 125, 131; 125
spoon 75 38, 39, 47, 56, 65, 113, 117, 121, 126, 129; 126

spoon 76 34, 39, 40, 41, 126, 131; 127
spoon 77 39, 40, 41, 119, 126, 131; 127
spoon 78 39, 40, 41, 47, 65, 113, 117, 119, 126, 129; 128
spoon 79 39, 40, 41, 42, 47, 113, 122, 129; 128
spoon 80 35, 40, 41, 47, 56, 65, 113, 117, 126, 129; 129
spoon 81 39, 47, 107, 131; 130
spoon 82 40, 41, 47, 48, 109, 125, 131; 130
strainer 47 53–54, 56, 65, 107; 106
strainer 48 53–54, 56, 65, 107; 106
strainer 49 15, 34, 53–54, 56, 65, 107; 108
container(s), evidence 13, 15, 34
condition, jewellery 11, 21; spoons 34
conservation 14, 33
inscriptions, 'handwriting' 41–42
wear, jewellery 21, 60–61, 70; spoons 35, 109
weights, jewellery 27–28, 68–69, 72–73; spoons 36–37, 41, 43, 68–69, 72–73, 117
valuation 14

Tiber Island 50
Timber building 13, 14, 15, 18
Tite, M. 9
Topaz 30
Torriano 81
Toynbee, J. M. C. 53
Traprain Law Treasure 34, 36, 37, 39, 44, 53, 54, 68, 107, 109, 121
Treasure Trove law 9, 14
Trier 43
Triton 28, 52, 58, 71, 107
Tuddenham, Suffolk 25, 72, 91
Tyche (of Antioch) 20, 28, 83

Valentinian I 39, 81, 91
Venus 20, 23, 28, 30, 31, 105
Vermand 37, 44, 79, 81, 83, 91
Verulamium 33, 131
Victory 30, 83
Virgil 44, 49, 51, 85
Vollenweider, M-L. 31

Walbrook 25, 53, 63, 97
Walls, R. 10
Water Newton coin hoard 27, 43, 69–70; Treasure 13, 43, 53, 54, 58, 68, 107
Waters, R. 10
Whiting, M. 30
Whorlton, Yorks 24, 58, 69, 72, 91
Wiesbaden 88
Williams, C. Ransome 62
Wilson, D. 10
Wilton, Yorks 70
Wincle 63, 64, 99, 107
Wire, technology 62–64
Witch cult 52
Wolters, J. 65
Wolves 49, 50, 51
Woodpeckers 28, 50, 51, 71, 74, 85, 95
Wroxeter 43

X-ray diffraction 59, 60
X-ray fluorescence 56, 60, 77

York 99

Zolforata 50

PLATE 1

PLATE 2

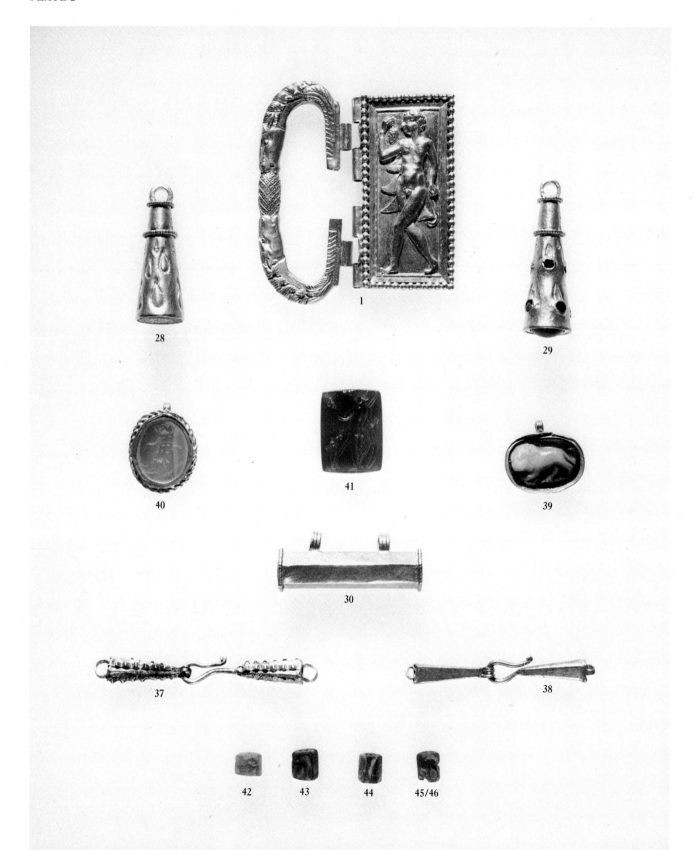

28

1

29

40

41

39

30

37

38

42   43   44   45/46

PLATE 3

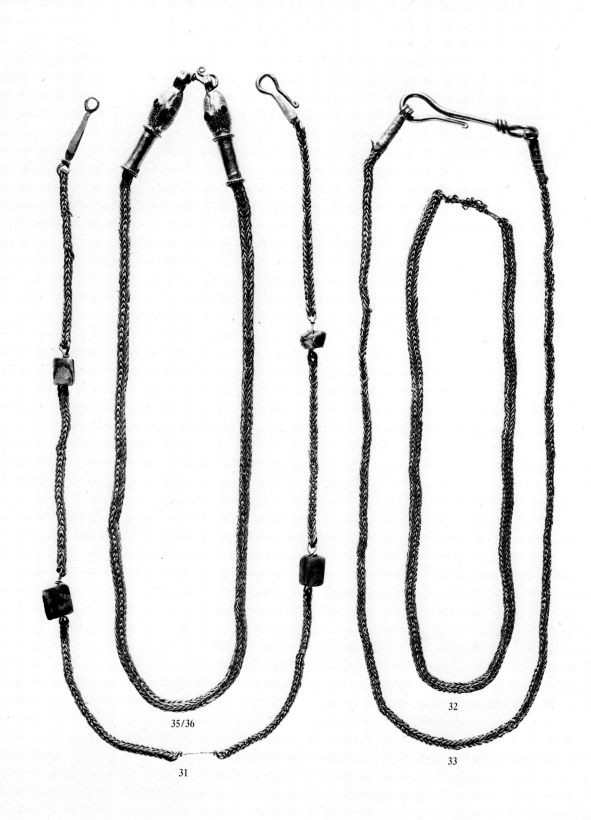

35/36

31

32

33

PLATE 4

24   25

26   27

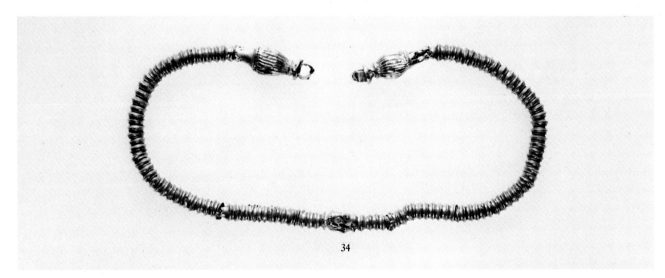

34

PLATE 5

48   47   49

PLATE 6

PLATE 7

PLATE 8

PLATE 9

PLATE 10

PLATE 11

73

74

75

76

77

PLATE 12

78 79 80 81 82

PLATE 13

83

83 *Reduced*

PLATE 14

PLATE 15

23 *Enlarged*

1 *Enlarged*

PLATE 16

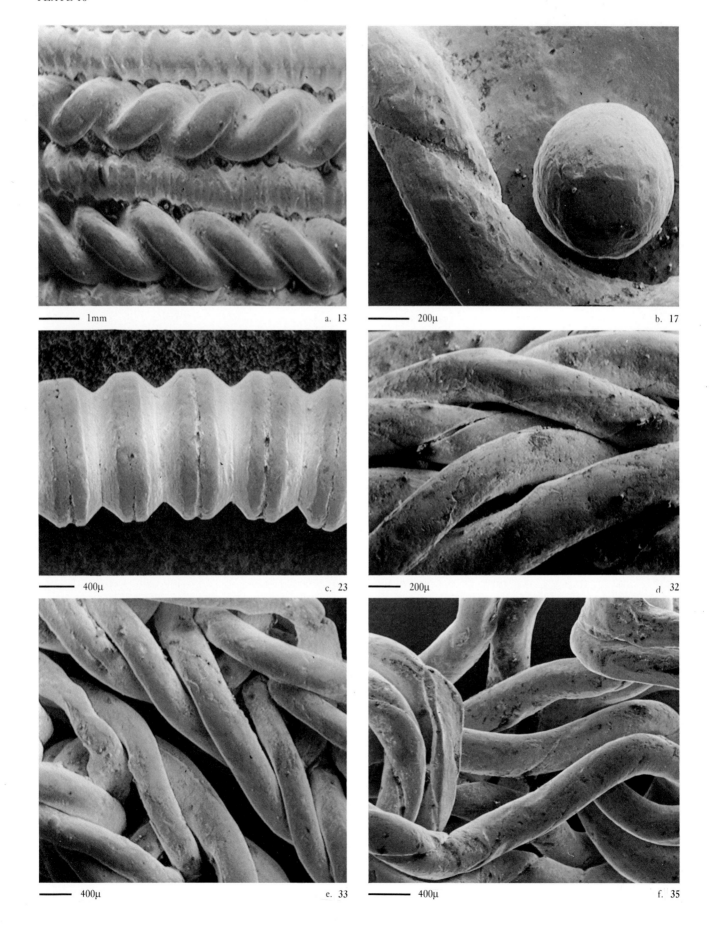

a. 13 — 1mm

b. 17 — 200μ

c. 23 — 400μ

d. 32 — 200μ

e. 33 — 400μ

f. 35 — 400μ